Dr Kevin Meares is a consultan accredited cognitive behavioural therapist. He works for the Northumberland, Tyne and Wear NHS Foundation Trust at the Newcastle Cognitive and Behavioural Therapy Centre. He offers therapy to adults with a range of complex psychological problems, specializing in anxiety disorders, and has a particular interest and expertise in the assessment and treatment of post-traumatic stress disorder. He is an experienced supervisor and trainer and he regularly leads workshops on CBT. His research interests focus on rumination and worry.

Professor Mark Freeston is the Head of Research and Development at the Newcastle Cognitive and Behavioural Therapies Centre where he was director of the Newcastle Diploma in Cognitive Therapy for ten years until 2010. He is also Professor of Clinical Psychology at the University of Newcastle. He divides his time between NHS duties and the University of Newcastle. He has published over a hundred scientific articles, mainly in the field of intrusive thoughts and worry and on the formulation and treatment of Obsessive Compulsive Disorder and Generalised Anxiety Disorder. He regularly provides workshops on the cognitive behavioural treatment of these disorders. His current research investigates intolerance of uncertainty, how it manifests in everyday life, how it may help to inform the treatment of problems like Obsessive Compulsive Disorder and Generalised Anxiety Disorder, and how it may help us understand anxiety among children and adolescents with autism spectrum disorders.

The aim of the **Overcoming** series is to enable people with a range of common problems and disorders to take control of their own recovery programme.

Each title, with its specially tailored programme, is devised by a practising clinician using the latest techniques of cognitive behavioural therapy – techniques which have been shown to be highly effective in changing the way patients think about themselves and their problems.

The series was initiated in 1993 by Peter Cooper, Professor of Psychology at Reading University and Research Fellow at the University of Cambridge in the UK, whose original volume on overcoming bulimia nervosa and binge-eating continues to help many people in the USA, the UK and Europe. Many books in the Overcoming series are recommended by the UK Department of Health under the Books on Prescription scheme.

OVERCOMING WORRY AND GENERALISED ANXIETY DISORDER

A self-help guide to using
Cognitive Behavioural Techniques

Kevin Meares
and
Mark Freeston

ROBINSON

ROBINSON

First published in Great Britain in 2008 by Robinson
an imprint of Constable & Robinson Ltd.

This revised and updated edition published in 2015 by Robinson

9 10 8

Important Note
This book is not intended as a substitute for medical advice or treatment.
Any person with a condition requiring medical attention should consult a
qualified medical practitioner or suitable therapist.

A CIP catalogue record for this book
is available from the British Library.

ISBN: 978-1-4721-0742-8

Typeset in Bembo by Initial Typesetting Services, Edinburgh
Printed and bound in Great Britain by Clays Ltd, Elcograf S.p.A.

Papers used by Robinson are from well-managed forests
and other responsible sources

Robinson
An imprint of
Little, Brown Book Group
Carmelite House
50 Victoria Embankment
London EC4Y 0DZ

An Hachette UK Company
www.hachette.co.uk

www.littlebrown.co.uk

Contents

Acknowledgements to the First Edition

We owe an incalculable debt of gratitude to the individuals we encountered in our clinical work who suffered with excessive worry; their collective experience is the principal source for this book. As this is a self-help book we have limited the number of references to research but acknowledge that the information is based on the silent yet generous contribution of many. We would like to thank all of those who have contributed to the pool of knowledge from which we have drawn. With this in mind we would like to thank all those who contributed to the programme of research at l'Université Laval, leading to the development of the model of Generalised Anxiety Disorder that forms the foundation for this book. We would especially like to thank Robert Ladouceur, Michel Dugas and Eliane Léger.

We thank all our colleagues at the Newcastle Cognitive and Behavioural Therapy Centre for their good humour, support and friendship, with special thanks to Dr Stephen Barton, for his generosity with both his time and his ideas, particularly related to the chapter on the heart of worry and on goal setting. Many thanks also to Dr Andrew Wilkinson, Dr Tracy Thorne, Dr Douglas Maisey, Jenny Shannon,

Emma Thomas, Carol Thackery and Dr Jen Lane for their helpful feedback on early drafts. Thanks to Peter Armstrong for many helpful discussions. Thanks to Karen Lysakowska, Anita Allinson, Jo Thomas and Jon Chapman for their contributions. In addition, we thank the numerous supervisors, supervisees, trainees and students who have contributed along the way.

Finally, we thank our families and friends for putting up with the absences, both physical and mental, the long hours, the late nights and the inevitable worry, both real and hypothetical.

Acknowledgements
to the Second Edition

Since writing the first book there are a number of people who have helped develop our ideas and who have encouraged us to write the second edition. First, thanks to all the people who have provided formal or informal feedback on the first edition and told us what they like about it and where it could be improved. Second, there are people who have contributed in various ways to the development of the ideas. There are colleagues, both clinical and academic, who have questioned, challenged and stretched our understanding and the model, including Dr Andrew Wilkinson, Dr Jacqui Rodgers, Professor Sue Leekam, Theresa Marrinan, Dr Gioia Bottesi, Dr Nick Carleton, Dr Sean Perrin. Numerous students at Newcastle University – both postgraduate and undergraduate – have revisited, reviewed, critiqued and investigated specific aspects of our understanding of both worry and intolerance of uncertainty and, most importantly, brought in new perspectives and original ideas. Once again our colleagues have been supportive, with a special mention for Dr Vivien Twaddle. Finally, we would like to thank our families again for recognizing that this is an important part of what we do and for supporting us to do it.

Preface

Is this book for me?

There are an overwhelming number of self-help books about all sorts of problems, so the first point that needs to be addressed is whether this book will be of use to you. Here are some simple questions that may help you answer this:

Have you always been a worrier?

Yes ❏   No ❏

If there is nothing to worry about, do you still find yourself worrying?

Yes ❏   No ❏

Do minor everyday things spiral into major concerns?

Yes ❏   No ❏

Once it starts, is your worry hard to stop?

Yes ❏   No ❏

Does worry stop you enjoying life?

Yes ❏   No ❏

Do your friends or family often suggest that you worry too much? Or, do they repeatedly tell you to stop worrying?

Yes ❏   No ❏

If the answer to at least two of these questions is yes, and if your worry is having a significant impact on how you function at work, at home or in social settings or is causing you distress, then this is probably the book for you.

How can this book help me?

This book will help you to build your understanding of worry step by step. If we can help you to understand what leads you to worry and what keeps you worrying, then we are a good step closer to helping you overcome it. With each step we will introduce new ideas that add to the picture of worry, and with these ideas you will find questionnaires, exercises and tasks to help you understand and then challenge unhelpful habits and beliefs that keep you worrying.

The nineteen chapters roughly divide into three parts. Chapters 1–3 set the scene: they introduce everyday and problem worry using some case stories, give some facts and figures about worry, and offer advice about how best to use this book. Chapters 4–7 look at how cognitive behavioural therapy can help us to understand worry and start the process of building up the picture of worry. They teach us to become aware of our worry in a new way, standing outside, rather than living within. With this new awareness, you will then learn to think about what you would like to achieve and set yourself realistic goals. Chapters 8–18 explain the areas you will need to focus on to overcome your worry, namely, learning to tolerate uncertainty (Chapters 8–11), learning about ideas that lead us to worry (Chapters 12–13), how to solve problems (Chapters 14–16), and how to face ideas or thoughts that we would much rather avoid (Chapters 17–18). Don't be concerned if these are unfamiliar – we take time to make sure that we explain each area thoroughly. Finally, we tie up the loose ends in Chapter 19.

We sincerely hope that you find this book useful. With very best wishes.

Kevin Meares and Mark Freeston,
Newcastle Upon Tyne, 2014

Introduction

Why a cognitive behavioural approach?

The approach this book takes in attempting to help you overcome your problems with worrying is a 'cognitive behavioural' one. A brief account of the history of this form of intervention might be useful and encouraging. In the 1950s and '60s a set of therapeutic techniques was developed, collectively termed 'behaviour therapy'. These techniques shared two basic features. First, they aimed to remove symptoms (such as anxiety) by dealing with those symptoms themselves, rather than their deep-seated underlying historical causes (traditionally the focus of psychoanalysis, the approach developed by Sigmund Freud and his associates). Second, they were scientifically based, in the sense that they used techniques derived from what laboratory psychologists were finding out about the mechanisms of learning, and they put these techniques to scientific test. The area where behaviour therapy initially proved to be of most value was in the treatment of anxiety disorders, especially specific phobias (such as extreme fear of animals or heights) and agoraphobia, both notoriously difficult to treat using conventional psychotherapies.

After an initial flush of enthusiasm, discontent with

behaviour therapy grew. There were a number of reasons for this. An important concern was the fact that behaviour therapy did not deal with the internal thoughts that were so obviously central to the distress that many patients were experiencing. In particular, behaviour therapy proved inadequate when it came to the treatment of depression. In the late 1960s and early 1970s a treatment for depression was developed called 'cognitive therapy'. The pioneer in this enterprise was an American psychiatrist, Professor Aaron T. Beck. He developed a theory of depression which emphasized the importance of people's depressed styles of thinking, and, on the basis of this theory, he specified a new form of therapy. It would not be an exaggeration to say that Beck's work has changed the nature of psychotherapy, not just for depression but for a range of psychological problems.

The techniques introduced by Beck have been merged with the techniques developed earlier by the behaviour therapists to produce a therapeutic approach which has come to be known as 'cognitive behavioural therapy' (or CBT). This therapy has been subjected to the strictest scientific testing and has been found to be highly successful for a significant proportion of cases of depression. However, it has now become clear that specific patterns of disturbed thinking are associated with a wide range of psychological problems, not just depression, and that the treatments which deal with these are highly effective. So, effective cognitive behavioural treatments have been developed for a range of anxiety disorders, such as panic disorder, Generalised Anxiety Disorder, specific phobias, social phobia, obsessive compulsive disorders, and hypochondriasis (health anxiety), as well as for other conditions such as drug addictions, and eating disorders like bulimia nervosa. Indeed, cognitive behavioural techniques have been found to have an application beyond the narrow categories of psychological disorders. They have been applied effectively, for example, to helping people with low self-esteem, those with weight problems, couples with marital difficulties, as well as those who wish to give up smoking or deal with drinking problems. In relation to the current self-help manual, over several years effective CBT techniques have been developed for helping people overcome their problems with distressing and disabling worrying. The current manual provides a detailed analysis of the nature of worry and the problems associated with tolerating uncertainty, together with specific techniques for overcoming the associated difficulties.

The starting point for CBT is the realization that the way we think, feel and behave are all intimately linked, and changing the way we think about ourselves, our experiences and the world around us changes the way we feel and what we are able to do. So, for example, by helping a depressed person identify and challenge their automatic depressive thoughts, a route out of the cycle of depressive thoughts and feelings can be found. Similarly, habitual behavioural responses are driven by a complex set of thoughts and feelings; and CBT, as you will discover from this book, by providing a means for the behaviour, thoughts and feelings to be brought under control, enables these responses to be undermined and a different kind of life to be possible.

Although effective CBT treatments have been developed for a wide range of disorders and problems, these treatments are not widely available; and, when people try on their own to help themselves, they often, inadvertently, do things which make matters worse. Over the past two decades, the community of cognitive behavioural therapists has responded to this situation. What they have done is to take the principles and techniques of specific cognitive behavioural therapies for particular problems, of proven effectiveness, and present them in manuals which people can read and apply themselves. These manuals specify a systematic programme of treatment which the person works through to overcome their difficulties. In this way, cognitive behavioural therapeutic techniques of established value are being made available on the widest possible basis.

The use of self-help manuals is never going to replace the need for therapists. Many people with emotional and behavioural problems will need the help of a trained therapist. It is also the case that, despite the widespread success of cognitive behavioural therapy, some people will not respond to it and will need one of the other treatments available. Nevertheless, although research on the use of these self-help manuals is at an early stage, the work done to date indicates that for a great many people such a manual is sufficient for them to overcome their problems without professional help. Sadly, many people suffer on their own for years. Sometimes they feel reluctant to seek help without first making a serious effort to manage on their own. Sometimes they feel too awkward or even ashamed to ask for help. Sometimes appropriate help is not forthcoming despite their efforts to find it. For many of these people the cognitive behavioural self-help manual will provide a lifeline to a better future.

Professor Peter J. Cooper,
University of Reading, 2014

1

The experience of worry

What is worry?

Worry is often experienced as a chain of negative thoughts, images and doubts about things that might happen in the future. In essence, worriers tend to be concerned by what's 'around the corner' rather than what's here right now. So, for the most part, worry is not about things where the outcome is *certain*, it's about things where the outcome is *uncertain*. Worrying about one thing often tends to lead quickly and easily to worrying about something quite different. As a result, worriers can get caught up in a whirlwind of thoughts about bad things that *might* happen. Often these are either highly unlikely or about very distant possibilities, but, when caught up in a chain or spiral of worry, they seem very real.

Once people are caught in this whirlwind, they often feel as if they can't stop worrying. The worry seems uncontrollable, and attempts to stop or divert it may not appear effective or may even seem to make it worse. People often report feeling tense, nervous or panicky, or they describe feeling overwhelmed, helpless or paralysed with uncertainty. Worriers tend to have an overriding sense that they cannot cope with the problems and situations the world throws at them. They may feel inferior, with low confidence and self-esteem. During the whirlwind, the predominant feeling is anxiety, but once the storm eases off, worriers often feel demoralized and exhausted.

People caught up in this whirlwind often show various other signs of anxiety. These signs or symptoms appear as a product of excessive worry. Those experienced most often are muscle tension, restlessness (being unable to relax), tiredness, irritability, difficulty in getting to sleep or staying asleep and difficulty in concentrating or focusing one's attention. As well as these main symptoms, other types of experiences can also develop, such as palpitations, butter-flies, a knot in the stomach, digestive upset or headaches. Once these intense physical sensations appear they can trigger more worry, and perhaps the worrier may start to worry about their health in response to them. Attempts to avoid the worry by pushing it away can work for a moment, but then these very real physical sensations act to remind the worrier about the very things they were trying to avoid thinking about in the first place! The whirlwind can be so much part of the way we think that we may not even notice it is happening, but we may notice the headaches, the tension or the irritability.

Worry may also circulate at the back of our minds, coming into sharper focus every now and again. When this happens, the often repetitive and usually dreadful content of our worry can force us to try to submerge it deeper in our minds. So worry becomes a vague, hazy experience punctuated by sharp, distressing thoughts that emerge from the fog of our minds, only for us to try to push them back again. This only leads us to worry all the more. Just like a whirlwind, worry moves fast, and we can quickly get lost in its labyrinth. It can be a confusing experience where reality and worry merge. The speed of thought gives us the impression that our thoughts are chaotic and lack any pattern or order. This sense of chaos yet further adds to the idea that our thoughts are out of control, causing us to worry all the more.

Worry is a little like the fun-fair game where a player has to hit with a mallet the heads of plastic puppets, usually rats or moles, which pop out of holes. Each time they hit one, another appears somewhere else on the board, and when they hit that one, another appears, and so it goes on and on. The 'game' is impossible to win: the rats and moles are always victorious. If you have ever watched people play this game you may have noticed how frustrated and tense they become.

Often we worry late at night or in the small hours of the morning, or at other times when we are 'alone with our thoughts'. We tend to keep worry to ourselves, as a private experience – even close friends may be unaware of our worrying, and if we admit to worrying about the children or our finances, we rarely reveal the distressing drama that has been playing out in our minds. This very personal experience has a profound impact on how we relate to others. For instance, our worry may motivate us to be over-protective: we may continually check on our loved ones, who may interpret this as intrusive or nagging. We may avoid situations or people that we know will set off worry. Sometimes worry drives us to seek reassurance from those around us, 'checking out' our fears with others in subtle or obvious ways. If we share our worries, it may only be because they are getting too much for us, and even then we may worry about burdening or bothering others. More usually, we worry about what people will think of us, concerned that others might see us as odd, weird, weak, stupid or even crazy.

Worriers also tend to focus on what *may* happen and so 'live' in the future. For example, while meeting friends their focus might be on whether they will be able to make time next week to meet up; or, at a football match, rather than enjoying the game, they think about whether they will be able to get their bus home. Living in this way has a profound effect on the capacity to simply live and enjoy life in the moment. Whatever the circumstances, their worry transports them away from the here and now to a tense, often bleak and anxiety-provoking future.

Worry can be likened to a mirage in the desert. Classically, in the 'comic book' image, a man is crawling across the desert in search of water when he observes what appears to be an oasis close by. Convinced that what he is seeing is real, he believes that salvation is at hand. He may start to feel euphoric, and even more thirsty at the thought of water. He may, for a moment, suspect that what he is seeing can't be true, but because his life depends on it he pushes this idea away. Thinking that the oasis is within reach, he runs and throws himself into the water. Alas, the oasis is hundreds of miles away; the mirage disappears and all he grasps is sand.

So what are the parallels to worry? Both mirages and worry are real: mirages are not imaginary, they're actually there – we can photograph them, but they're distorted and 'bend' reality. In the same way, when worry develops it is distorted and takes on the *illusion of being true*. Our worries seem *very real* and *convincing*. Even if we doubt them to some extent, they twist and turn around important personal issues such as the loss or death of a loved one, or what is important to them, or a sense of inadequacy. Like the thirsty survivor who starts to run on seeing a mirage of an oasis, worriers have a tendency to believe their worries and then act on them. For example, José (who appears in the case stories below) worried about how his children would manage his new relationship after his divorce. His worry seemed so convincing that he felt sure they would not cope and would end up rejecting him. He tried to win his children's affection by buying them gifts, even though he had no evidence that they thought badly of him. Like the mirage, his worries seemed real and they loomed menacingly over his future relationship with his children. This motivated him to try to stop them coming true, but his actions were based not on facts but on worries, for which he had no evidence.

Once the worry has passed, the worrier is often left feeling exhausted and demoralized. Having braved and fought the experience, we then take stock. Often it is only then that we start to feel tired and drained, and only then do we reflect on how the whirlwind has impacted on our lives. This exhaustion is both emotional and physical. The brain uses up about 20 per cent of the body's total energy supply, so if you're wondering why worrying is so exhausting then reflect on this: during a bout of worry you burn more energy than usual, since mental activity demands energy too. Imagine you are running within a giant hamster wheel for all the time you spend worrying – how exhausting would that be? The sense of demoralization is also influenced by an internal commentary on their worry. Worriers often 'beat themselves up' mentally after the whirlwind has passed; they might berate themselves for having wasted time worrying. Or, if their worry has got in the way of solving a problem or stopped them from doing something important, this can leave them feeling useless and down and full of self-loathing.

Understanding worry – a traffic metaphor

One of the important steps towards overcoming worry is getting a better understanding of what worry is and how it sticks around as a problem. When teaching health professionals about worry, we have found that thinking of worry as a stream of traffic is helpful. We will refer to this traffic metaphor throughout the book.

Learning to manage worry is like trying to manage the flow of traffic at rush hour. Imagine that you have been asked to solve the traffic problems of a major city. How would you go about doing this? Would you head out at each rush hour to direct the traffic? Would you focus your attention on each car or driver and ask them to do things differently? Would you try to understand the things that cause traffic congestion or that make congestion worse?

Would you try to introduce new laws or rules to help people behave differently? You would probably want to start by getting a good idea of what the problem is, so it would make sense to monitor the traffic and understand when, where and what causes the major problems. You could also find out whether particular problems were caused by particular types of vehicles.

As we have said, worry is a chain of thoughts or images that quickly spirals out of control. Trying to stop the flow of worry and to pick on an individual worry is difficult, because once you have worked one worry through another appears hard on its tail. Imagine trying to solve traffic problems by stopping each car and talking over the problem with each driver. What might happen? Would it solve the problem or would it actually make the problem worse? Given that there are thousands of cars, buses and trucks, it is doubtful that this strategy would work.

To understand and improve traffic flow, it appears we have to begin to recognize that we cannot do this by focusing our attention on each car, bus or truck. Instead, we have to think about what influences the flow of traffic, such as types of vehicles (buses or cars), drivers' strongly held beliefs (e.g. that driving is much less hassle than public transport) and other factors such as the school run, the influence of 9–5 working hours, the weather, roadworks, holidays and so forth. By doing this we can begin to understand the ebb and flow of traffic. The crucial message is that we cannot solve traffic problems by focusing our attention on each car. This is also true of worry. Like traffic flow, in order to overcome worry we must attend to the flow of worry and the factors that influence this, rather than focusing on each individual worry (each individual car).

Influences on traffic flow

Living with uncertainty. Uncertainty is an inherent element in travelling, including unforeseen delays, breakdowns, accidents, slow-moving traffic, punctures, debris on the road and so forth. When the flow of traffic is very heavy or if conditions are bad, as in heavy rain, these other factors act together to increase the level of uncertainty, making journey times even more unpredictable. Living with the uncertainty that driving creates is something we have to learn to tolerate in our modern world if we are to get to our destinations without blowing a gasket. Despite having satellite navigation and radio broadcasts telling us where the traffic problems are, we are still in the lap of the gods when driving from A to B. The bottom line is that we have to learn to tolerate the uncertainty.

Driving rules. Other factors that influence traffic flow are the general rules that govern a driver's actions. For example, *If I keep up with the flow of traffic I am less likely to have an accident*; this idea might mean that drivers keep up with the flow of traffic, even when conditions are such that they'd be safer slowing down. *I should never be late*; this idea might result in drivers trying to make up time by speeding when they have been delayed by roadworks. You may believe that *no one should get by me* or that *no one should cut in front of*

8

me; this belief might make you an irritable driver. General rules seem to influence the flow of traffic just as much as weather or roadworks. So, to manage traffic problems we would need to work out which rules were problematic and try to change them.

Types of vehicle. In trying to manage traffic, it also helps to think about vehicle categories. Each type of vehicle may require different traffic-management solutions – the introduction of bus lanes, lower speeds for trucks or crawler lanes on long slow hills, for example.

Unhelpful attitudes to traffic problems, and avoidance. Finally, when trying to approach the problem of traffic management we may be resigned to the idea that traffic problems will never be solved; we may be pessimistic about any solution and intimidated by the size of the problem. This unhelpful stance towards the problem of managing traffic might leave us feeling frustrated or depressed, meaning that we avoid trying to do something about the problem. We might simply *avoid thinking about it* or avoid things that remind us that there is a problem: we may just *bury our head in the sand*.

So how does this help us understand worry?

The nature of worry. First, just as with traffic flow, in order to overcome worry we must attend to the flow of worry and the factors that influence this, rather than focusing on each individual worry. Traffic jams and congestion call for our attention, but to solve them we must concentrate our efforts elsewhere, rather than focusing solely on the traffic itself. With worry this is also true: some of the products of worry might seem to be the things to focus on – for instance, irritability, sleep problems, concentration problems and more – but our attention should be on the things that generate these problems in the first place and on what influences and 'tells' us to worry.

Worries, like traffic problems, do not just appear from nowhere, although they often feel like they do. To overcome your worry you need to be more aware of when and how your worry develops into a whirlwind of worry.

If traffic is blocked in one lane, it finds another way of moving, by changing lanes, using rat runs and short cuts, which also tend to suffer from more and more traffic. Often these rat runs develop on roads that are completely unsuitable, or take us miles out of our way. So, like traffic, worry also has a tendency to spread, change topic and shift, transporting us away from the idea or problem that triggered it in the first place. You will learn to understand more about what triggers your worry and how it develops in Chapters 4 and 5.

Living with uncertainty. There is inherent uncertainty in driving that we have to learn to cope with. Many worriers find uncertain situations intolerable and tend to avoid uncertainty if they can. They often have a series of ideas that suggest to them that uncertainty is a stressful and hazardous experience and should be avoided if possible. We end up deploying worry as a strategy for dealing with all of life's uncertainties, even when worry might be an unsuitable solution to the problems or events we face. In order to overcome your worry you will have to learn to deal more effectively with uncertain situations, by finding other things to do instead of worrying. We will turn to the issue of uncertainty in Chapters 8–11.

Worry rules. Just as there are rules and assumptions that influence drivers and thus the flow of traffic, worriers often have particular rules and ideas that influence their tendency to worry. For example, *If I worry about my family, then it shows I care*, or, *If I worry I will be able to spot problems before they happen*. These rules or beliefs support and maintain your worry, and in order to overcome this you will need to experiment with breaking these rules. We will turn our attention to these rules and assumptions in Chapters 7, 12 and 13.

In trying to fix traffic problems we may frequently do things that seem to improve the situation in the short term, but tend to make the problem worse in the longer term: for example, if you take a short cut to avoid a busy junction, you may be caught in a jam along with all the other drivers who did exactly the same, or heavy traffic might try to use small neighbourhood roads, making them more dangerous. With worry, we often try to manage our worry using 'sensible' strategies. Unfortunately, these have a tendency to backfire and make the worry worse. So we have to help you to recognize how you manage your worry and then ask if this is one of those things that make it worse. We have outlined these unhelpful strategies throughout the book.

Different types of worry. Just as with different types of vehicle, different types of worry require different management strategies. In general, there are two categories of worry

11

to consider: worries about events that have happened (*Real Event Worry*) and worries about things that have not happened yet (*Hypothetical Event Worry*). Again, this reminds us that to overcome our worry we must become much more curious about what types of worry make up the flow. Are we worrying about real events that have happened, or about things in the future that have not happened yet? We will return to this distinction later, when we turn our attention in Chapter 5 to recognizing the different types of worry, but just keep this in mind for now.

Unhelpful attitudes to problems and avoidance. In order to begin to solve the problem of traffic flow, we have to engage with the problem. Worriers tend to have an unhelpful attitude towards problems. Typically, they see problems as threatening; they doubt their ability to cope with them and, even if they do try to engage in problem solving, they are pessimistic about the outcome. So in order for us to help you overcome worry, you will need to adjust your view of problems and remind yourself that you have the capacity to solve them successfully. You will learn more about problem solving in Chapters 14–16.

Worriers tend to avoid situations that might trigger worry or they try to block the worry out of their minds. Like many other things, if worry is not dealt with it will keep coming back, since unfinished business has a tendency to keep popping up into our minds. We will turn our attention to facing your fears in Chapter 17–18.

Measuring change. We need to monitor what happens when we try to change things. Throughout this book there are rating scales, questionnaires and ideas to help you do just this.

Summary. Ultimately, to solve the problem of traffic flow, we will need to reduce the number of vehicles using a particular lane or road. So the problem needs to be solved in a different way than by using short-term strategies. It is the same with worry: we need to stop the worries 'getting on the road' by finding new and better ways of working with them.

Stories of worry

The following stories describe how excessive worry can impact on people's lives. They illustrate the way worriers tend to think, some of the consequences of their worry and some underlying themes. It might be worth making notes and asking yourself the following questions as you go through them; Exercise 1.1 may help you do this (see pages 20–21).

- Is there an aspect of this person's story that reminds me of myself? If so, what is it?
- Which story feels closest to home and why?
- What has been going through my mind as I read these accounts?
- What links these stories together?

These stories are based on the worriers we have worked with in our careers. They are not modelled on any one person but have been put together to describe the typical patterns we see in our clinics.

ALISON

Alison is in her late forties. Her three children are still living at home. She feels tense the whole time and worries about her blood pressure. She loves her job, but finds it very stressful and from time to time too much to cope with. She has recently been promoted to a senior administrative role, and heads up a small but talented team. She finds it hard to delegate and does too much of the work herself. It's not that she doubts the quality of her colleagues' work but she knows that *even good people can make mistakes*. She checks her own work repeatedly and never sends an email without reading it several times. She worries especially on a Friday night and will often drop in to work at the weekend to check things over.

Recently she wanted to buy a new digital camera to take pictures at her son's twenty-first birthday, but she couldn't decide which one to get. She visited nearly every shop and received conflicting advice. She worried: *What if I make a bad decision? If I do, I may not understand the instructions, and if I take the photos I could annoy everyone by being intrusive.* Her worries went on and on. Paralysed by them, in the end she gave up on buying the camera. She regretted this and felt ashamed that her worry had got the better of her. She always phones her husband to check he is on his way home, and worries if her husband or children are late. Often she builds horror stories in her mind as her worries take hold. She is a lovely woman and is loved by her family and friends; but they get annoyed with her because she's very protective of them and she often needs reassuring that they are OK. When she gets worn out with worry her concern turns out the wrong way; her kids feel she is intrusive, her husband feels he is alternately nagged and asked to be a rock of security.

JOSÉ

José is a divorcee with two children, aged ten and twelve. He has a new relationship with a younger woman called Jane, who wants to have a family with him. His job is secure, but he gets very tense and agitated when he hears rumours about how things might change. Since his divorce he has lost confidence and worries about his ability to cope with his busy job, his children and his new relationship. Jane is great with his kids, but he is concerned that she will leave him in the same way his wife did. He feels tense and notices that he is snappy with the kids. He finds himself daydreaming about his future, when all he can see is catastrophe after catastrophe: *What if the kids don't manage the divorce? They may start to fail at school, and then they'll start to take drugs; they'll wind up in jail; they'll hate me and never want to speak to me again. And then Jane will leave me and I'll lose my job* . . . His worries whirl on and on and leave him anxious and upset. Although José knows that these are 'just' worries, he sometimes feels they are real, which makes him anxious that he is losing his mind. He is confused because he thinks if he didn't worry about

15

his children he'd be a poor father. He knows he is starting to spoil his children by giving them too much, but
he can't help himself. Spending extra money makes
him worry about his finances and he becomes irritable
with himself, which spoils the time he has with his children. He never used to worry; before the divorce his
life was planned out and he knew where he was going.
His divorce really unsettled him, and at the moment he
doesn't think he can really rely on anything. He hates
his life being so uncertain.

ALEX

Alex is twenty-three. He's full of nervous energy and
rarely sits still for long. He makes impulsive decisions
that sometimes work out for him but usually end up
badly. As a consequence, he has debt problems: he
bought warranties he didn't need, and he is locked
into an expensive mobile phone contract. When faced
with a decision, he would rather act than live with the
overwhelming sense of uncertainty. He is good at his
job. He is never late for work, but all the way there
he thinks about what will happen if he is late: *What if
I'm late? I'll miss that meeting and lose my job*. His anxiety triggers more worries and he starts to worry that
he will miss his stop. He listens to music on his MP3
player, but pulls the headphones off to make sure he
hasn't missed anything. He checks his ticket for the
number of the bus, even though he knows he's on
the right one. By the time he gets to work he's

exhausted. His worry follows him throughout the day, into the office, into meetings, into telephone conversations, at lunchtime and breaktime. He has avoided promotion at work because he doesn't think he could cope with the new challenges this would bring. He recently started to worry more about terrorist attacks and put off going on holiday with his friends, not sure if he'd be safe at the airport. Nor does he think he could cope with being severely injured or burnt. He hates himself for worrying so much, but also thinks that his worry helps him to spot dangers, keeps him safe and solves problems.

MAYA

Maya is fifteen and lives at home with her mum and younger brother. She is bright and could do well at school but worries about her work and about fitting in. She describes herself as a perfectionist and works really hard to make sure that her worries don't come true. She makes a great friend and helps others when she can. She tells her friends about her worries, but, at the same time, fears that her friends won't want to know her if she keeps bothering them. She feels confused and alone. Worrying helps her to plan and prepare for exams; she says it keeps her motivated. However, worrying also makes her much less efficient because she worries much more than she actually works, though her friends say she spends too much time working. She doesn't want to stand out and so she never goes out without texting her friends, to make sure she is wearing the 'right' clothes. When she is out, she worries about lots of things, including whether she is in the right place to meet her friends, about her studies, about what her friends might think of her and about finding her way home. All these worries make it almost impossible for her to enjoy being with her friends.

PAUL

Paul recently turned sixty and retired from work. He was a successful engineer and is in a supportive, solid marriage. He planned wisely for his retirement and has sound investments and a good pension. Despite being financially secure, he worries about whether he has chosen the best investments and has recently taken to continually comparing his investments with others on the Internet. His children are grown up and he has several grandchildren; some he sees regularly, the others live too far away. He is fit and well but since his retirement his mind has started to focus on his health. He has also been thinking more about his family and how he should make more effort to hold them together. At night he spends hours worrying about them, his health, his financial situation and about being a burden to his children. He recently took out more insurance to cover the gaps that his other insurance policies didn't cover. He worries about whether his kids will look after one another, and about the health of his grandchildren. Although his children are in good relationships, he has doubts about how long their relationships will last. His worries go round like a carousel, one after the other, and lead him to some very dark places; to him they seem out of his control and he drinks in order to sleep. He keeps his worries to himself, because he fears burdening his wife and making her ill.

Getting better

We know from research that roughly two-thirds of worriers get much better when they follow the treatment programmes that use the type of approach found in this book; the other third will also get some form of relief. Furthermore, the gains made can be long lasting and, with careful follow-up plans, worry can become a thing of the past rather than a current problem. While we recognize that one-to-one therapy is different from a self-help approach, in our experience as therapists nearly all the people we see report some benefit from taking a closer look at the things that start them worrying and keep them worrying. So keep this mind. Is this something that you would want to have a go at? The book will draw your attention to worry, which may feel uncomfortable, but by understanding worry you will be better placed to overcome it.

Exercise 1.1 is the first step in bringing your mind to think about your worry. As you read the stories above, aspects of the stories may have hit home for you. Table 1.1 will help you to think about this further and about what life might be like if you worried less.

EXERCISE 1.1: REFLECTIONS

Use a notebook to write down your answers to these questions.

My reflections on the case stories

Which story feels closest to home? Why is this? Which aspects of the stories remind you of your own experiences?

Do these stories tell you anything about your worry? If so, what?

What has been going through your mind as you read these stories?

Are there things that tie these case stories together? What themes or commonalities stand out for you?

Thinking about what you have written so far, do you have any ideas about what you might want to try to change?

If you did change the things mentioned in the question above, what difference would that make to your life? Is that something you want to invest time in?

Complete the following sentences:

If worry was less of a problem for me then . . .

It would mean . . .

I could . . .

I would be able to . . .

I might be able to . . .

I want to . . .

We asked a number of non-therapists to read these stories and give us feedback on what they thought tied them together. We thought you might like to see their responses. They appear more or less as they were given to us, edited only to make them clearer. Responses that seemed to us particularly important are in italics. Do these responses add to your understanding? What have they picked up on? Do any of the features feel like something close to home? You may want to revisit your own responses and add to them. Have your goals changed as a result?

Table 1.1: Responses to the case stories

Response 1:

All want to be in control, but can't quite manage it.

Low personal confidence.

Their focus seems to be on what they can't control rather than what they can.

No direction for the future (no positive goal to aim for).

Personal insecurity (not having the courage of their convictions).

Social expectations – how to meet them? (Alex was a salesman's dream, Paul and Alison had to provide for extended family, Maya wants to be perfect, etc.).

Obsession.

Expanding range of worries (i.e. one building on top of another).

Rather than addressing the root concern, focusing on ways to manage (e.g. drinks in order to sleep, looking for issues that don't exist).

None is happy or content.

Loss: they each stand to lose (family, friends, job) if their worry comes true.

Response 2:

Worries/concerns about decisions seem to be the manifestation of the problem (whether it be investments, what to wear, what to buy, or what bus they're on . . .).

So, probably associated with a lack of confidence in their own decisions, and maybe even low self-esteem or the belief that they are not valued.

That nothing will ever be OK, no matter what one does.

Sometime this is associated with major changes (e.g. José's divorce, Paul's retirement), sometimes just with the stresses of everyday life (Maya, Alison, José).

So much is triggered by major or minor life changes (or the fear of them), which shows that life is not stable or predictable. Their response to this is to try to cover all possibilities to ensure nothing bad happens, which no one can ever do.

Trying to control outcomes to minimize risk (e.g. cross-checking everything, not sharing responsibility with others).

All rob the individual of the ability to live in the moment even if something is not going wrong at the time; their worries are about what might be.

They all start out as good or reasonable values (e.g. Paul's care and responsibility for the family, Alison's care of friends, family and high standards at work, Maya's 'motivation' to do well, José's concern for his children, his wanting to do his job well) but they end up being motivated by fear, not positive outcomes, and their worries become generalised and spiral out of control.

Response 3:

Seeking reassurance.

Extremely high personal standards.

Difficulty in making decisions.

Looking for info from lots of sources.

Critical of self for being like this.

Low expectations of others.

Chain of thoughts leading to catastrophizing.

Something about uncertainty.

Living in the future, not in the here and now.

Response 4:

Uncontrollable nature of worry.

Worry is event-related and its content is related to experience and future-orientated.

There are positive and negative aspects of worry.

Individuals' perceptions of worry and how this feeds worry.

Lots of *what ifs*. Dislike of vagueness. Feels a burden.

The silent burden of worry

As can be seen from the above, worry can have extensive and often devastating effects on people's lives. Worry is a burden. It is like living each day as if carrying the weight of one's own world on one's shoulders. Worry saps our energy and leaves us feeling tense. It interferes with our lives: we have to plan for it, we give in to it, we accommodate it, and it pushes us to avoid situations where we know it will get worse. For some, it stops career plans, it interferes with relationships, and life goals are suspended as a consequence. Often we are so used to carrying the burden of worry that we forget how much it is impacting on our lives – it has become a damaging habit that we no longer even notice.

Pinning our colours to the mast

Well, we all would worry about that, so what's the problem? He's a worrier – he's always like that, he's not happy unless he has something to worry about.

Does this sound familiar? Worry is normal. We all worry. But we would also like to make clear a few key messages. First, we believe that excessive worry should not be accepted as a normal response to all life events, nor should it be accepted as part of someone's personality. Second, excessive worry is not something that just happens: the process of worry can be understood. We can understand it and we can outline the factors that start us worrying and those that keep us worrying. Third, for individuals who suffer with excessive worry these processes have usually become automatic. Fourth, once people understand the processes, they can begin to change how they think about and react to worrisome situations and thus learn to worry less. Finally, in order to modify the habitual way of reacting (i.e. worrying), individuals need to be willing to try out new things, to learn to focus their attention on what keeps worry alive, to reflect on the experience of worrying and then, once they understand how it works, to adopt a new way of reacting: then to *practise* these processes over and over until new more helpful patterns are firmly established.

You **can** overcome your worry. You **can** learn to worry less. You **can** lessen the burden of worry you carry.

Pit stops

Throughout this book you will find pit stops. These are to encourage you to get into the habit of stopping and reviewing what you have read. Do this as often as you need to. The pit stops will prompt you, but if you are confused, then stop and think about what you understand and what you don't understand. Write it down and return to it once you have read further. In order to get things clear in your mind, take your time and reread passages if necessary.

Here is the first one:

PIT STOP

Let's stop and think about what you have just been read-ing. Can you summarize the key ideas you have taken on board? What is sticking in your mind? Maybe write them down. If you have any questions, jot these down too. You can return to them once you have had a chance to digest the information.

What is sticking in my mind from my reading so far?

1.

2.

3.

Using this book

How can I be sure the advice given is good?

The National Institute for Health and Care Excellence (NICE) is an independent organization responsible for providing national guidance on the promotion of good health and the prevention and treatment of ill health in the UK. In 2011 NICE updated their guidance on anxiety, and recommended that high levels of worry, or Generalised Anxiety Disorder (GAD), its medical name, should be treated by using a psychological therapy called cognitive behavioural therapy (CBT). You will find more information about CBT in Chapter 4. NICE also recommended using self-help approaches based on CBT principles, especially as a first step; this self-help book on worry is based on CBT principles. The way that worry is described in this book, and the ideas the book suggests to help you overcome it, are also based on up-to-date research and the best psychological understanding of GAD or worry. *Overcoming Worry* is the product of several different groups of researchers from around the world who have worked on worry, some of them for nearly thirty years.

Worry is very common among the general population and so not everyone who worries will have all of the symptoms of GAD (you will find more about the diagnosis of GAD and facts about worry in Chapter 3). This book aims to help both those who suffer from this clinical disorder and those who feel that they are worrying more than they would like to.

How to use this book

1. Getting this book is a good first step to overcoming your worry. However, reading and then applying the ideas it contains are crucial. This may well sound obvious, but from our personal experience it is very easy to feel as if we are *doing* something about our problems by *thinking* about them. So the first piece of advice is this: once you have a copy, make sure you read this book and then follow the advice it contains. This book will help you to: engage in new experiences to overcome your worry; learn to be curious about your worry and observe it; develop a better understanding of your worry; and to do things differently to overcome your worry. The crucial step is putting new ideas into practice, doing things differently and reacting in new ways to your worry.

2. Don't try to read this book all at once – pick a chapter or a few pages and focus on these. If you are worrying a lot this often makes concentration very difficult. If your worry makes you hop from one thought or subject to the next, then having a small goal is better than trying to read a whole chapter at

once. You may find it helpful to ask yourself, *What was I doing* [e.g. reading] *before I started to worry?* And then return to doing it.

3. Make notes: have a pen and a notebook with you as you read. Drawing pictures or diagrams may also help. If this is your copy then allow yourself to scribble notes and underline the sentences or sections that are most relevant to you. This book is a tool and needs to be used and engaged with.

4. Is there someone you can read the book with? Some of us find talking about ideas and having conversations more effective than trying to understand things on our own.

5. Plan some time alone with the book. Are there quieter times in your day or week? Is there somewhere you can go where you will not be disturbed? Maybe take the book out for a coffee! Are you a better reader in the morning, afternoon or evening?

6. Is now the best time for you to try to overcome your worry? If there are difficult life events such as births, marriages, new jobs, promotions, or moving house, then it might be better to wait until you have some stability in your life before attempting change. However, our lives are full of challenges and big events, and waiting for a quiet moment may be ill-advised, so be aware of the tendency to avoid facing your problems. Ask yourself these questions: *Am I putting off starting because I am worried about the outcome? Am I putting 'imaginary problems or issues' in the way of*

30

trying something new? What would you advise a friend to do, if they were considering trying to overcome their worry now?

7. Write down the advantages and disadvantages of overcoming your worry. When you consider what you have written, where does the balance lie?

Can I use this book if I am taking medication?

Family doctors and psychiatrists often prescribe medication to help with anxiety and worry. Many people we meet in our clinical work have taken or are currently taking medication to help with their psychological problems. We would generally offer them psychological treatment even when they are on a prescribed medication, and the effect of this drug is taken into consideration when developing the treatment plan. So, in short, you can still use this book even if you're taking medication. If you're concerned, then have a conversation with your family doctor or other health professional; it might be helpful to take this book with you to show them. Together you can decide on what is the best course of action.

If you are already on medication, then it's probably better to continue with it and work on your worry until it starts to improve. Once this has happened, then might be the time to visit your family doctor to review your medication. On the other hand, if you have just started taking medication, this may not be the best time to begin working on your worry. Stability is the link here; it is better to hold one thing constant while you change the other than to try changing everything at once. Or, put another way, it is best not to widen the roads, put in traffic lights, start a bus lane, introduce congestion-charging and a new one-way system all at the same time. One step at a time, one problem at a time.

You may also want to visit the website of the National Institute for Health and Care Excellence (NICE), where you will find more information about GAD and drug treatments (see also Appendix 6).

If you are really not coping, please visit your family doctor.

Your approach to this book

This book is about learning to do things in a different way. When we are learning new skills or tasks, it is not unusual to feel unsettled or nervous and you will worry about change. These things are not the signs of progress, however; the new experience or learning or opportunities that improve our lives are the real signs of positive change. Anxiety or nervousness can close down our mind by drawing our attention to worrisome thoughts, which in turn makes learning much harder. So, trying to *keep your mind open to new ideas is important*. As Sir James Dewar, a Scottish chemist and physicist said, 'Minds are like parachutes, they work best when open.' Keeping your mind open means being prepared to listen to new ideas or trying new skills even if they make you feel anxious. Another way of keeping your mind open is to become more aware of your worry and to pay attention to it rather than just being 'in' it; this is like stepping out of the traffic flow and sitting on a bridge to observe. Self-observation enables the development of new perspectives, which in turn will help you to understand your worry and overcome it. In following this book you will become better at self-observation and consequently become more aware of your worry. We will help you to develop a better understanding of worry and will then suggest exercises, ideas and practical advice for overcoming worry.

This book does not offer a miraculous cure. Remember – worry is normal and we all worry from time to time. So trying to rid your life of a normal, everyday mental activity is impossible. What we can try to do, however, is 'turn down the worry dial', so that you worry less. This book is about helping you deal with your worry in an effective way. As a rule of thumb, the more you apply yourself to the ideas found in this book, the more you will get out of it. The journey you are about to embark on will require hard work, but if you apply yourself then the least that will happen is that you will understand more about worry, and at best you may learn to worry less. Is this something you would value?

The consequences of worrying less

In our clinical work we find that some people, when they start to get better and their worry becomes less of a problem, begin to look back on their lives and feel sad for the time they have lost through worrying. It's almost as if they are grieving for a life that could have been, a life without worry. Worry has such a pervasive and eroding effect that, once it is less of a problem, we see more clearly how our lives have been affected. This phase will pass as you learn to accept your past and embrace your future. This is something to bear in mind particularly if you have worried and tended to avoid change; it is not a sign of things getting worse, or a sign that you have traded one problem for another, but a natural consequence of moving on.

PIT STOP

Let's stop and think about what you have just been reading. Can you summarize the key ideas you have taken on board? What is sticking in your mind? Maybe write them down. If you have any questions, jot these down too. You can return to them once you have had a chance to digest the information.

What is sticking in my mind from my reading so far?

1.

2.

3.

Everyday and problem worry – introducing Generalised Anxiety Disorder

Worry is a normal process

All of us worry. Worry is a normal process. Research suggests that whether we worry a lot or a little we all worry more or less about the same kinds of things. From time to time we may worry about our families, relationships, our working or school lives, health or finances. For people who worry excessively, though, the problem is not so much what things they worry about – these are common to us all – but more the ease with which they fall into worrying. There are some subtle differences between people who worry excessively and others. For example, people who worry excessively worry much more about minor things – catching the bus or train, minor car repairs, forgetting groceries, being late, a glass of wine, a rare sugary treat, buying a small gift – the list of minor, everyday things that people worry about is endless and these minor experiences can quickly telescope into major worries of disastrous proportions. A Swedish proverb captures well this idea: it tells us that 'worry gives small things a big shadow'. Worriers also tend to worry more about remote or unlikely events: for example, a father worrying about how he would cope with his grandchildren, even though his own children were still in nappies; or a woman worrying about the possibility of rain ruining her daughter's wedding even though the wedding was still seven months away; or someone worrying about the possibility of a flight being cancelled, while sitting at home booking a summer holiday in January. Sometimes worriers can worry about the future with no specific threat in mind, just a sense of impending doom.

'Big occasion' worry

Chronic or habitual worriers need to learn to keep worry for the 'big occasion', when it can be of some use. With big events, worry may help to anticipate danger, solve problems, motivate to action, protect, or show caring. With these types of events, the downside of worrying – namely the high degree of preoccupation with it and the inability to turn it off, the muscle tension, the inability to sleep, the uncomfortable feelings of anxiety – may be an acceptable price. This type of worry means that we are engaged in trying to deal with a situation that really is there and can't be dealt with by ignoring it or running away. It normally means that something important to us is being threatened in some way. It may be possible to meet big occasion problems with calmness and detachment, but most people, even those who are not worriers, will worry in these situations.

The muscle tension means that we are ready to act, the preoccupation means that we are engaged in thinking about the situation, and the disturbed sleep tells us that this is top priority stuff. We find concentrating on other tasks difficult: the big occasion worry demands our attention, and since we are in a state of alertness so we feel restless. Being on guard and ready for action means that we are prepared to act, but also means that we are overly alert and sensitive, which often translates into irritability.

The problem for worriers is that they use worry as a way of reacting to everyday life events as well as these big occasions. In these everyday incidents using worry can be thought of as using a sledgehammer to crack a nut. Worry is therefore a mismatch for events that are highly unlikely, or that are so far in the future that we can't do anything about them, or for things that are not really here right now or just around the corner.

Most people will automatically worry when it really matters, but the worried mind is unfortunately hyperactive, unfocused, repetitive and undermining. To get the better of worry we have to learn to save it for the big occasions and not use it as a *one-size-fits-all* approach to everything in life. The goal of overcoming worry is to get to this point where worry is no longer an omnipresent, costly and exhausting approach to life, but a state of mind that is active, focused, creative and commanding when the situation truly demands it. We want to enable you to apply worry in short bursts for the big occasions at the right time, rather than for long periods at the wrong time.

Differences between excessive worry and everyday worry

In general, the difference between excessive and everyday worry is a matter of degree rather than outright difference. Unsurprisingly, chronic worriers tend to worry more often and for longer periods of time than people with everyday worry, and they tend to believe that their worry is more out of control. However, worry is a common, everyday experience, and from time to time each of us might feel we worry too much, or that worry has taken over. This suggests that everyday worry and excessive worry run on more or less the same tracks. We can begin to think of worry as existing on a continuum or dimension, and whether you worry a little or a lot, the same underlying processes are at work. This idea is also a central principle of cognitive behavioural therapy or CBT, which suggests that psychological problems are exaggerated or extreme versions of everyday experiences. In Figure 3.1, worry is demonstrated on a worry gauge. This diagram illustrates that worry exists on a scale or dimension from 'no worry' to 'severe worry'. At times we all can experience the severe end of worry, and our worry gauges are constantly fluctuating in response to life events and how we think about them. For example, most people suffer a bout of severe worry (spiking into the 'red') before an important exam, job interview or tough meeting; they may also have a fitful night of sleep beforehand. In these cases, severe bouts of worry tend to appear before and during major life events. Those who suffer with excessive worry not only worry in response to these major events but also about minor events.

Such minor events are usually much more frequent, and as a result their worry gauge is often in the 'red'. If they notice that their worry gauge is not in the red (i.e. that they are not worrying), further worry may also be triggered, yet again pushing their gauge up into the red. It is not surprising that worriers suffer with other signs of anxiety as well, such as restlessness, irritability, difficulty in sleeping, fatigue, muscle tension and concentration problems.

When worry tends to stray and stay in the red, and when worry feels more out of control and couples with other signs of anxiety, the individual may be given a diagnosis of Generalised Anxiety Disorder, or GAD for short; the symptoms of GAD are listed on pages 41–3.

Figure 3.1: Worry gauge

- Where would you put your average worry on this gauge? Put a line there.
- Where would you like it to be (remembering that worry is normal)? Put a second line there.

Please remember that worry is normal and that this book will not eliminate worry completely. But it can help you to turn down the worry dial.

The diagnosis of Generalised Anxiety Disorder (GAD)

Classifying a problem like worry with a psychiatric label (a diagnosis) can be considered either helpful or frankly unhelpful, depending on your viewpoint. There is much controversy and debate about the usefulness of diagnosis. However, in our clinical experience we have found that, for the most part, the people we have worked with have been relieved or found it helpful to find a label or name for their problem – often because their problem had been previously missed or, worse, dismissed. For the clinician, a diagnostic label may also be a guide to the right kind of treatment. On balance we think it's worthwhile spending time in helping you to understand what GAD is. Below you will read an extract from the fourth edition of the *Diagnostic and Statistical Manual of Mental Disorders* (DSM-5, 2013, American Psychiatric Association). This is a handbook for mental health professionals: it lists different categories of psychological problems and the criteria for diagnosing them. The American Psychiatric Association published the previous version in 1994; it has recently been updated as our understanding improves and as we get better at describing psychological problems more accurately.

In brief, and as we have stated above, the key features

of GAD are excessive and uncontrollable worry about a number of different subjects, together with other symptoms of anxiety. Take a moment to read through the criteria. Which statements apply to you?

Diagnostic Criteria for Generalised Anxiety Disorder

- Excessive anxiety and worry (apprehensive expectation), occurring more days than not for at least six months, about a number of events or activities (such as work or school performance).
- The person finds it difficult to control the worry.
- The anxiety and worry are associated with three (or more) of the following six symptoms (with at least some symptoms present for more days than not for the past six months).
    - ° Restlessness or feeling keyed up or on edge
    - ° Being easily fatigued
    - ° Difficulty concentrating or mind going blank
    - ° Irritability
    - ° Muscle tension
    - ° Sleep disturbance (difficulty falling or staying asleep, or restless unsatisfying sleep).
- The anxiety, worry, or physical symptoms cause clinically significant distress or impairment in social, occupational or other important areas of functioning.
- The disturbance is not attributable to the physiological effects of a substance (e.g. a drug of abuse, a medication) or general medical condition (e.g. hyperthyroidism).

41

- The disturbance is not better explained by another mental disorder.

Source: reprinted with permission from the American Psychiatric Association. *American Psychiatric Association: Diagnostic and Statistical Manual of Mental Disorders*, Fifth Edition. Arlington, VA, American Psychiatric Association, 2013.

Of course, you may not have full-blown GAD, but you may still worry a lot. For example, research has shown that not everyone who suffers with excessive worry will have three out of the six required symptoms for the required time. In fact, research using questionnaire data and informal observations of people who attend for treatment suggests that a significant proportion of worriers can have the typical psychological profile (such as excessive worry and a belief that their worry is out of control) but do not suffer the associated physical symptoms. Some people tell us that they worry infrequently, say once a month, but when they do worry they do so severely, sometimes worrying for days at a time. Furthermore, the profile of worry can shift and change over time; so, one week or month a particular symptom such as sleeplessness is dominant, the next week or month another comes to the fore, such as irritability.

Of the associated symptoms found in chronic worriers, muscle tension seems to be more specific to GAD than any other and may be the best current unique predictor of excessive worry. However, muscular tension may not improve in everyone when worry decreases; so it's not a foolproof marker for everyone who worries. A wide range of other physical symptoms has been reported in worriers; these appear in the lists below. Although these are linked to GAD and can be common, they are not symptoms that contribute towards the diagnosis.

Other common physical symptoms linked to GAD

- Upset stomach
- Headaches
- Dry mouth
- Peeing more often

- Being very jumpy
- Feeling shaky
- Nausea
- Diarrhoea

- Heart flutters
- Sweating
- Tremor
- Difficulty swallowing

Other common experiences linked to GAD

- Feeling tuned out
- Unable to focus
- Nail biting

- Feeling isolated
- Feeling jittery
- Sense of impending doom

- Feeling alone
- Alcohol problems
- Pacing the floor

Although the formal diagnostic criteria are helpful, they are essentially a guide – many people with disabling and distressing experiences of worry fall outside the diagnostic framework.

SUMMARY BOX

GAD = **G**eneralised **A**nxiety **D**isorder

GAD = EXCESSIVE, UNCONTROLLABLE WORRY ABOUT SEVERAL SITUATIONS OR EVENTS

Worry and other psychological problems

Anxiety problems tend to hunt in packs, and the vast majority of individuals with GAD will have at least one other coexistent psychological problem. 'Pure' GAD is therefore rare. Like salt, probably the most common ingredient in recipes, worry appears as the most common extra ingredient in other psychological problems. The most common problems that coexist with worry are depressive disorders, and about 70 per cent of people with GAD will report depressive problems at different times. Many people with GAD may also suffer from another anxiety problem such as social phobia, panic attacks or health anxiety.

Other anxiety problems that coexist with GAD

There are three main types of coexistence. The first is where GAD is the main or primary problem and the other anxiety problems are secondary. The second is the other way round, when GAD is secondary to other primary anxiety problems. The third is when it is hard to tell which problem is the primary or secondary problem and the problems appear as equals. It is worth bearing this in mind while reflecting on your difficulties, because knowing whether your worry is primary or secondary will help you to know which problems to work on first. We will explain this further below.

Let's take the first of these. For many people, moderate to severe GAD may be accompanied by other mild to moderate anxiety problems such as social phobia (fear of what others think of you) or specific phobias (fear of spiders, dogs, heights). These secondary problems are more likely to get better on their own during successful GAD treatment. So the simple message is this: if GAD is the main problem, then work on this and the other problems will, in all likelihood, disappear. However, for some worriers these secondary problems may require attention in their own right.

The second way that GAD coexists is as a secondary problem. In this case it makes sense to focus on the more problematic difficulty first. For example, in situations where someone is suffering with moderate to severe obsessive compulsive disorder, post-traumatic stress disorder, panic, agoraphobia or social phobia, with secondary GAD, we should treat these primary problems first. (There are self-help books written for each of these problems in the *Overcoming* series.) It is worth mentioning that often, as these primary problems are treated, the person with GAD may feel that their worry problem is getting worse. However, this is a case of being able to see more of an object as the tide recedes; the object was always a certain size, but as you see more of it, it looks bigger. So, in these cases, worry *feels* as if it's getting worse but is not *actually* getting worse. Of course, once the first problem has been addressed then we would expect to turn our attention to treating the GAD.

The third coexistence pattern is when neither problem appears to be the main problem. In these cases, the problems have equal weight and we have to try to make a decision about which one to tackle first. We may decide to work on the one that will shift more easily or address one problem and see how this affects the second.

If this is hard to follow, then drop in to see your family doctor to talk it through.

Depression and GAD

Depressive symptoms are normal in moderate to severe GAD. When depression appears as a secondary problem it is often typified by exhaustion and demoralization rather than clinical depression. Worry is an extremely tiring activity; just remember the last time you worried about and then attended an interview. While the interview may have lasted only twenty to thirty minutes, afterwards you may have felt exhausted. Without the focus, drive or energy of the worry, you may also have felt deflated. When we are trying to separate the typical type of depression that comes with GAD from clinical depression we have to look closely at some of the specific symptoms of depression that may not fit with GAD. For example, individuals suffering from clinical depression may experience sadness or weeping, a generalised loss of interest, loss or gain in weight, a noticeable and significant change in their appetite, over-activity or under-activity, poor self-worth, excessive guilt and suicidal thoughts.

Another feature of depression, which is very similar to worry, is rumination. When cows chew the cud, they are essentially re-chewing grass they ate earlier. (They are called ruminants, and this is where the word comes from.) Put simply, rumination is going over and over *past* events or negative experiences, whereas worry is more often about *future* events or things that have not happened yet, but seem as if they could or will. Rumination is mostly associated with low mood or depression, and worry with anxiety. It appears that people who worry will also probably ruminate on past events. It might be that we flip-flop between worry and rumination, moving from thinking about past events to then thinking about how these events might influence our future. As we move from one to the other, the signature emotion may change from depression to anxiety and back again. Both rumination and worry are like our thoughts going round and round in a washing machine, and both can be intensified or 'put into a spin cycle' by other thoughts, such as *I'm losing my mind*, or *I'll feel like this forever.* see the diagram below.

Figure 3.2: The relationship between rumination and worry

If you're feeling depressed and you're not sure whether it's because of your worry or whether it's a problem in its own right, then we would suggest you visit your family doctor and discuss these ideas further.

Irrespective of where your worry sits on the worry gauge, we hope this book will have something in it to help you. In short, a diagnosis is not needed for you to get something from this book. When we talk about chronic worriers or people with severe worry, we are referring to people whose worry is interfering with their lives, irrespective of whether they have been given a diagnosis of GAD.

The DSM-5 criteria are used to formally diagnose GAD. On pages 50–51 is a questionnaire based on the DSM. This has been developed to make it easier to spot whether worry is a significant problem. Please spend a few moments completing it. We will discuss what it reveals in due course.

Problems with spotting GAD

One of the main difficulties in spotting problematic worry is that health professionals may not ask the right questions at the right time. This happens for many reasons, but a principal cause is that people with chronic worry tend to worry more when stressful life events happen (e.g. a daughter's wedding, job deadlines, exams). At these stressful times, worriers suffer with more worry, which produces anxiety symptoms (e.g. muscular tension, sleep disturbance or concentration problems). The increase in these symptoms eventually leads them to visit their family doctor or other professional. Unfortunately, the worry is commonly seen as normal because the health professional assumes that everyone worries about such stressful events. As a result, clinically significant worry is often overlooked. If worry as the central problem is overlooked, the person's problems go unrecognized and they fail to find the help they need to target their problem. The person may begin to think that this is something they have to just live with. Alternatively, they may blame themselves for worrying, or they may begin to view their excessive worry as normal or as part of their personality. It's almost as if the belief that *I am a worrier* is the only answer. As we have mentioned, worry is often a 'silent problem', like carrying a heavy weight; worriers may simply just get used to carrying the burden, but the impact on the lives of worriers is immense.

Getting better at spotting worry as a problem

Remember the questions posed at the beginning of this book (see pages xi–xii). These are the critical questions we ask in our clinical assessments to help us work out if someone is suffering with excessive worry or full-blown GAD. These need to be taken together with the diagnostic criteria to reach a formal diagnosis, but they are helpful, straightforward questions that will help you to assess whether worry is a significant problem in your life. Please review them.

You may need to help your doctor or other health professional to understand more about your experience of worry. On the next page is a questionnaire developed by a group of researchers in Canada. It is designed as a quick way of spotting excessive worry and helping to diagnose GAD. If you want help to work on your worry, you may want to take it along with you to show your doctor or health professional.

It is worth bearing in mind that mental health professionals are often anxious about accepting the idea that we have a particular problem without investigating the problem for themselves. They may be a little sceptical, but that is probably helpful. They will help you to stand back and think carefully about what is going on for you and consider all the things that are having an influence on your problems. Don't be put off by this: overall, health professionals think it is better to be careful and thorough than obliging and potentially careless.

WORRY AND ANXIETY QUESTIONNAIRE

For numbers 2 to 4 and 6, circle the numbers most relevant to you.

1. What subjects do you worry about most often?

    a)   d)

    b)   e)

    c)   f)

2. Do your worries seem excessive or exaggerated?

0	1	2	3	4	5	6	7	8
Not at all excessive				Moderately excessive				Totally excessive

3. Over the past six months, how many days have you been bothered by excessive worry?

0	1	2	3	4	5	6	7	8
Never				One day out of two				Everyday

---

4. Do you have difficulty controlling your worries? For example, when you start worrying about something, do you have difficulty stopping?

0	1	2	3	4	5	6	7	8
No difficulty				Moderately difficult				Totally difficult

5 Over the past six months, to what extent have you been disturbed by the following sensations when you were worried or anxious?

Rate *each* sensation with the following scale:

0	1	2	3	4	5	6	7	8
No at all				Moderately				Very severely

_____ Restlessness or feeling keyed up or on edge

_____ Being easily fatigued

_____ Difficulty concentrating or mind going blank

_____ Irritability

_____ Muscle tension

_____ Sleep disturbance (difficulty falling or staying asleep, or restless unsatisfying sleep)

6. To what extent does worry or anxiety interfere with your life; for example, your work, social activities, family life, etc.?

0	1	2	3	4	5	6	7	8
No at all				Moderately				Very severely

How to review the Worry and Anxiety Questionnaire

This questionnaire has been used extensively in research and has been found to be a good way of working out whether someone has a problem with worry or not. You will notice that all the questions on the Worry and Anxiety Questionnaire are scored on a 0–8 scale. If you have scored 4 or more on most of the items, then this suggests that excessive worry is a problem that you may need to face up to. If you score between 2 and 3 on most items, then it still may be helpful for you to learn more about how to turn down your worry dial.

What questions did you score most highly on?

Which symptoms of anxiety do you experience most severely?

Getting a snapshot of the level of your worry

Below is one of the most widely used questionnaires for assessing worry; it is called the Penn State Worry Questionnaire. Professor Tom Borkovec and his colleagues at Pennsylvania State University developed this question-naire in the late 1980s and early 1990s. It measures an indi-vidual's tendency to worry and enables comparisons to be made with other people who worry excessively. You may wish to fill it in at regular intervals to track your progress (once every two weeks perhaps: see Appendix 4 for a form to help you with this).

Please see below for the instructions – in particular the importance in reversing score items 1, 3, 8, 10 and 11. Take a notebook and write down your responses. What is your total score? What thoughts were going through your mind as you completed this questionnaire? Note these down too.

Your score can be anywhere between 16 and 80; higher scores indicate higher levels of worry. People with GAD tend to score over 57, so our target is to help you get your score below this, but getting a lower score than this is even more encouraging. Of course, some people may score less than this but still have a problem with worry.

Note that some items are reverse scored **(R)**. On these items, if you scored 5 (i.e. very typical) then your score changes to 1, 4 changes to 2, 3 remains the same, 2 changes to 4 and 1 changes to 5. Once you have 'reversed' the scores, write in the new number and cross out the old one. To find your score, add all the numbers up.

THE PENN STATE WORRY QUESTIONNAIRE

Enter the number that best describes how typical or characteristic each item is of you, putting the number next to each item.

1	2	3	4	5
Not at all typical		Somewhat typical		Very typical

1. ____ If I don't have enough time to do everything, I don't worry about it **(R)**.
2. ____ My worries overwhelm me.
3. ____ I don't tend to worry about things **(R)**.
4. ____ Many situations make me worry.
5. ____ I know I shouldn't worry about things but I just can't help it.
6. ____ When I'm under pressure, I worry a lot.
7. ____ I'm always worrying about something.
8. ____ I find it easy to dismiss worrisome thoughts **(R)**.
9. ____ As soon as I finish one task, I start to worry about everything else I have to do.
10. ____ I never worry about anything **(R)**.
11. ____ When there is nothing more that I can do about a concern, I don't worry about it any more **(R)**.
12. ____ I've been a worrier all my life.
13. ____ I notice that I have been worrying about things.
14. ____ Once I start worrying, I can't stop.
15. ____ I worry all the time.
16. ____ I worry about projects until they are all done.

Source: Meyer, T. J., Miller, M. L., Metzger, R. L. and Borkovec, T. D., 'Development and Validation of the Penn State Worry Questionnaire', *Behavior Research and Therapy*, 28 (1990). With permission from Elsevier.

Figure 3.3: Gauging the level of your worry

Fear and worry – an evolutionary perspective

Fear and worry help us deal with danger: either real and immediate danger in the case of fear, or anticipated or future danger in the case of worry. Short bursts of fear and its accompanying anxiety occur in response to physical danger, and they help us to deal with that danger through three main mechanisms, namely, fight, flight or freeze. These responses are 'hard-wired' and are linked to the parts of the brain that developed relatively early in an evolutionary sense (the reptilian part or limbic system). When an event is perceived to be life threatening, the body's systems react incredibly quickly, often without our awareness. Through millions of years of evolution our bodies have been 'hard-wired' to react to and deal with threat, preserving what is most important: ourselves and our group. At these moments of threat, the more primitive part of our brain takes over to protect us. What we end up doing depends to a large extent on the interaction between the event and the chemical processes in our brains. In simple terms, the

55

adrenal gland (found just above the kidneys) will, in danger-ous situations and under instruction from part of the brain, pump chemicals into your body. These are called adrenalin and noradrenaline and they work together to prepare your body for either 'getting the hell out of there' (flight) or 'get-ting ready to rumble' (fight). The freeze reaction is less well understood, but has many similarities to the fight and flight responses. This reaction is also influenced by other brain chemicals, which have an impact on memory and our per-ception of time, place and what's real. The freeze response might be linked to a sense of dissociation; this is a symptom of anxiety where the person might feel 'spaced out' or 'not really here'. The freeze response might 'take us out of a situation', almost as if, when things get to be too much, our mind decides to shut down from our body. We can't really predict which of the fight, flight or freeze reactions will happen to us in any given situation; they can all have adaptive or evolutionary value and can help us to survive.

For example, in North America, in the very rare event of being attacked by a brown bear – a medium-sized omnivore – if you have exhausted all the options available to you, the advice is to fight and fight for your life. A well-aimed blow to the nose with a stick might just do the trick and save you. However, if confronted by the much larger grizzly bear, then the best chance of survival is not just freezing, but playing dead. This tactic doesn't guarantee your survival, but there's little hope in doing anything else, like fighting or running. Indeed, there are survivor accounts in which playing dead is exactly what people have done and lived to tell the tale. If you are reading this book while hiking in North America, then the other thing you need to know is that both types of bear are quick – so don't run. Nor would we advise you to throw this book at them, partly because bears can't read, but partly because there's no evidence that they worry, and such an action may make them angrier!

Why do we anticipate danger and why do we worry?

If fear is a way of responding to immediate danger, worry is a way of dealing with possible danger at some point in the future. In other words, worrying is planning to make sure that you don't meet the bear, or that, if you do meet one, it won't attack you, or if it does, then you know how to get away, and if all else fails, you know what to do, depending on whether the bear is black or brown!

Some anthropologists have argued that the emergence of language and living in complex social groups were two of the main influences on how our modern brains developed, particularly the frontal lobes. Looking after our social group and our position within the group thus became a critical element for survival. At the same time, humans were evolving problem-solving skills and developing the capacity to think and plan ahead. As planning ahead became more important, they also learnt to live with uncertainty. It was important that at least some people were looking ahead: *We've had a poor harvest. What if we don't have enough grain to get us through winter? Maybe we could trade some cattle for*

57

grain with our neighbours? Worry might be considered useful in this context, as it allowed our ancestors to think ahead and run through in their imagination what might happen next, with multiple endings and possibilities. So, when we worry, our frontal lobes are thinking through the possibilities and looking for solutions to manage and prevent real or likely threats from happening. It is no accident then, given that we are largely social animals, that within the general population roughly one-third of all worry is focused on the breakdown of social relationships. And, through adaptive problem solving, we try to ensure that the social groups we live in, such as our families, friendships or social networks, survive or stay together. Worry seems to have been around for at least as long as modern humans. It appears that even in the first century AD worry had a dramatic impact. The Roman poet Ovid (43 BC–AD 17) told us that 'happy is the man who has broken the chains which hurt the mind, and has given up worrying once and for all'.

Brain research has shown changes in blood flow in different parts of the brain when people worry. An American team has shown that during worry in people who do not worry excessively there is increased blood flow that indicates increased brain activity in the fronto-orbital regions, the parts of the brain associated with language and attempts to integrate information and look for solutions. There is also less activity in the limbic system, parts of the brain associated with more primitive fear responses. So it would seem that, although related, fear and worry have two different functions and have developed at different times in human evolution.

The fear response system evolved very early and is shared with many animals, even quite primitive species with tiny brains. The worry system evolved much later and required the large forebrain that evolved with language, problem solving and planning. Its basis is probably shared only with higher mammals or the most advanced primates, and even then it is likely to be far more evolved in humans. When the worry system is more active, the fear system is less active, and rather than reacting with flight, fright or freeze, the brain goes into *What if?* and *What could I do then*? mode. We all need some of this ability; the question is, how much do we need?

So to worry is to be human. But to worry excessively is to try to be superhuman – that is, to be able to anticipate, prevent, deal with, make better or pick up the pieces after anything and everything that could possibly go wrong at anytime and anywhere. What kind of superhero would we need to be able to do this? What special powers might they need? Do you have them?

How many people worry?

If to worry is to be human, how many of us worry excessively or have a diagnosable problem with worry? Between March and September 2000, trained psychologists working for the National Psychiatric Morbidity Survey randomly interviewed over 8,000 adults living in the UK. This survey aimed to find out how widespread psychological problems were in the UK population. The survey found that in every thousand adults, forty-four reached a diagnosis for GAD.

GAD was second only to mixed anxiety and depression in terms of how commonly it occurred; indeed, GAD was found to be more common than depression. Furthermore, research in many different countries has suggested that roughly between 2 and 4 per cent of a population will have enough symptoms to receive a diagnosis of GAD in one year, and 4 to 7 per cent of people will develop GAD at some point in their lives. Between 2 and 4 per cent may not sound very many, but with the use of these figures, of the 60 million people who live in the UK, this equates to between 1.2 and 2.4 million people with diagnosable GAD, that is, 1.2 to 2.4 million people who suffer with excessive worry. If you included people who worry a lot but who do not have enough symptoms to reach a diagnosis of GAD, the numbers will be even greater. Playing it safe, that's roughly about one person in every twenty-five. Next time you are sitting in a café watching the world go by, think about this statistic. So you are not alone!

When does GAD usually begin?

Worry can occur at any time, and this is also true for GAD. If there is life stress, or if our lives have changed in a major way, or if we have increased responsibilities, then we will be more susceptible to worry. Consider the example below.

Abby was fifteen weeks' pregnant. Prior to her pregnancy she would not have considered herself a worrier. However, her pregnancy and the uncertain future of her baby triggered worry about her partner and her baby. She worried about her partner having a car crash and her baby not having a father; she started checking on him to make sure he arrived at work. She tried to make sure that he spent as little time in the car as possible, offering to do trips so that he did not drive as much. She did this to control uncertainty as far as possible, so that, rather than not knowing where he was, she could keep tabs on him. She became irritated when he ate unhealthy food since she was convinced that this would lead to ill health and sudden death. She felt keyed up and couldn't sit still. In an effort to manage the uncertain situation she found herself in, she searched the Internet for information about pregnancy. She found more and more information, some of which contradicted other information. This fuelled her sense of uncertainty and thus generated more worries. She worried about whether her child would be born early and whether it would develop normally. She worried whether, if it did develop and grow to be as smart as she hoped for, she would be able to help with the homework at secondary school. When she wasn't worrying about the child taking a wrong turn in life and ending up dropping out of school, she was worrying that the child would go to university, succeed and leave her behind. These worries triggered more *what if* statements, leading to more worry and so on.

Research tells us that roughly two-thirds of clinically significant worry tend to appear early in a person's life span, between the ages of eleven and our early twenties. This phase of our lives is important, when we are laying the foundations for the years to come. As a teenager our world starts to open up, peers become more important, we may become interested in romantic relationships, we are expected to develop autonomy, accept more responsibility for ourselves and our actions, and then start to think about who we are, what we want and how to get it. As we move through adolescence into young adulthood, we are increasingly expected to do these things by ourselves. It is a time fraught with uncertainty as we try to find our feet in an increasingly complex world, and the fact we may feel we have relatively little control can make these transitions much harder. Worry appears at these early moments as a result of many subtle influences; it may not to be triggered by a major life event or trauma. It might simply be linked to some of the normal developmental hurdles we all have to cross but that are experienced differently and that affect us in different ways during adolescence.

The other time that worry tends to appear is much later in the life span, during middle age. This is the time of life that is often typified by stability in a number of areas of our lives. We might be more certain of who we are, and where we fit in the world. We may have an established career and home life. So why would worry tend to appear at this time? One possibility is that it is linked to some significant change, such as bereavement, trauma or disaster, or a major shift in the way we live our lives, such as divorce or retirement. This might challenge the status quo and generate doubt and uncertainty, fuelling worry. In mid-life, one – and often more than one – of the following may happen. We may now be more likely to be caring for or worrying about our parents as they age. Our children may no longer be under our direct scrutiny and 'control' as they learn to develop their autonomy by trying things out, and perhaps getting it wrong (more than once!). Even when they are older, they may not be completely independent until their mid- or late twenties. We may also realize that although still young, we are not as young as we once were; retirement is no longer out of sight now and routine niggles from our bodies let us know we are getting older. We may also be in jobs that we find very demanding because we have progressed, or we may find ourselves in jobs that we find frustrating and stressful because we cannot see other options. We may be financially supporting parents and children, while trying to have a life of our own and plan for retirement. And all of these things may be happening to our partners, siblings and friends! In our mid-life years we can find ourselves in the position of worrying for three generations, or even more if we still have grandparents alive or have become grand-parents ourselves.

Hence, worry is *more likely* to appear at these times; that is, either during our early development to adulthood or later, in middle age. But it is important to remember that worry can appear at any point in a person's life, given the right circumstances, just as Abby's experience above demonstrates.

What causes GAD?

First of all, worry is a normal and helpful process when we are faced with real situations where the outcome is uncertain. But why do some people come to worry excessively or why is their worry gauge turned up so high so much of the time?

A precise cause of GAD is not known. There are several factors involved in its development, including biological influences, such as our genes, or the levels of certain brain chemicals. The biological view of GAD suggests that we can treat it by using medicine to alter the levels of brain chemicals. While there is always merit in considering other approaches, this book is written from a psychological perspective and as a result we will focus next on some of the psychological pathways to excessive worry.

According to our clinical experience there are many pathways to worry, but our experiences while growing up seem to be important. Why this should be so is a very complex question. There is no set pattern and an infinite number of influences. Below are some themes that might be important; they are not in any particular order and there will be others we have not listed.

1. Growing up with a parent who worried, and learning to worry from them.
2. Growing up in a very unstable or uncertain household, where someone in the household was affected by illness or unemployment or some other stress, without being able to do very much about it.

3. Being told by someone important that there was no way that you could cope with life, and believing them.

4. Taking on too much responsibility at an early age, because the person who should have done so couldn't.

5. Being over-protected and never learning to deal with life's uncertainties.

6. Living in a household where no one worried, but someone had to.

7. Being left alone to cope.

8. Trying to make sense of a situation that you could not make sense of and no one talked to you about it.

9. Experiencing a traumatic event as a child or teenager.

10. Losing a loved one, such as a parent, unexpectedly.

11. Trying to referee the arguments between your parents or between a parent and other siblings.

12. Being bullied and trying to find ways to deal with it by yourself.

13. Having an unpredictable parent or carer (negligent, abusive, aggressive, drunk or violent).

14. Big disruptions to what was expected at key moments (such as school transitions, 'rites of passage') due to other events such as moving house, illness, parental divorce, family health, etc.

Any of these experiences can leave people with a sense of uncertainty and the idea that bad things can happen. This is often associated with a lack of confidence in their ability to cope or deal with everyday problems, coupled with a sense that they should be able to do so – although most worriers in fact deal very well with problems when they arrive.

Sometime worriers build on past experience to build a sense of future threat. An example of this is seen in José's story (see pages 15–16). His previous relationship did not work out and there was a set of circumstances that influenced the break-up of his relationship. José's worry is about whether something similar could happen again. This worry makes him more aware of events or issues within his new relationships that match those within his failed marriage. In psychological terms, he is hypervigilant, or on the look-out for any matching features between his failed marriage and his new relationship. This would encourage him to imagine that the same thing could happen in his current relationship; he would see his new partner and his ex as one and the same, ignoring any information that suggested otherwise.

EXERCISE 3.1: EXPLORING EARLY INFLUENCES

This exercise aims to help you think about how your past has influenced your tendency to worry. Again, write down your answers in your notebook.

1. If your early life had uncertainties, how did you deal with them? What did you say or do to manage these uncertainties?

2. What were you protected from? Were you over-protected or under-protected?
3. Who else worried in your home? Who did you learn to worry from?
4. What were the family sayings about worry?
5. What were you told were good or bad things to worry about?
6. What responsibilities did you have? Did you ever feel overwhelmed with responsibility, but still managed to cope?
7. What messages did you get about your ability to cope with life? Who gave them to you?
8. What were you praised for, and what were you criticized for?
9. When you worried, how did others react? When you worried, how did you react?
10. What memories come to mind when you worry?
11. If you focus on the feeling that you get when you worry, when do you remember feeling this for the first time?
12. When did you notice that you were a worrier? What was going on for you at the time?

How CBT makes sense of the past

There are many different ways worry can appear, and no fixed set of circumstances that will definitely lead to worry. In CBT, however, we are often interested in understanding how our early and later experiences influence the development of our ideas about worry. For example, growing up in an unstable household might lead us to think, *If I work out what might go wrong, then I will be able to stop it from happening*, or, *If I am certain, then nothing bad will happen*; *If I tie up the loose ends, everything will be OK*; or, *Worry helps me deal with uncertainty*. These ideas guide us and influence how we act. We discuss this further in Chapter 7. However, although it is interesting to find out where this way of thinking comes from, in CBT we are much more interested in seeing how it keeps worry going; and our greatest interest is in finding out how we might change things.

What is a normal amount of worry?

This is very difficult to answer – it's like answering the question *What is normal weight?* or *What is normal height?* In just the same way, a 'normal amount of worry' will vary for each individual. This does not mean that hours and hours of uncontrollable worry should be normal for anyone, nor that those who have a greater natural tendency to worry cannot learn to turn down the worry gauge to more everyday levels. However, research gives us an idea of the range of normal worry. In a questionnaire study on 128 students in the early 1990s, Frank Tallis and his colleagues at the Institute of Psychiatry in London found that nearly all the students said that they worried. About 40 per cent of them worried at least once a day, 20 per cent worried every two to three days, and about 15 per cent worried about once a month. In terms of how long a worry episode lasted, they found that about a quarter said their worries were fleeting, about 40 per cent said their worry lasted between one and ten minutes, 18 per cent said it lasted ten to sixty minutes, and 20 per cent said that it lasted over one hour. The students who reported the most worry would probably have been diagnosed with GAD. In this number of people (128), it is likely that five or more of them would have GAD and ten or more would have shared many of the other features. The students also said that they worried more in the late evening or in the small hours of the morning. Of course, people who have GAD tend to worry more than those without it; one study found that people with GAD worried for about 60 per cent of the day. Some people with GAD report worrying in every waking moment and some that they worry even while sleeping, with worry themes appearing in dreams. On the other hand, others report that their worry is on the 'back burner', simmering away, and it will 'come to the boil' rapidly when something sparks it off.

Another way of thinking about normal levels of worry is to reflect on the average scores on the Penn State Worry Questionnaire (see page 54). You might expect the average to be very low, somewhere around 20–25, but this is a long way from the truth. The average score on this questionnaire is around 40 (including adults, older adults, students and others). This reminds us that worry is normal and that everyone worries.

People who worry also seem to have a *worry box*. No matter how small or large their problems are, the box is always full. Worry seems to expand in the space and fill it, no matter how small the worry is to start with; indeed, if there is nothing to worry about, this concern will fill the box . . . *what if I have missed something* . . .? The author of the *Mr Men* and *Little Miss* series, the late Roger Hargreaves, captures this beautifully in *Mr Worry* (which we use when training therapists!). Mr Worry meets a helpful magician who asks him to provide a list of all the things he worries about. The magician makes sure none of these things ever happens. Mr Worry is happy for a week, stops frowning, smiles and sleeps soundly. But after a week, he goes to see the magician because he is worrying again . . . about not worrying.

What do people worry about?

People with GAD tend to worry about the same kinds of things as people without GAD – they just worry more. Because of the hundreds of worries that race through our minds when we worry, and because we rarely stop to observe or step out of the stream of worry, it can often seem that there is no pattern or order to our anxiety. However, research on people who worry and those who worry less suggests that worries tend to cluster around particular themes. These include social-, financial-, work-, illness- or death-related themes, and even worrying about worrying. This last theme is exactly what you imagine it to be, namely that as a consequence of worrying so much, worriers tend to start to worry about the consequences of their worry. Typically, worriers might think that their worry will drive them out of their minds, or that not worrying is a bad sign.

Roughly one-third of all worry is focused on the family and interpersonal relationships. This type of worry is usually focused on the breakdown of the family circle, friendship or other important relationships. It usually revolves around real or imagined events such as illness, death or other life events such as children leaving home, friends moving away or anything that could potentially disrupt social relationships. Financial worries tend to revolve around what might happen if bills aren't met, or if money becomes tight, or if one is unable to meet changes in interest rates, and so on. The implications of financial difficulties are often social, since the worrier is concerned by what their friends or others will think of them. They may worry about how to tell their children they can't afford the school trip and then how to face the school and other parents. Their worry also projects them into the future, and they may see themselves losing their home, needing to downsize or even ending up on the streets. With illness- and death-related worries, the worrier often thinks about how they might fail to cope with the pain or discomfort of a crippling, usually life-threatening illness, and, even more likely, about how close friends or family might suffer or fail to cope following their death, or who will look after their loved ones.

Worry themes are typically related to the stage of life we find ourselves in. For instance, as children the worries are usually linked to childhood fears such as losing one's parents, getting in trouble with authority figures, being hurt or getting ill, etc. As teenagers we seem to worry most about school, our peers and fitting in. Some research has suggested that as we approach adulthood we begin to think about and worry more about adult themes such as romantic relationships, money and one's future. As young adults our worries concern education, jobs and finding a partner. As adults they are over job and financial security, relationships and whether we want or have a family, our children and parents. In middle age we start to be concerned about the changes that occur with age and changing roles. As older adults we worry about our health and death. Interestingly, some research shows that with adults aged over seventy-five, worry tends to decrease, perhaps because our social world is shrinking as we lose our parents and start to lose our peers, and we are more likely to be cared for than in a position to take care of others and so can start to let go of our worries (there may be much to be learnt about life from the over-seventy-fives). Because of the link between life stage and worry themes, our worry is often seen as normal for the relevant life stage. For instance, what teenager doesn't worry about fitting in? Another problem is that the worry seems all the more believable and likely to happen, since it fits neatly to the life stage, making it harder to spot and to challenge.

So although worry feels like a whirlwind with an unpredictable course, there are patterns and rhythms to it because it tends to circle around a number of themes that reflect the things that are important in a person's life at the stage they are at.

Types of worry

Broadly speaking there are at least two different types of worry. Some of the problems we worry about already exist; these are called *Real Event Worry*. And there is worry about problems that *could potentially* exist at some point in the future (although there is no evidence now that this is the case), otherwise known as *Hypothetical Event Worry*. This second type of worry may never exist in the sense that it is imagined, but it can have the feel of a nightmarish daydream. This type of worry is often set in the distant future and is usually very unlikely to ever happen.

For example, if I worry about a letter I am writing, then this problem exists and my worry is *Real Event Worry*. However, if I worry about the idea that I may develop cancer although there are no signs that I am unwell, then while the thoughts of worry are real, the cancer itself does not exist except in imagination. This kind of worry about things that do not exist yet is called *Hypothetical Event Worry*. Let's consider another example: my wife has been in a car crash and I am worried about how she will cope with her pain; this is *Real Event Worry*. On the other hand, I may worry that my wife *could be* involved in a car accident; this is *Hypothetical Event Worry*, the second type of worry. We will return to this distinction later.

PIT STOP

Let's stop and think about what you have just been reading. Can you summarize the key ideas you have taken on board? What is sticking in your mind? Maybe write them down. If you have any questions, jot these down too. You can return to them once you have had a chance to digest the information.

What is sticking in my mind from my reading so far?

1.

2.

3.

4

What is CBT?

The 'C' in CBT refers to *cognitive*. Cognition essentially refers to what we think and how we think. It includes all the different things our minds can do, like planning, problem solving, decision making and drawing conclusions. Cognitive behavioural therapists, however, are usually most interested in the thoughts (or cognitions) that pass through the mind – literally, what a person is thinking. The 'B' in CBT refers to *behaviour* and includes our actions, what we do and what we avoid doing. It includes subtle actions like where we look or how we stand and more obvious actions like which places we tend to avoid. A central idea of CBT is that the perspective or view we take of an event or situation has a profound influence on how we feel and act. In other words, how we think about an event is vital in helping us understand why we feel and act in particular ways. One of the great teachers of CBT in the UK was the late Dave Westbrook. Dave was a clinical psychologist who worked in Oxford and he found a very clear way of explaining the principles of CBT. The diagrams below are an adaptation of his ideas and his genius at making things clear and simple. Let's consider Dave's 'common sense' model. Here events lead directly to feelings. For example, if someone lost their job, you might expect them to feel down.

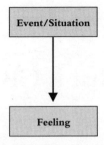

Figure 4.1: The 'common sense' model

However, we also know that the same event can have different emotional consequences for different people. For example, losing a job could leave people feeling anxious, angry or even relieved (see below). So, how can we explain this and what does it tell us about the common sense model shown above?

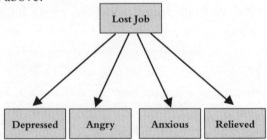

Figure 4.2: The 'common sense' model expanded

First, it tells us that we cannot assume to know what people feel when something happens to them. Second, it shows that in order to better understand how they feel, we must pay close attention to what they are thinking. We could ask, *When you felt this way, what went through your mind?* Below is a diagram showing the cognitive model. Here the thinking or cognitive element is added. Does this make sense to you? It may be helpful to pause to reflect on this fundamental point by thinking of a time when you noticed strong feelings (such as anger, anxiety, guilt or depression) and then ask yourself, *What was going through my mind just before I started to feel this way?* or, *What was I thinking that might have led me to feel like this?*

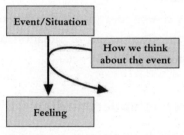

Figure 4.3: The cognitive model

Now let us return to the original event and see if we can make sense of the feelings expressed by those who lost their jobs. You will see that by paying close attention to their thoughts we can better understand why they feel what they feel. See if the links between each person's thoughts and feelings make sense to you.

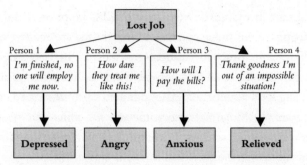

Figure 4.4: Adding thoughts into the 'common sense' model

In summary, a central idea of CBT is that the perspective or view we take of an event or situation has a profound influence on how we feel and act.

The next step in understanding CBT

Now let's add two more elements, namely bodily sensations and actions or behaviours.

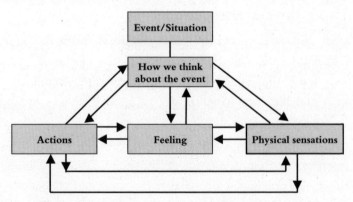

Figure 4.5: Adding sensations and actions in the model

Let's take the actions first. In the CBT approach there is a strong relationship between our thoughts, feelings and actions. For example, when we feel frightened because we see danger, our feelings motivate us to act – perhaps keeping us away from the danger. Or, when we feel annoyed, possibly because someone has offended us, this may prompt us to ignore them. In CBT the interaction between our thoughts, feelings and actions is seen as central in keeping our problems going. Finally, our thoughts, actions and emotions also have an effect on how our body feels. Each element – thoughts, feelings, physical sensations and actions – interact with one another. A worrier might suffer with muscular tension and headaches (physical sensations) and they might feel irritable (feeling) and start to worry about their health (thoughts), which in turn might result in booking an appointment with their family doctor (action).

Using the cognitive model

Let's take an example to illustrate the principles described overleaf. If you saw a friend in the street and they ignored you, what might go through your mind? How might you feel and what might you do as a consequence? Would you notice any physical sensations? You'll find a worked-out example below, but, for a moment, just reflect on these questions and see if you can get a sense of how you might think, feel and act.

EXERCISE 4.1: STARTING TO USE CBT

Event/Situation: You see a friend in the street and they apparently ignore you.

Elements	Questions	Your Answers
Thoughts (Cognition)	What would go through your mind?	
Feelings	How might you feel?	
Actions (Behaviour)	What might you do?	
Bodily sensations	What bodily sensation might you notice?	

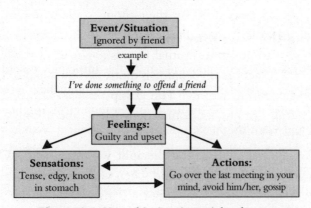

Figure 4.6: How this situation might play out

How to read the diagrams

The arrows are there for good reasons. See if you can work out what the arrows mean for each person. Sometimes they mean *leads to*, sometimes they mean *influence* and sometimes they illustrate connections. The important thing is that we begin to recognize and separate thoughts, feelings, actions and bodily sensations and then get curious about how they fit together, what connects to what and how.

In the example above, the person felt guilty and upset as well as physically tense and edgy – both the feelings and the physical sensations were motivated by their thoughts. They started to replay their last meeting, reviewing in their mind what they could have said to cause such a reaction. Their focus is entirely on what they may have done wrong and they fail to think of other explanations; this reinforces the idea that they have done something to offend their friend. Rather than approaching their friend to ask them, they are so convinced by their thoughts that they avoid them. In order to get their own side of the story in first, they start to gossip to mutual friends about what has happened. The action of gossiping is motivated by the idea 'I've done something wrong'. The gossip pushes them further away from simply contacting their friend and asking how they are.

A cognitive behavioural therapist will often ask, 'What was going through your mind when you saw your friend?' And then, 'When you thought this, how did that make you feel?' They may follow this question with, 'When you felt or thought this then, what did you do?' These questions make the thoughts explicit, make clear the relationship between thoughts and feelings, and then link them to actions. The therapist will also ask you to reflect on what sensations you felt in your body and how these connected with thoughts, feelings or actions.

Supposing you thought this instead: *My friend looks really preoccupied, there must be something going on with him.* How might you feel and what might this thought motivate you to do? Again, what if you thought, *How dare he ignore me, after all these years!* What would you do, and what would you feel both emotionally and in your body, as a consequence?

As you can see, changing the thought has an impact on how we feel and act. So, in summary, how we think about an event is vital in helping us to understand why we feel and act in particular ways.

Building on CBT to help us understand worry

As already mentioned, in CBT we are interested in how and what people think and how this influences their feelings, actions and bodily sensations. In the examples above, a situation triggered thoughts that led to strong emotions. In worry the same is true, although there are some minor differences. What follows are the first steps in developing your understanding of worry; it's worth spending some time on them and reflecting. Let's take an example.

Tom has yet another meeting today and he's at home watching the TV news when there is a vague hint of travel disruption 300 miles from where he lives. He wonders, *What if my train is late and I'm late for work?* This thought opens up doubt and uncertainty, and he starts to worry. He thinks about the implications of being late for work, how this will impact on his job, his relationship and his life. His worry quickly turns into a nightmarish daydream. His worries feel very real, they arrive thick and fast, which generates more doubt and uncertainty, and he worries all the more. His worry feels out of control. He is barely aware of where he is as his worry carries him further away. He starts to *feel* anxious, tense and restless and he looks about nervously. He is snappy with his partner because she is 'taking an age to get ready' and he needs to leave early to make sure he has time to get to work. He arrives at the station, his train is on time, so he is relieved, but he and his partner are not speaking as she is annoyed about his irritation. He then starts to worry about his relationship . . . *What if she leaves me?. . .*

He has been worrying much more recently and it's taking its toll. The negative tone of his worry starts to impact on his mood and his worry begins to drag him down. Going through these whirlwinds of worry is so often draining; he feels exhausted and demoralized as a consequence.

Track this example through on the diagram below: please note that you should read the diagrams from now on from the bottom up. We have only added key arrows; there may be many more. For instance, the worry generates muscular tension in the worrier's body, this motivates pacing and checking, which further cranks up the anxiety. From now on when the diagram talks about anxiety this includes more than just the feelings; it also includes actions and physical sensations. These are all seen as the product of a whirlwind of thoughts, namely worry. The worry is itself often triggered by a thought.

There are a number of points we'd like to make clear. Worry can be triggered by external, observable events, like hints of bad weather (hundreds of miles away), or by internal events, such as a physical sensation – like palpitations – or a mental event – like a thought that pops into your mind. These situations tend to trigger *what if* questions or their equivalent (*supposing that*, *imagine if* and so forth). Worry has a particular quality and is often triggered by a particular kind of question; usually these are phrased as *what if* questions. The *what if* questions can be thought of as a signal or sign that some form of uncertainty or doubt has been 'spotted' by the worrier within the situation they face. In Tom's case, the uncertainty centred on the possible delay of his train by a mere hint of travel problems in another part of the country some 300 miles away! And each *what if* question leads to a chain of worry or further *what if* questions. As you can see from the spiral in the diagram, worry is a chain of thoughts that spirals out of control; one worry follows closely behind the others. In addition to *what if* statements there are other trigger thoughts including, *Wouldn't it be terrible if* or *Supposing this happened I wouldn't be able to cope*

What is CBT?

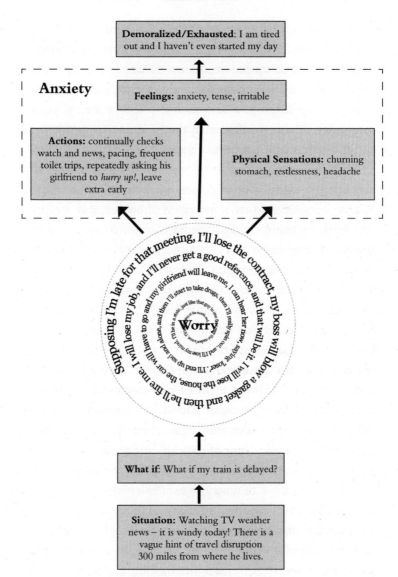

Demoralized/Exhausted: I am tired out and I haven't even started my day

Anxiety

Feelings: anxiety, tense, irritable

Actions: continually checks watch and news, pacing, frequent toilet trips, repeatedly asking his girlfriend to *hurry up!*, leave extra early

Physical Sensations: churning stomach, restlessness, headache

Worry

Supposing I'm late for that meeting, I'll lose the contract, my boss will blow a gasket and then he'll fire me, I will lose my job, and I'll never get a good reference, and that will be it. I will lose the house, the car will have to go and my girlfriend will leave me, I can hear her now, saying 'loser', I'll end up sad and alone, and then I'll start to take drugs, then I'll really spiral out, and I'll lose my mind, I'll be in a state, just like that guy in see in the street corner on a bus, and I'll lose my...

What if: What if my train is delayed?

Situation: Watching TV weather news – it is windy today! There is a vague hint of travel disruption 300 miles from where he lives.

Figure 4.7: Developing the picture: Tom's example
(read from the bottom upwards)

and even if I did, then . . ., or *Imagine if it turned out like this* or, *Say, if this happened, then . . .* Each of these statements functions to open up doubt and uncertainty and leads to the spiral of worry. The product of all this worry is anxiety. And now in our emerging understanding of worry this includes the bodily experiences of anxiety, the emotions produced and the actions the worry motivated.

The *what if* questions open up uncertainty, which in turn sets off worry, which in turn 'ratchets up' uncertainty. Worry is comprised of a chain of thoughts and images whose sheer numbers and the rapidity with which they appear – combined with the fact that the topic of the worry can shift and change – mean that trying to reason with each worry is impossible. So, to overcome your worry, we have to focus not on each individual worry but on factors that provide conditions that stimulate worry. We have to learn how to spot different types of worry, as each type of worry needs a different solution. It can help to think about the stream of worry as if it were an action our mind performs. Anxiety is the short-term or immediate emotional consequence of the stream of worry. As we have said, anxiety includes the physical experience of worry, like muscular tension and stomach upset, as well as the psychological experiences, like difficulty in concentrating or irritability. Anxiety also includes what we end up doing, so for Tom he was checking his watch and hassling his girlfriend. Anxiety and the other physical symptoms appear as the products of worry, so rather than trying to focus on the results of worry, we should focus on what causes worry to spiral and grow. Low mood, demoralization and exhaustion are the longer-term consequences of worry and, unfortunately, if you worry a lot then feeling moderate depression is a likely side-product of chronic worry. Again, the solution to these symptoms is to address the causes of worry rather than trying to work on these symptoms directly (see Figure 4.7).

Tom's experience is a little like riding the Cresta Run (the 1,200-yard toboggan run in Switzerland). Once the *what if* triggers his worry, it transports him away, twisting and turning, building speed and anxiety as it goes, eventually spitting him out at the other end, exhausted. As we worry more, the links and chains of worry become increasingly elaborate and far-fetched, bringing with them even more uncertainty and chaos. But even at these moments there is the potential of finding a new way of being, of accepting uncertainty and letting go of worry – and thus freeing us from our burden.

Now turn to the worry diagram below. Remember, 'anxiety' in this diagram now includes feelings, actions and physical sensations. Think back to the last time you worried. Can you track through your worry by using this diagram?

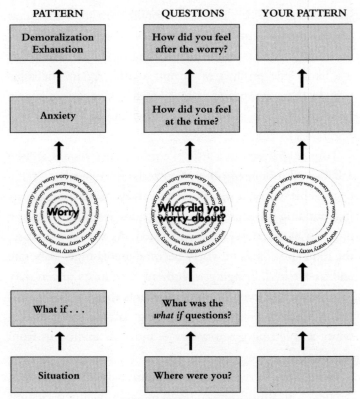

Figure 4.8 Your worry diagram

Think of the last time you worried. Can you fill in the blank boxes in the right-hand column?

EXERCISE 4.2: QUESTIONS TO HELP DEVELOP YOUR WORRY DIAGRAM

Situation	What ifs	What you were worrying about?	What were the products of your worry?	How did you feel after you stopped worrying?
Date and Time Where were you? What were you doing? Who were you with?	What went through your mind just before you started to worry? Can you spot the 'what if' statements (or equivalents) that triggered your worry?	Briefly describe what you were worrying about. Could you spot other *what ifs* within this bout of worry? Where did they take the worry?	What physical sensations did you experience? How did you feel while you were worrying? How strong was this feeling? (0 = not very strong 100 = intense feelings) What did your worry motivate you to do?	How strong was this feeling? (0 = not very strong 100 = intense feelings) Did you notice any other sensations?

The importance of practice

The aim of CBT is to enable you to develop new ways of thinking about your worry and to help you to break out of the vicious cycles that keep you worrying. CBT can help you to make sense of your experiences by looking in detail at how you think, feel and act in situations that trigger worry. With the help of this book, you will explore how the interactions between your thoughts, feelings and actions can keep your problems going. You will be encouraged to develop skills that help you to feel better and keep you feeling better. These skills can also be applied to other difficulties that you may encounter in the future.

CBT techniques may be difficult to grasp at first, but most people can learn them with practice. *Practising the skills in this book is vital to improvement.* If you signed up for a Spanish course and attended every week but never spoke or practised outside of your lessons, how much progress would you expect to make? Compare this with practising an hour a week, or, even better, an hour a day. The same is true of CBT; without repeated practice, you will not notice or feel any improvement. Practising new skills feels unnatural, deliberate and conscious at first, almost like wearing someone else's shoes. This is especially true if you started worrying when you were very young and the 'worry shoes' are familiar, even if they have never been that comfortable. But as we internalize new ideas they become our own, and this instils confidence.

Practise, practise, practise!

As far as possible we will offer you good explanations for the tasks we suggest in this book. It's essential that you understand why we're asking you to engage in particular tasks before trying them out. Our aim is to enable you to learn what you need to keep you feeling better.

Finally – in CBT we treat GAD differently from other anxiety problems

Cognitive therapy self-help books usually suggest spending time weighing up the evidence for a particular idea or thought. There are many reasons why this might be helpful. For example, it may open our field of view to consider things we had not thought of before; it may shift our perspective with the aim of enabling us to develop new ways of thinking, or it may aim to get us to reflect on what is at the heart of our concern by focusing in on underlying meaning. Another general aim is to help us realize that the likelihood of our fears coming true is very slim and even if they did we would probably be able to cope with the outcome. For many people with anxiety problems this is a very helpful process. For example, a man believed that he would bump into a workplace bully in a local pub, and that if his fear came true he would not be able to cope and would go to pieces. Furthermore, he felt sure that this was highly likely to happen even though the bully lived miles from his home. Understandably, he felt anxious and started to avoid his local pub. Using cognitive therapy, we first aimed to help him work on the likelihood that the bully would walk into his pub. Second, we discussed what he would do if the bully did appear. He quickly realized that, because he was among his friends, he'd feel more confident, and began to see that, even if the bully turned up, he'd be able to cope. His anxiety reduced as a consequence. To help him we focused on guiding him to think through the following questions: *How likely is it that this will happen? And even if it did, would it be as bad as you think?* Helping him to see that the probability of his fear materializing was very low, and that, if it did, his worst fears would not be realized, enabled him to overcome his fear and return to the pub.

The problem we face with the whirlwind of worry is that this idea of looking at the evidence for and against this stream of thoughts may not work. This is for several reasons. First, worry is phrased in terms of '*what if*' statements, and we cannot reason out a question; we need a statement to do this. Second, worry is a chain of thoughts that shift and change, so once you work with one, another will take its place. Third, people who worry have sensitivity to uncertainty. As a result, worriers tend to need absolute certainty to feel better, which is impossible. Think of the man mentioned above: as he learnt that the chances of the bully's appearing were very low and he recognized that he could cope he felt more confident and less anxious. If he were a worrier, however, then this *weighing of the evidence* would not be enough, because even a *splinter of doubt* would trigger off worry – *What if he comes into my pub?* – leading to other worries – *What if he talks to me? What if I don't know what to say? What if my friends side with him? What if I get to know him and like him?* – and so on. In worry, one worrying thought can lead on to thousands of others. To help a worrier, it would be impossible to *weigh the evidence* for every worry so rather than work with their multiple worries we should focus on other things, like enabling them to cope better with uncertainty, which removes one of the things that fuels worry.

PIT STOP

Let's stop and think about what you have just been reading. Can you summarize the key ideas you have taken on board? What is sticking in your mind? Maybe write them down. If you have any questions, jot these down too. You can return to them once you have had a chance to digest the information.

What is sticking in my mind from my reading so far?

1.

2.

3.

5

Becoming more aware of your worry

The last chapter outlined the situations or events that triggered *what if* statements (or equivalents), which then led to worry. As we have seen, worry is a chain of thoughts that shifts and twists as it develops; the whirlwind of worry then generates anxiety. Anxiety includes physical and emotional sensations such as butterflies in the stomach, muscular tension, being unable to relax, irritability, or a sense of impending doom. Furthermore, in the longer term we tend to feel exhausted by our worry, because it is simply an exhausting activity. Our worry often leaves us feeling demoralized, since we fail to act to solve problems that trigger our worries, or because we are 'cheesed off' with worrying so much. Below you'll find a quick summary.

**Trigger → What if . . . ? → Worry → Anxiety →
Demoralization and Exhaustion**

This chapter will help you to become more aware of your worry and enable you to spot the different types of worry that come to mind. As the traffic metaphor suggests, one of the first things we have to do when trying to understand

and improve traffic problems is to define the problem and work out a way of measuring it so that we can track change. We also need to develop different solutions for different kinds of traffic (for example, bus lanes for buses, cycle lanes for push bikes). We can easily tell the difference between buses and bikes and we need to help you to become as good at spotting the different kinds of worry you have.

It may sound a little odd for us to suggest that you turn your attention to your worry, as this is probably the last thing you want to think about. You may also feel that your worry already takes up far too much of your time, and turning your attention to it might seem to be doing the wrong thing. We have also suggested that to overcome your worry you have to attend to the things that keep it going rather than to each individual worry, so you may be rightly thinking that this does not add up. We recognize that there is a slight contradiction in what we are saying, but we hope the value of doing what we suggest will become clear as we go through this chapter. In essence, we are asking you to begin to pay attention to your worry and begin to try to work out what type of worry it is. To become good at this you must focus on your worry. This is like stepping out of a stream and sitting on the bank and watching the worry flow past. This is important, as it allows you to reflect on worry rather than being in it; from the 'river-bank' you are in a better place to recognize the different types of worry that float past.

Real Event and *Hypothetical Event Worry*

As you will have read in the last chapter, there are usually several themes that underpin worry – money worries, worries about children or family, or worry about friendships or work. So your first task is to get a feel for what you worry about. Second, you need to think about the type of worry that you experience on these themes. Remember that there are broadly speaking two different types of worry. There are real problems we worry about, which exist; these we have called *Real Event Worry*. In addition, there are worries about problems that *may* exist, which we have called *Hypothetical Event Worry*. This second type of worry may never actually exist except as imagined by an individual, but it can have the feel of a nightmarish daydream. It is often set in the distant future and is usually very unlikely to ever happen. For example, while many of us dream about winning the lottery, worriers would also worry about winning it – about what they'd buy, how they'd deal with all the requests, even what to do when all the money had gone! This is classical *Hypothetical Event Worry* – they may not even have bought a ticket yet, let alone had the life-changing jackpot win. Here are another four everyday examples:

> *Real Event Worry*: My central heating system is making a funny knocking noise, and I worry about when I can get the serviceman around.
>
> *Hypothetical Event Worry*: If the central heating system is making a funny noise, I will get carbon monoxide poisoning, and it will then blow up and then the

house will burn down (despite the heating system being serviced every year and only being a couple of years old).

Real Event Worry: My credit card bill *has arrived* and I'm worrying about whether to pay it all off this month and leave myself short of cash or pay some interest but have enough cash to take my mum out for dinner for her birthday.

Hypothetical Event Worry: My credit card bill is *due to* arrive and I'm worrying about being able to afford the monthly instalments. If I can't pay my credit card bill then I'll have to go to court, I'll have the bailiffs round and they'll kick in my door and throw all my stuff into the street, and everyone will see what a loser I am.

So what is there to be gained from separating our worry? In short, *Real Event Worry* you can do something about, by problem-solving the situation – even if you are not quite sure how to go about it, or not confident that you will succeed. In fact, worriers are rarely confident about their true abilities. *Hypothetical Event Worry* events, by definition, are not real and are both so unlikely and so far in the future that problem solving will *never* work. So, with this kind of worry, we focus on the worry itself and study the underlying message that it contains. You will learn more about this later. But for now consider the following quote from *Shantideva*, an eighth-century Indian Buddhist scholar, who said:

If you *can* solve your problem, then what is the *need* of worrying? If you *cannot* solve it, then what is the *use* of worrying?

This quotation illustrates why it is important to become more curious about the type of worry you are experiencing. To recap, you can work on *Real Event Worry* by problem solving rather than worrying, whereas with *Hypothetical Event Worry*, which is often far removed in time and highly unlikely to happen, there's no use in worrying. In this case we investigate and confront the 'awful truth' that we think lies at the heart of our worry. So, again, we must do something other than worry.

In the diagram below, the whirlwind of worry is made up of two shades, representing the two types of worry, namely *Hypothetical Event Worry* and *Real Event Worry*.

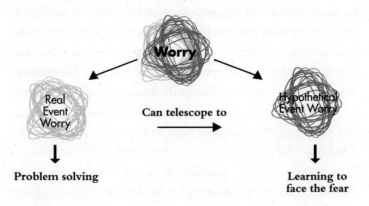

Figure 5.1: Splitting *Real Event* from *Hypothetical Event Worry*

You may also find it helpful to reflect on the Serenity Prayer, which asks for:

the serenity of mind to accept that which cannot be changed; the courage to change that which can be changed, and the wisdom to know the one from the other.

Of course, this is not always easy to do, especially when we have been caught up in worry and struggle to access the wisdom that might help us to tell one type of worry from another. *Real Event Worry* and *Hypothetical Event Worry* are often mixed together and to separate them requires some effort. To complicate things further, worry can have both hypothetical and real aspects and so the distinction is not absolutely clear (see the exercise on pages 106–7). We have to learn to live with the uncertainty that this might trigger in us. However, doing your best to separate the two types of worry is important, as each type requires a different solution, just as solving the traffic flow problems requires different strategies for different modes of transport. In practice this means we need to become skilled at recognizing the different types of worry. The reason for being interested in this will become clearer later in the book (see Chapters 14–17).

Sometimes it's not possible to change *Real Event Worry*. For example, when someone is in deep poverty or living with serious illness, or working in a situation where there is real uncertainty, the solutions may lie elsewhere (such as in seeking practical help) – working with your worry alone may not be enough in cases like these.

'Telescoping' worry

In Table 5.1, below, you will find examples of each type of worry and how they tend to overlap. Worry also has the tendency to telescope to the future, so that *Real Event Worry* will evolve into *Hypothetical Event Worry*. Let's take the first example. Here the person starts to worry following an argument with their partner:

> Although most of the time we get on well, I have just had an argument with my partner and we are not talking. I start to worry about the consequences of the argument. *What if* we stop talking completely, and then my partner finds someone else? And what if they have an affair and I never know, but then stumble across them together? And supposing I lose my rag and do something stupid, and then I'll have to leave and I'll lose the house. I'll go to pieces, I won't cope and my life will go down the tubes, the trial will go on for months and I'll end up in jail, and I'll be left with nothing. My partner will have it all and I'll never find anyone again. And my partner could take out a court order and I break it because I want to see the kids; then I'll be arrested for harassment. Where will this end?

In this example the worrier is transported by worry away from the issue at hand to an imaginary and nightmarish future which at the time feels very real and is very upsetting. He or she worries about whether they can cope with the outcome of the trial and can see themselves disappearing into a hole. Like a whirlwind, the worry leaves a trail of emotional devastation in its wake. At some level the worrier *knows* that their worry is not true, but at another level it *feels* very, very real and produces many of the emotions that you would expect to have if this were happening for real.

Does this pattern seem familiar to you? Notice how the worry, like an *express elevator*, takes the person away from an event or situation that they might be able actually to *do something* about, in this case an argument with their partner. This part of the worry is potentially solvable, by, for example, waiting for a quiet moment and sitting down together and talking things through.

Table 5.1: more examples of *Real Event* vs *Hypothetical Event Worries*

<u>May</u> telescope to →

Real Event Worry	*Hypothetical Event Worry*
I've just had an argument with my partner and we're not talking.	Things will get so bad that I'll break the court order (see above) and the trial will go on for months and then I'll be left with nothing, my partner will have it all.
I have to meet my boyfriend at the airport and I'm worrying about how to get there.	There could be a terrorist attack.

My wife is late home from work and we have some tickets for a show later.	My wife could have had a car accident.
I have a fever and feel dreadful.	I might become seriously ill and die alone.
I've lost the passwords to my Internet banking account.	Somebody will 'hack' into my account and take all my savings.
My child has a temperature.	I'll be interviewed on local television about how I failed to spot a serious illness.
My youngest is not wearing his cycle helmet to school.	He'll fall off his bike and get a head injury and then go off the rails and end up in care.
My neighbours are noisy.	I'll never be able to sell the house, I'll be stuck here for ever.
My car was stolen.	It will be used in a bank raid and I'll be prosecuted for this and end up in jail. Alone.
The drain outside the house needs fixing; there are two inches of water everywhere whenever it rains.	The house might be flooded or there could be a landslide.
We've been invited to have dinner with my partner's boss, and I don't want to go.	My partner will go without me, meet someone, have an affair and leave me.

I fell out with my neighbour.	They'll make a complaint and I'll get into trouble with the police and be forced to move.
I have an itchy rash and the doctor doesn't know what it is.	I will die from some horrible illness.
My child is disobedient and getting into trouble at school.	I'll be visiting him in prison; how will I fit the visits in with work?
I can't concentrate on work.	I'll lose my mind if I keep worrying.
I have too much work to do.	I'll lose my job and end up on the streets.
My three-year-old watches too much TV.	I'll have a twenty-stone teenager.

What do you make of the table above? Does the pattern seem familiar to you? Does it give you any clues as to what you might do to overcome your worry?

Hypothetical Event Worry can lead to *Real Event Worry*, although the route is less direct. The *Hypothetical Event Worry* may lead to real physical symptoms of anxiety, such as irritability or concentration problems, which then become the subject of *Real Event Worry*. In these cases we need to work out which type of worry comes first and work with this: if the root worry is a *Real Event*, then we move to problem solving, but if the root event is hypothetical, then we move to face the fear at the heart of our worry. Each of these will be covered in more detail in Chapters 14–18.

The inclination to 'get on' the express elevator might begin to tell us something about what separates worriers from those who worry less. With 'big occasions' most of us have had the experience of the express elevator, but with everyday events, people who worry less might be more able to catch themselves before they reach the tenth floor or they get to the fiftieth and come straight back down – either by saying to themselves, *Come on, where are you going with this?*, or by recognizing that they are 'in' the *elevator* and saying to themselves, *Slow down a minute, I'm getting ahead of myself*, and then getting back to either solving the problem or getting on with life. Worriers may reach the fiftieth floor before they know it and may not have noticed the ride up, or the fact that they are on the fiftieth floor, locked in and panicking while the problem or situation that triggered their worry remains on the ground floor, unresolved.

When our worry telescopes or we ride the *express elevator* of worry the level of uncertainty that we feel increases greatly. This is not surprising. When we launch ourselves into the future everything becomes hypothetical and uncertain because none of it has happened. All the potential problems, the solutions to the problems and the potential problems within the solutions (every silver lining has a cloud) are all possible. The imaginary or hypothetical future is indeed uncertain because none of it is real! However, it also feels scary, and we learnt in Chapter 3 that we have evolved with the capacity to feel fear because if the threat is real, rather than hypothetical, fear readies us for appropriate action. This uncertainty, and the scary, doom-laden feeling that go with it, in turn triggers more worry.

To overcome your worry it is important to become much more aware of when this 'telescoping' happens so that you don't 'get ahead of yourself' in your worry. To help you with this there are some exercises and questions in the next section. But recognizing the pattern is a first step.

Separating *Real Event* and *Hypothetical Event* Worry

'When I look back on all these worries, I remember the story of the old man who said on his deathbed that he had had a lot of trouble in his life, most of which had never happened.' Winston Churchill

For now let us consider how we can separate out the two types of worry. The questions below aim to help you to see when your worry has become much more hypothetical. The first few questions ask you to think carefully about the context of your worry, in particular where and when the things you are worrying about are taking place. With *Hypothetical Event Worry* the feelings of uncertainty and anxiety created are very real, so when this happens reflect on the content of your worry and ask when and where this worry is happening. If the answers suggest that your worry is set in the future (tomorrow, next week, or especially at some indeterminate time in the future) and the worry has transported you somewhere else (not where you are right now) then you are much more likely to be dealing with *Hypothetical Event Worry*. The 'time code' (some time in the future) will give you the strongest clue. If you get a sense that you are dealing with a *Hypothetical Worry*, then track this back to the start (press ground floor in the express elevator). What first triggered this chain of worry? Was the trigger a *real event* or was it *hypothetical*? Is it something you can do something about?

In order to take this further, the next question to ask is how real the worry is. In very concrete terms, could you 'show it' to someone else? For instance, would they see the bailiffs knocking at your door, or would they just see your credit card bill? Would they see your partner talking to a divorce lawyer or just your partner in a huff? Would they see a doctor rushing you into hospital or just telling you to come back next week if it doesn't clear up?

The last question is about taking action; if the worry is about a real event, then can you actually *do* something about it rather than *worrying* about it?

EXERCISE 5.1: SEPARATING *HYPOTHETICAL EVENT WORRY* FROM *REAL EVENT WORRY*

Bring a current worry to mind. Sit with a notebook and pen and try to answer the following questions.

* Where is your worry set? Is it in the present or the distant future? What is the 'time code'? Have you taken a ride on the Tardis? Or shot up in the Great Glass Elevator?

- Compared to where my worry has taken me, where am I right now? What day is it, what year? (Bring yourself back to the present.) What was I doing just before my worry took hold?
- Have I got ahead of myself? Where did this line of worry start? Did it start with a real event (then track back), or did it start with a hypo-thetical event (imagined concern)? *Where did I get on the express elevator?*
- Is the thing that I am worrying about something that *actually exists now*? Can I describe the issue that I am worrying about in concrete terms, with a time, date and a place? Would someone else be able to 'see' the issue? Would they see the boss firing me or the pile of work to do, the social workers turning up or the kids being difficult, and so on?
- Could something be done about it? Could someone else solve this even if I don't currently have the confidence to say that I could? (In theory, is this issue solvable?)
- If yes, then could I do something about it (even though you may worry that you may not be able to do it right)?

As we have said before, sometimes it is possible to find worries that are about real events that have hypothetical implications. For example, if I attended a meeting and my workmates rejected my proposals, this is real; but I may then go on to worry about whether I'll lose my job or if I'll ever get another job again, which is more imagined. Or my financial worries could well be real, but I also worry that I'll never be able to find my feet again financially and that I'll live a life of ruin in an imagined and desperate future. Hypothetical events can also trigger further hypothetical worry. For example, if I worry (without any evidence) that my partner will leave me, this may lead to the worry that I'll die alone and in poverty. We will learn more about solving these kinds of difficulties in Chapters 17–18. To make sure that you have got the idea, think about the following examples and try to decide whether the worry is *real* or *hypothetical* or a bit of both.

EXERCISE 5.2: SPOTTING *REAL* vs *HYPOTHETICAL EVENT WORRY*

Think about *Real* vs *Hypothetical* first. What makes this item hypothetical? What makes it real? Is there a bit of both? Can you separate out each element? Tick to indicate which type of worry you see.

Worry	Real	Hypo-thetical	Both
1. I've completed a piece of work that I've never done before and I'm worried about whether my boss will like it.			

---

2. I'm about to go on holiday and am worried that my plane will be delayed, although the weather is fine, and there have been no security alerts or baggage handler strikes.			
3. I've been to the bank, and there is less money in there than I expected.			
4. There are new streetlights in my road and I'm worried that I won't be able to get to sleep at night.			
5. I'm having a baby and am worried about whether my employer will allow me the extra maternity leave I want to take.			
6. My daughters are two and four years old: I'm worrying how I will cope with them as teenagers with boyfriends.			
7. The double-glazing is old, the frames are cracking and there is condensation between the window-panes: we need to replace it.			
8. We need to get the plumber in to fix a leaky pipe. How will I be able to pay if the leaky pipe damages all the electrics?			
9. I need to make a minor insurance claim of £200. I'm worried about filling the forms in correctly and that the company may not process the claim properly and my premium will go up, or that they will refuse to pay and accuse us of submitting a false report.			

Possible ways of answering

1 = Mostly Real.

2 = Hypothetical: I haven't even got to the airport.

3 = Real: I could show this to the bank manager.

4 = Hypothetical or Real: if I haven't spent a night in bed with the new lights then this is Hypothetical, but if I have and I couldn't sleep then this is Real and I could do something about this.

5 = Mostly Real: the baby is not the issue; the response of the employer to my pregnancy is as yet unknown. It's not a given (and things would be complicated if he doesn't agree – Hypothetical), but I could ask and find out (Real).

6 = Hypothetical: set in the distant future.

7 = Real: anyone else can see the condensation too.

8 = Both: we have a leaky pipe (Real problem), with a Hypothetical ending (what if the leak damages the electrics?).

9 = Both: similar to 8. We are worrying about completing a form (Real) and this leads to a Hypothetical Worry where the company messes up our application, even though it has not been sent (time code and place offer clues).

By now you will have a better idea of what you are trying to spot in your worry. It's time to turn your attention to your own worry. In order to help you do this you will find a Worry Diary below (see also Appendix 3), which you may like to use. If it's too small, then why not copy it out onto a larger piece of paper? You will need to keep this diary for at least a week and record your worries three to four times a day (see the 'Practical tips' in the next section if you need to).

Before you start recording your worry consider the following questions and write down your answers.

- What do you think you are likely to find if you do this?
- What worries do you have about doing this? What predictions might you make?
- What do you worry about most?
- Can you spot themes in your worry already?
- How much time do you think you spend worrying?
- Is there any pattern to your worry?

Once you have kept this diary for a week, ask the following questions:

- What have you learnt about your worry?
- Did anything surprise you?
- If so, what was it?
- When and where do you worry the most?
- What are the things that you worry about most often? What are the recurring themes? What do you make of this?
- Do you get a sense of how long you spend worrying?
- Does one worry lead to another?
- Do your worries represent real events?
- Do your worries ever predict the future?

WORRY DIARY

Day	Time	CONTENT	DISTRESS	WORRY TYPE
		What was the worry about?	How intense was the worry? How uncontrollable did it seem? Scale 0 = mild; 100 = very severe	Is the worry about a real, current problem: does the problem actually exist? Yes/no. If no, is it hypothetical? Have I got ahead of myself?

- How often do your hypothetical worries come true? What does this tell you?

You may like to make a list of the bad things that you 'see' in your worry. How many of these actually come true?

Practical tips

The following tips apply to all the exercises that appear in this book, so read this carefully and return to it if you need to.

Keeping a diary is difficult, so it's worth thinking about what might help you to remember to write it up and what might get in the way of completing it. The bottom line is that the sooner you sit down to write things down, the clearer your memory will be. The longer you leave it, the worse your memory. And it's often better to have the raw material rather than the processed version – a bit like the difference between fresh and tinned strawberries. So the sooner you sit down to record, the better the quality of the information.

If you need to record information three or four times a day then you might find it useful to link up the diary to events in the day such as morning tea, lunch, the six o'clock news or a daily soap. Some people decide to record their worry at four-hour intervals. If you use a computer during the day, then you might want to copy the diary sheet onto the desktop. Mobile phones usually have an organizer function that 'bleeps' when it's time to do something. It can be helpful to carry a notebook or diary to jot down a few quick notes, before returning to the diary sheet a little later.

The pattern that you decide to work with and how you remember to complete the diary has to work for you. The important thing is that you start to reflect on your worry more often. So have a think about what is realistic and achievable for you.

Despite the best-laid plans, our lives often have a habit of interfering with our goals. What might hinder, interfere or put you off completing the Worry Diary? Are you concerned about keeping it from the eyes of others? You may also worry about losing it, and then thinking, *What if someone reads it?*, leading to another bout of worry. Thinking these issues through beforehand will help, but beware of avoiding putting pen to paper because of worry – and, let's face it, you probably will worry about this.

The information you start to collect here will be used in many of the exercises throughout this book, so it will help if you start to get into the habit of recording your worry.

PIT STOP

Let's stop and think about what you have just been reading. Can you summarize the key ideas you have taken on
board? What is sticking in your mind? Maybe write them
down. If you have any questions, jot these down too. You
can return to them once you have had a chance to digest
the information.

What is sticking in my mind from my reading so far?

1.

2.

3.

6

Marking out the route to feeling better – setting goals

Goals

In Exercise 1.1 (pages 20–1) there are some questions aimed at getting you to think about what you want from this book; more specifically, what are your goals. Setting goals is an important step in overcoming worry and there are many good reasons for this. For example: if, in our work as cognitive behavioural therapists, we start working with clients before we have set ourselves clear goals, we don't really know where we are going, or what we are trying to achieve. Furthermore, although emotional or psychological change can sometimes be quick, usually it is slow and steady. Or think for a moment about how your hair grows; you know it is happening, but it is not something you notice or can see. But if you took photos two months apart, then you would notice the difference. Psychological change has this quality: it's measured and sure, and it can go unnoticed unless reviewed and assessed. In our clinical experience, it is as if people quickly get used to the new way of being, almost as if they can't see where they've been, and this can make it much harder to 'see' progress, just as your 'new' hair length becomes just the way your hair is. So setting goals is crucial: goals motivate us, they help us to recognize change, they give treatment a direction and purpose and, critically, they also tell us where the finishing line is. As someone once said, 'If you aim at nothing, you will hit it every time.'

In this chapter we review the advantages of setting personal goals and then review the things that can make goals more effective.

Worry gets in the way of getting things done

To set goals is to challenge life's uncertainties but will in itself trigger worry. You may ask yourself, *What if I don't have any goals?* or, *What if I don't know how to achieve them?* or, *What if I have too many goals and don't know which to focus on?* and so on. One of the key problems you may face is how to step out of worry in order to begin work on it, without worry hijacking your efforts to get better. There is no easy answer to this. However, we need only a small ledge to get a first foothold: you need only to step outside of worry *enough* to start dealing with it. Understanding how worry works is also very useful, and will help you feel more in control of your worry.

The frameworks found in this book, the tables and diary sheets, suggest ways to help you find your feet and organize your thinking. For instance, writing things down means that you can come back to them if you are hijacked by worry. When thinking about your worry, see *it* as the problem, not yourself. Worry is only a tiny part of who you are. Treat yourself with compassion, just as you would treat anyone else struggling with worry.

To reach your goals you have to try out new things; goals are all about what you are *trying* to do, and simply *trying* is achieving, since you are moving towards your goals. As Samuel Beckett wrote, 'Ever tried. Ever failed. No matter. Try Again. Fail again. Fail better.' It doesn't matter if you do not achieve your goal, as long as you are trying to achieve it.

In Chapters 14–16 we will turn our attention to problem solving, which may help you to think about how to overcome some of these difficulties. There, we begin to think about things to do other than worrying. When thinking about setting yourself goals, you may say to yourself, *I can't cope with this, things will go wrong*, or, *I can't manage to do this*. This chapter will also address such thoughts. You may wish to read on and come back to this point, but it can be very useful to have set some personal goals before embarking on overcoming your worry. Remember, a goal is a two-fingered salute to worry and uncertainty. *You can do this!*

Advantages of setting ourselves goals

If we are looking for good reasons to break the seemingly impossible into manageable chunks, we should look no further than the story of British mountaineers Joe Simpson and Simon Yates. In 1985 they climbed Siula Grande, a 20,814-foot mountain in the Peruvian Andes. On the

118

descent, disaster struck. They had run out of fuel, food and water, and the weather conditions deteriorated, and, to cap it all, Simpson broke his leg. Together they decided that the best and quickest way down the mountain was for Yates to lower Simpson by rope in 300-foot stages, which they continued to do into the night. During the attempt to get off the mountain, Yates, blinded and deafened by blizzard conditions, lowered Simpson over an ice-cliff and there he hung in mid-air. Yates had neither the strength to pull him up nor enough rope to let him down. Simpson was equally stuck on the other end of the rope, unable to help himself. Neither could communicate with the other. Yates was being pulled over the edge, and finally he made the agonizing decision to cut the rope. Later, when he could clearly see the ice-cliff and the crevasse below it, he was convinced that his friend must have died.

Unknown to Yates, Simpson had survived the 100-foot fall; he had come to rest on a small ledge within the crevasse. Alone, with a very badly broken knee, in excruciating pain and without food or water, Simpson took three days to crawl, scramble and drag his broken body for five miles and down 3,000 feet to their base camp, where Yates was just setting off, with another friend, Richard Hawking, to face the world to explain what had happened. Following his experience Simpson wrote the best-selling book *Touching the Void*, and a film of the same name followed. You may like to see the film or read the book.

There is much more to the story, but our focus is on Simpson. He clearly described how he motivated himself to get down the mountain. Given his situation, he knew that if he thought about or focused on the whole tortuous journey ahead, he would have probably given in and died. Instead, he set himself small achievable goals such as, *I'll get to that rocky outcrop in thirty minutes* (an easy task had he been able to walk), and he defied excruciating pain to meet his goal. Or, *I'll get to the edge of that crevasse in twenty minutes*, and so on. His survival was truly remarkable, and by breaking this impossible journey into manageable, achievable stages, or goals, he was able to defy the odds and survive. Unsurprisingly, he is now a motivational speaker, helping others to find a way to overcome their problems. (Incidentally, another factor that motivated him was his reluctance to die with a song he hated ('Brown Girl in the Ring' by the 1970s pop group Boney M) playing over and over in his mind. Fair enough!

So why are goals so important? First, they contain within them the idea that things can be different, that change is possible. Second, they help us to focus on future possibilities, rather than the problems that impede us; they help us to 'think outside the box'. Third, they help us to become a more active part of the process of change, and, in so doing, help us to feel more influential in, or responsible for, change. Fourth, they impose structure on the seemingly unwieldy. Fifth, they give us targets that we can achieve, offering a taste of success and building up motivation. Sixth, they give a sense of meaning to our endeavours: they enable us to find out more about ourselves, which drives personal growth and development. Finally, and probably most importantly, they hold out hope and can carry us through the toughest times.

Can you see how Simpson's story illustrates these factors?

Getting better at setting goals

Our goals should aim to be **SMART** goals, that is:

Specific
Measurable
Attainable
Realistic
Time-limited

The SMART criteria are the ones to concentrate on. However, we would also ask you to read the SMART-COPER Refining Goals section and reflect on the points raised here to help you refine your goals.

Compassionate
Ordered
Positively framed
Engaged
Reviewed

There are no right or wrong ways of thinking through your goals. At the end of this chapter is a table to help you develop them. Like many of the tasks suggested in this book, you may worry about doing this at first, which may stop you from doing it; but, once the worry has passed, return to the task, and if worry interferes again, wait for it to pass, and again return to the task, and so on, until it is done. Ask yourself, *What was I doing before I started to worry?* and then go back to it.

SMART goals

SPECIFIC

Goals should be clear and focused. Often people have a 'headline' goal, such as *I want to feel better, I want to be happy* or *I want to be rich*. Such goals are about where we want to get to, but they tell us little about how to get there. So we need to explore them a little further to unearth a more focused and detailed version. You can do this by asking a few extra questions to make the goal more specific and break it down into manageable chunks. More specific goals give us clues about how to go about achieving them. Reflect on the questions in Table 6.2 (p. 131) to help you define your goals.

MEASURABLE

With the best goals we can measure our progress. Think of your goal as a goal on a football field: you know when you have scored, or when you have achieved your goal, when the ball is in the net. So, for instance, if you wanted to worry less, how would you know that you were worrying less? You may wish to use some of the questionnaires or diary sheets found in this book to help you measure your progress. Or, more simply, use a scale of 0–100 and ask where you are on the scale at any given moment. For example, you could record on this scale how much your worry interferes with your relationships (see below). There are limitless ways of measuring change in this way: the key is to find targets to measure that make sense to you. Using these scales you can decide on what and how to measure progress. For example, you could measure intensity, frequency, degree of uncontrollability, level of worry and so on.

Example of rating scale

How much does worry interfere with my relationships?

Date ....

Not at all   Interferes a great deal

| 0 | 10 | 20 | 30 | 40 | 50 | 60 | 70 | 80 | 90 | 100 |

What problems does this cause?

ATTAINABLE AND REALISTIC

Are the goals you have set doable? Are they feasible? Can you reach them? Are they sensitive to your situation? If you have a busy life, or have little time to think and reflect, then your goals should be in tune with this. Imagine you're setting these goals for a close friend who worried in similar life circumstances; from this point of view, are your goals workable? Is there someone you trust with whom to chat through your goals? A few minutes a day together might be achievable (doable) and realistic.

Worry is a normal everyday process, so setting a goal such as *I never want to worry again* is completely impossible – we all worry. Furthermore, setting a goal to eradicate worry from your life would quickly lead you to failure and deflation. It's important to give yourself small tasks that are sensible within the practical limits. So, a headline goal might be, *I want to learn how to worry less*; a more specific, realistic goal might be, *I want to reduce my worry about my children by 30 per cent*.

TIME-LIMITED

Set a time frame for the goal. For example, *I want to read the next chapter within two weeks*. Time limits help to maintain focus and momentum. Setting a time limit that is too brief may lead to more anxiety or a poor job since you rush to complete the goal. On the other hand, time limits that are too far away may not offer the sense of urgency that helps us to complete goals. For some of us, a deadline offers something to work towards, it motivates us and helps us plan what we need to do and when we need to do it. Broadly speaking, we know that worriers can do one of two things: either they put things off for as long as possible or they dive in without thinking. Both these styles are influenced by how worriers react to uncertain situations (we will talk more about this later). If you recognize the first of these traits in yourself, then it might be worth giving yourself tighter deadlines; if you recognize the second you may need to give yourself more time.

SMART-COPER Refining Goals

COMPASSIONATE GOALS

Goals are not cold-hearted things; they represent how we would like to see ourselves in the world and, as such, they encapsulate our intimate thoughts, feelings and aspirations. As the Irish poet W. B. Yeats wrote, 'I have spread my dreams under your feet; tread softly because you tread on my dreams.' Engaging in goal setting is a deeply personal experience; it can make us feel extremely vulnerable. Consequently, it can be very difficult, because of the anxiety and concerns that bubble to the surface the moment change is invited into our lives. This book is about change, and no one finds that easy; so be thoughtful and sensitive to your needs in the way that you are to others. Change requires courage, but goals can help.

ORDERED – SHORT- AND LONG-TERM GOALS AND STEPPING STONES

When you have worked out some goals, ask which can be achieved in the near future and which are longer-term goals. To help you with this, answer the following questions:

- Which of these goals are easier to meet?
- What might give you a sense of success early on?
- What can be achieved right now?
- What can be left for later?

Think of goals as a series of stepping stones: to get to the third stone you have to walk across the first and the second.

If one goal is dependent on another, you may need to ask which goals *have* to happen first. For example, if your goal is to reduce worry about finances by 50 per cent, this will be dependent on another goal that focuses on developing a better understanding of your worry. Or, if your goal is to fly a helicopter, this will be dependent on a goal of attending training sessions and another one of passing exams.

POSITIVE REFRAMING – AVOIDANCE AND APPROACH GOALS

Goals framed in a way that means we are trying to get away from something bad or negative are called avoidance goals. Goals that are moving us towards something positive are called approach goals.

Let's start with an unusual example: imagine running away from a tiger. Compare the goal of avoiding being eaten with the goal of finding safety. The first is an avoidance goal, the second an approach goal. While both are reasonable, the first keeps your mind and eyes focused behind you, on the tiger – on all that is frightening and scary – while the second forces you to focus on the solution, not the problem. Now stop for a moment and try this suggestion.

Imagine you are being chased by a tiger. Keeping the first goal in mind (to avoid being eaten), what pops into your mind, what pictures do you see? Spend a few moments with this. Then, with the tiger still there, your goal is now to find safety. Ask the same questions. What happens?

Our reasonable goal of avoiding the tiger may bring to mind all that could go wrong, all that is horrible, images of blood and gore. However, the second part of the exercise may have brought to mind images of safety, an elephant lifting you on to its back or a helicopter lifting you away from the danger. Avoidance goals tend not to lead us anywhere in particular; they may even leave us running around in circles. On the other hand, having approach goals tends to mean that you are looking out for a particular feature to head towards. This is not to say that avoidance goals are unhelpful, it's just that approach goals may be more helpful – they don't keep reminding us of the problem. And it's more likely that by pursuing an approach goal (finding safety) we will also achieve the avoidance goal (not being eaten) because it leads to active plans that involve actually doing something.

How can I identify which is which? We can 'hear' avoidance goals in the words people use to describe them, such as 'reduce', 'get rid of', 'prevent', 'avoid', 'escape', 'quit', 'forget'. For example, *I want to reduce my worry*, or, *I want to avoid feeling anxious*. Again, these goals sound very reasonable, but at the heart of them is the idea of worry or anxiety (the tiger). Take the worry goal. Worry is a negative experience (the tiger), and trying to escape this experience provides the energy or drive for the goal. In trying to reduce worry, we are in essence trying to move away from it. However, the goal tells us little about where we should move to, and, if we succeed, we don't really gain anything positive, except to escape from the clutches of our negative feelings (the tiger). Researchers suggest that goals framed in this way are less likely to be achieved. As the exercise above has shown, such goals keep in mind the idea of threat, of what could go wrong, and, as a result, they may make our worry or anxiety worse. They also put the energy for change outside of ourselves: we are fleeing or escaping something awful, rather than heading towards something positive.

On the other hand, approach goals lead us towards something positive; the goal provides direction and has an implicit reward. So, rather than saying, *I want to lose weight* (an avoidance goal), an approach goal would suggest, *I want to eat more vegetables.*

Here are some examples:

Table 6.1: Examples of reframed goals

Avoidance goal	Reframed or approach goal
I want to give up smoking.	I want to be able to run up two flights of stairs without stopping.
I want to lose weight.	I want to go for a twenty-minute walk five times a week for the next month.
I want to stop giving all my work to my boss for her to check.	I want to handle routine things more independently.
I want to get rid of worry.	I want to spend more time reading.

I want to stop telephoning my husband when he's on his way home.	I want to write some emails and catch up with my friends.
I want to reduce the number of times I look into things before I make even small decisions.	I want to manage my uncertainty by making quicker decisions.
I want to reduce worrying about my kids by 30 per cent.	I want to spend at least twenty minutes a day playing with my children.

There is still much to be discovered by research about the different types of goals and their impact on us. But it would seem to be common sense to begin to think of our goals as representing the hope of a new way of being, rather than as an escape from the old. But reframing requires some work. A tip: think about adding new actions or behaviours, rather than reducing or stopping existing actions or behaviours: about what you can do and will do, not what you are trying to stop doing.

Usually the avoidance goals spill out first – and that's OK. Goals are often framed in avoidance terms in the early stages, since our focus is then understandably on the problems themselves. However, it may help to stop and think about your goals and ask if reframing them could offer some advantage. Having a mix of avoidance and approach goals is OK, since, as with all things, balance is the key. And you may include both approach and avoidance aspects in a goal. The bottom line is that any goal is better than none.

ENGAGED

A tip: keep a postcard or credit card–sized paper in your wallet or purse, and write on it the reasons why it is important for you to keep *engaged* with your goals, so that when the going gets tough you can remind yourself of the reasons why you are trying to change. Alternatively, find something that visually symbolizes your positive approach goal. Keep this somewhere in your mind or, better still, find something to remind you of it – a picture from a magazine, a postcard, an object, a word, a phrase, anything that keeps your approach goals in mind.

REVIEW

It will help to set a series of review dates to reflect on your progress. You may want to put a note on the fridge or use the organizer on your mobile phone to remind you when to review your progress. What would help you to remember to review your progress?

Our goals should not be set in stone. It is helpful to review and renegotiate them as things change. As this happens you will access new information and experiences, which will alter your goals, so that reviewing and renegotiating become part of the process. As Doug Larson, an English Olympian, suggested, 'Establishing goals is all right if you don't let them deprive you of interesting detours.'

Below, you will find a series of questions and an exercise (Table 6.2) to help you to set better goals. Sit with a notebook and write down your responses. There are many questions: not all of them will be relevant to you, so read them through and decide which questions work best. Take time, but beware of investing too much time and energy in this; are you avoiding starting to put your goals into action? And remember, having any kind of goal is better than none; so don't get hung up on trying to find the perfect set of goals.

Table 6.2: Developing better goals for overcoming your worry

A: Questions to help you clarify your goals
- If worry were less of a problem in my life, how would things be different?
- What would I do with my time if I worried less?
- What would I notice if I worried less?
- What activities have I avoided because of my worry?
- Is there anything I would like to start doing if I worried less?
- Is there anything I would like to stop doing?
- What would we see you doing if you worried less?

B: Questions to help organize your answers
- Which goal would give me a sense of achievement?
- Which of the goals gives me an emotional buzz?
- Am I picking an issue that is too tough; is there anything easier I could attempt now?

C: SMART goal questions
- Is this goal **s**pecific? Can it be broken down further?
- How can I **m**easure progress towards this goal? How will I know when I have achieved it?
- Is this goal practically possible or **a**chievable?
- Is this goal **r**ealistic?
- How long will I realistically need to complete this goal? (**t**ime-limited)

D: COPER goal questions

- Is your goal compassionate?
- Which are short-, medium- or long-term goals?
  - ° Which goal needs to be done first?
  - ° Which can I ignore for now?
- *If my goal is an avoidance goal, would reframing it into an approach goal help?*
- *For when things are tough:* What are your reasons for continuing to engage with your goals?
- Is there a picture or an object that could remind you of your goals?
- Can I set a date to review my progress?

PIT STOP

Let's stop and think about what you have just been reading. Can you summarize the key ideas you have taken on board? What is sticking in your mind? Maybe write them down. If you have any questions, jot these down too. You can return to them once you have had a chance to digest the information.

What is sticking in my mind from my reading so far?

1.

2.

3.

7

Learning about rules

As we mentioned in the traffic metaphor earlier (Chapter 1), there are other things that influence the flow of traffic, such as drivers' beliefs or rules: *If I keep up with the traffic flow, I'm less likely to have an accident.* For a moment, consider what would happen if you rigidly held this rule. Suppose there is heavy rain and the traffic is moving much too quickly, or imagine everyone else is going well above the speed limit – what would you do? Would you break the rule or would you keep it? Our life experience helps us to know when it is best to either update or break our life rules. It is this flexibility that allows us to adapt and adjust to new experiences or situations.

It seems that our emotional wellbeing is based on beliefs or rules that are held firmly enough to give a consistent sense of who we are. Yet, at the same time, these rules and beliefs need to be fluid enough to enable us to adapt to new experiences. If you think about it, even so-called hard and rigid things, like bridges and tall buildings, move, flex and bend to wind and loads; without this ability they would soon break and fracture.

When people have psychological problems, often this flexibility is lost and their rules have become stuck and rigid. Our feelings can be considered to act like resin or concrete, setting the rules in place and making them harder to change. In this state, they are extreme and absolute, with no shades of grey. We can see these qualities reflected in the words used to make up the rules. For example, *I must <u>always</u> worry to solve my problems*; *I should <u>never</u> make a decision without checking it*; or, *If I can't predict what will happen, I'll <u>never</u> be able to cope*. If we think about these rules, would you consider them to be rules that everyone should hold? If not, why not? You may consider them to be unhelpful or extreme; you may also consider them to go beyond what is considered to be common sense.

We each have a unique 'rule book', which is a set of beliefs that guide our actions and help us to make sense of the world around us. If a Martian landed in your street tomorrow, using your rulebook he or she should be able to understand more about your world. The 'rulebook' helps us to make sense of the world because the rules are essentially predictions about what will happen next: for instance, *If I smile then others will smile back*; *If I hit my thumb then it will hurt*; *If I eat then I won't be hungry*, and so on. When we look at how people act we can begin to work out what rules might be influencing their actions. Usually we are unaware of these rules, but with a little attention and thought we can work them out. The first way to spot them is to become curious about what you or others do (or don't do) in a given situation. Our aim in this chapter is to reveal your 'worry rulebook' and then help you find ways of adapting the rules or even breaking them. The first section explores the different types of rule or belief that might be in operation, the second section moves on to helping you develop your 'worry rulebook'.

How to spot rules

Rules are often phrased as *if–then* statements, but they can also be *shoulds*, *oughts* or *musts*. They can be about many things – thoughts, feelings, actions, events, memories or even bodily sensations. We can use these phrases (*if–then*, *shoulds*, etc.) to help us work out the rules that might be active in any given situation. Take an everyday example such as why people form a line at a bus stop.

EXERCISE 7.1: WAITING AT A BUS STOP

How would you finish these statements? Write your answers on the dotted line.

If I stand in a queue **then**..................................
If I am at the front of the line **then**......................
If my feet are cold **then**....................................
If I am lost in my thoughts **then** ....
If I urge the bus to come **then** ....

For the first of these beliefs or rules you might say, *then I'll get on the bus*, or, for the fourth belief, you may answer, *I'll miss the bus!* For the final one, well, of course, *It'll be late!* Completing these phrases helps us work out what rules might be operating. Can you also see how these rules tell us about what might happen next, how they are essentially predictions? (Stop for a moment to think about this.) If my feet are cold, then we might predict that I'd stamp my feet. It works the other way round, too – if I notice someone stamping their feet, then I can guess that their feet are cold, although I can't be certain without asking.

Rules can also be phrased as *shoulds*, *oughts* or *musts*, and using these phrases can help us to work out other rules. For example:

> *I **must** not stand too close to the person in front. I **must** not talk to the driver when he is driving. Other people **should** never barge in. I **ought** to have the right change.*

Rules can be culturally specific. This means that bus queues in Bristol, Calcutta, Istanbul, La Paz, Toronto, Beijing, Paris and Nairobi are all influenced by slightly different rules, which means that different things happen. If you have travelled to new places, it might take a while to understand how the 'local' rules operate – this is part of the fun (or hassle) of travelling. When we learn about how others live their lives, we are essentially sussing out the rules that govern their actions.

We can also ask questions to help us detect rules, questions like, *Supposing you didn't queue, what would happen?* or, *What are the advantages and disadvantages of queuing?* These questions trigger us to reflect on the things that are important to us and bring us closer to understanding the rules that drive our actions.

How do your rules influence your actions at a bus stop? Before reading on, review your answers in the exercise above and try to imagine how these rules might influence your actions. You may also want to complete the following sentences:

- At a bus stop I should . . .
- At a bus stop I ought to . . .
- At a bus stop I must . . .
- At a bus stop others should . . .
- At a bus stop others ought to . . .
- At a bus stop others must . . .

What about your worry rules? Try completing the following:

EXERCISE 7.2: WORRY RULES

If I worry, then...

If I don't worry, then ....

I should worry because ....

Rules or beliefs? (Rules = Beliefs)

So far we have used these terms together or interchangeably. They are different ways of referring to the same thing. In CBT, rules are a type of thought and so we can call them beliefs.

What happens when the rules are broken?

When our rules are broken, or more usually when they look as if they might be broken, we often feel strong emotions. For example, if someone looks as if they are about to 'barge in' to a queue, then we may feel irritated or even angry. If someone is standing too close to us, we may feel uncomfortable. The fact that they are threatening to break or have actually broken the rules might lead us to do something about it, like moving to plug the gap, complaining, moving away or having angry thoughts of revenge.

Rules and worry

Worry is an everyday experience, and naturally there is a range of rules that underpin or support worry. Everyone holds some of these worry-supporting rules, but worriers probably tend to hold them much more rigidly than non-worriers. Research also tells us that if we target these rules in treatment then the symptoms of excessive worry may reduce. So it's worthwhile spending some time understanding them and then finding ways of adapting them. Rules appear in every chapter of this book; in some chapters they play a much more central role than in others, and some will be much more relevant to you than others. In the upcoming chapters note the sections that most closely describe the way you think, so that you can return to them. Many of the rules can be worked with by using *behavioural experiments*; we will tell you more about these later in this chapter.

Rules that support worry instruct us to worry in lots of different situations – when we face uncertainty or everyday problems, for example. Rules might also instruct us to do other things in addition to worry, such as avoid situations that trigger worry, seek much more information than we need, put things off so we worry later or seek reassurance. There are many others. If we are looking for signs that these worry rules are in action, then we need look no further than worry itself. The action of worry suggests that our worry rules have been activated. But these other signs – avoidance, putting things off and so forth – also give us clues as to the type of worry rule that is in action. In the forthcoming chapters you will learn how to spot the tell-tale signs that these rules are in operation.

Understanding what keeps problems going

A helpful analogy is to think about the time when the world was thought to be flat. This idea comes with images of the 'edge of the world', where great waterfalls cascade over from the rim of the earth into oblivion. If we truly believed this, then it would make good sense to avoid the edge of the world. But because we never go to the edge of the world, we never find out that this simply isn't true, so the belief that the world is flat lives on.

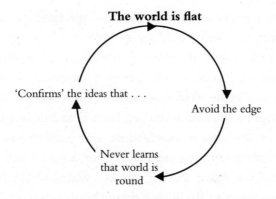

Figure 7.1: Flat world analogy

Now, imagine you hold this belief very strongly and that we turn up and tell you the world is round. Would you believe us? Probably not, given that you imagine that those foolish enough to sail to the edge of the world would fall into oblivion. Next we might suggest you come with us on a journey around the world and 'over the edge'. How would you feel? What would you do? You might decide to give us a wide berth, writing us off as con artists and troublemakers (and you might be right). But supposing we brought evidence that the world was round. What if we showed you pictures, diagrams and charts, brought gifts and treasures from beyond the known world; what would you think then?

What evidence would you need to take the risk? (Think about this before moving on.)

What if we asked you to think about the balance between the advantages and disadvantages of a flat earth, and then a round earth? What if we took you to talk with other sailors to find out what they knew? What if we watched a ship

140

disappearing over the horizon, hull first, masts last? What if we told you that you would see new constellations of stars if you travelled with us? What if we observed together a lunar eclipse and watched the curve of the earth's shadow as it passed over the moon? What if we provided you with detailed diagrams to help you see how it all might work? What if we told you of an island paradise just beyond the horizon with everything you could ever want in plentiful supply (we will leave this bit to your imagination)? You might just begin to think that there *may* be another way of seeing things (the world is round) and that there *may* be something to be gained from challenging your idea that the world is flat. Now that we have 'softened you up' with evidence and the promise of treasure, what would be the most convincing piece of evidence to prove once and for all that the world was not flat? The bottom line is that you would need to go over 'the edge' and find out for yourself.

In CBT this is what is called a *behavioural experiment* – doing things differently to find out something new. In our example, you might be beginning to think there may be something in this idea that the world is round, but you might still be doubtful. You might agree to come for a sail, and after an hour or so, we turn to you and say, *Look, the world is round*. But you are not convinced and you reply, *Yes, but if we sailed further then we'd really go over the edge; the edge is just beyond this horizon*. So we sail on for another hour and the same thing happens again. So we ask, *How long would we have to sail to convince you?* And you say, *A year and a day, and in and out of weeks*. And off we go. As we sail we might look up into the night sky to see how the constellations change, collecting evidence as we go. And finally, after a year and a day, we'd ask, *So how does this experience of sailing for all this time fit with the idea that the earth is flat?* If your flat world idea still remained then there would be nothing for it – we'd have to call NASA and get you a seat on the next space shuttle!

Why are we telling you this story? It helps to demonstrate the ideas that we will use for helping you to change. It shows how rules motivate actions, which in turn act to confirm the original idea. For instance, if I believe that worry helps to solve problems, then it makes sense to worry. In order to challenge the idea of a flat earth we needed to find evidence to gently rock the foundations of this idea. To do this, we used the same ideas and techniques used in the treatment of worry and other emotional problems.

Table 7.1: Flat world – worry rules comparisons

Strategies	Flat earth example:	Worrying example:
	If I sail over the edge of the world I will die.	Worrying helps me solve problems.
Information gathering	We found objects from beyond the edge of the world and information in the form of maps and charts	We might ask, how do people in general solve life's problems? What ideas/techniques are there to help/teach you to do this? Do good problem-solvers recommend worry as a technique to solve problems?

Developing an understanding of how the rules lead to actions and keep the problem going	We helped you to understand how your thoughts might be influencing your behaviour and keeping the idea of a flat earth alive.	We would show you that worry can get in the way of solving problems, particularly if the worry makes it hard to concentrate – the rule may end up causing more worry and prevent you from solving the problem.
Advantages and disadvantages	We reviewed the advantages and disadvantages of taking risks to learn new things.	We might review the advantages and disadvantages of worrying to solve problems. For instance, you may get some good ideas, but do you really want the emotional baggage that comes with solving problems in this way?
Evidence for an alternative view	We looked for good evidence that suggested that the earth was indeed round.	We would look for good evidence that worrying to solve problems was not as helpful as other methods. We might ask in what other ways, aside from worrying, you have solved problems. Which is the best way?

Surveys	We talked to the sailors and learnt from them.	We might ask you to survey several friends about how they go about solving problems. How many of them do you think might suggest worrying?
Goals	We spoke of the treasure that lay in wait for the brave explorer.	What do you stand to gain by solving problems in another way? Is this some-thing worthwhile to you?
Behavioural experiments	We took you over the edge of the world.	We might ask you to solve a minor problem by using problem-solving steps, rather than worrying; what's your prediction about what would happen? How can you push this idea?
Reviewing learning	Given all this inform-ation and experiences, what do you believe now?	What have you learnt about worrying as a method of solving problems?
What can you do now to push home the idea?	Sail alone around the world.	Solve bigger problems using problem-solving skills.

In the flat world example above, we used information gath-ering (charts, objects), we developed an understanding of the problem, we looked at the advantages and disadvantages of change, we provided evidence for the alternative idea of a round earth (stars, masts and eclipse), we surveyed other people (sailors) to find out their experience, and we reminded ourselves of the value of change (treasure). We then reviewed the idea in the light of these new experiences and the final step was trying something new. The last part is important, because doing something new normally leads to new information and ideas. It's as if you have a new piece of the jigsaw (new information), and you have to accommodate this into your existing worldview, which can be quite an earth-shattering experience. This new information can be like wearing someone else's shoes for a while; it might feel odd and take a while to wear them in. This is why it's important to follow up your experiments with others until it begins to feel like second nature. The acid test is whether you start to feel differently. While sometimes this happens quickly, mostly it's a question of chipping away and doggedly moving forward.

While the story above is about actions and thoughts, it is principally about feelings. In the flat earth example, fear is the main motivating emotion. If you believe that the world is flat, it makes absolute sense to feel frightened about going over the edge of the world! The test enabled new learning by trying something new, and as a consequence the fear of the edge was dissolved. Doing things differently requires courage, and these kinds of experiences are not easy, but the benefits are huge. Anxiety and fear can lock us into unhelpful patterns of thinking and action; behavioural experiments are the key, and enable us to unlock our mind and free it from anxiety.

Behavioural experiments are among the most powerful ways of enabling change and helping people to overcome their problems. We will outline in more detail how they work later, but first let's take the flat earth experiment a little further by looking at how some of the actions people use to keep themselves safe during experiments get in the way of learning something new.

Safety behaviours

As we have suggested above, rules and beliefs encourage or discourage actions. For instance, one way to prevent yourself falling off the edge of the world is simply to avoid sailing and never get in a boat, or at least never leave the port. However, if you do go sailing, there are some things that you might do to keep yourself safe. Let's imagine that we are in the boat and we are heading towards the edge of the world. If you are like us, then you may want to 'hedge your bets' and *do* something to make the experience less frightening. Because your safety behaviour makes you feel safe, it might be something you do every time you sail out into open water and consequently you may not notice it. The idea that the world is flat may encourage you to trail a rope back to shore, so you can pull yourself back if you *feel* you are too close to the edge. You may ignore the edge and pretend that none of this is happening and stare into the bottom of the boat (missing the evidence from the stars). You may feel safe only if you can see your homeland behind you (meaning that you sail in circles for days and not towards the horizon). These actions are logical, given the idea that the earth is flat, and they function to make us 'feel' safer. However, they are based on the idea that there is something 'real' to fear. If we manage to sail closer to the edge of the world while trailing a rope, we may think that the only reason we are safe is because of the rope; that is, *If I didn't have this rope then we really would have gone over the edge.* This turns the experience into a near miss – *Phew, I saved myself from certain death this time* – rather than allowing us finally to find out that there is nothing to be frightened of. Can you see how entirely logical and understandable this is? Breaking, or the potential of breaking, our rules or other beliefs produces strong feelings and motivates us to take action to find safety where we can. This cycle in turn serves to 'rubber stamp' our original unhelpful rule, as above. To drive this idea home, here is our version of a story told by Paul Salkovskis, Professor of Clinical Psychology and Applied Science at the University of Bath.

A man was sprinkling white powder in the fast lane of a very busy motorway. The police were alerted and arrived with blue lights flashing, stopped the traffic and arrested the man. They asked him, 'Why were you sprinkling white powder on the motorway?' The man replied, 'It's anti-elephant powder to keep the elephants off the road and stop awful accidents from happening.' The police officer exclaimed, 'But there are no elephants in Newcastle!' And the man answered, 'You see, it works!'

The things we do to keep ourselves safe (safety behaviours) have a number of unhelpful side-effects. They keep the idea alive in our minds that there is something to be frightened of (*that was a near miss, next time I won't be so lucky, be prepared*); they often make the situation or problem much worse (by being in the fast lane the man was actually putting his own and others' lives at risk rather than stopping accidents); and they keep our danger radar on, which means that we pick up on the tiniest signs of danger or see danger where there is none. There are many safety behaviours in worry. For example, asking someone for reassurance once a decision has been made is a safety behaviour aimed at reducing uncertainty and worry. Unfortunately, it keeps worry alive because the worrier never learns to trust their judgement. Each time a new decision or situation arises, the worrier doubts their ability to make a good decision and so seeks reassurance. If this is done enough times, then those close to them may start to get annoyed, which in turn triggers more worry, the very thing the worrier was trying to reduce in the first place. Also, because the worrier's 'threat radar' is on full, even decisions they are certain about trigger them to seek reassurance.

Safety behaviours and worry

Below is a list of typical safety behaviours, with a series of questions to help you explore your own. Spotting safety behaviours is helpful because they are important in keeping worry alive, and they also give clues as to what rules might be lurking beneath them. Review the list and then try to answer the questions that follow.

Table 7.2: Typical safety behaviours seen in worriers

Seeking reassurance for decisions	Checking on the whereabouts of loved ones (e.g. finding excuses to telephone them)
Trying to push upsetting ideas out of our minds	
Seeking out excessive amounts of information before making a decision	Checking and rechecking on decisions or tasks
	Over-protecting others
Avoiding certain types of information that trigger worry	Avoiding fully committing to things to leave an 'escape route'
Putting off making decisions	Distraction
Overanalysing problems	Being overly busy; throwing ourselves into activity rather than solving problems (e.g. cleaning)
Solving problems impulsively	
Making lists as a substitute for actions	Using lots of superstitious behaviours to avoid bad luck or create good luck

Take a notebook and try to answer the following questions:

- Which of these behaviours are typical of you?
- What other things do you do to reduce worry or uncertainty? Make a list of these.
- What rules might be driving your safety behaviours?
- Do other people hold these rules as strongly as you do?

- Supposing you didn't have or dropped your safety behaviour; what do you fear would happen?
- Supposing you 'amplified' your safety behaviour; then what do you think would happen? (For example, what might happen if, on purpose, you checked more often than you usually would? What effect might this have?)
- How might these safety behaviours make your worry worse?
- What are the advantages and disadvantages of these behaviours?

Summary

So far we have explored the rules (or assumptions) that underpin our actions; we have seen how they have an influence on how we feel and what we do, and how, unfortunately, these actions tend to backfire as they keep our problems alive and also make them worse. It is important, then, to find a way of challenging these unhelpful patterns.

Modifying our worry rulebook – behavioural experiments

If worry is a problem for you, then we have to help you to challenge the rules that underpin your worry. We do this by taking the stance of a scientist wanting to explore and work out how things relate to one another or how things happen. Like a scientist, we want to set up experiments to see if we can learn something new when we change what happens. We want to look for evidence or facts to test the validity of particular rules. You, and more specifically your worry, will be the subject of these experiments and so it's very important that you understand why we are suggesting them, how these experiments might make things better and what to expect when you are doing them. Behavioural experiments are all about predictions; that is, *what we expect to happen vs what actually happens*. If what *actually* happens is very different from what we *expect*, then we would do well to update the way we think in the light of this new information. Behavioural experiments are powerful because they help us change by giving us *an experience of doing something new, rather than just thinking or talking about it*.

Planning behavioural experiments

What follows is a series of steps that offers a blueprint to show you how you can start challenging some of the rules. You will find a table summarizing the key points at the end of this chapter. In each chapter there will be further signposts towards what behavioural experiments you might want to engage in. We have put the blueprint here because it offers some basic principles that apply, no matter what kind of experiments we do. Nearly all the techniques within CBT can be thought of as attempts to examine the helpfulness of particular rules or beliefs, or, put another way, to find out what is really going on. Behavioural experiments and other techniques try to help answer this question by bringing all the information into play, rather than just information selected by the filter of our emotions, habits, avoidance, safety behaviours, unhelpful thinking styles or other processes. In order to bring a more helpful perspective into play, we have to approach the experiment with an open mind, ready for new learning. We have to become curious about previously unexplored information and, like an explorer, we need to seek out, discover and then understand new or previously ignored or avoided experiences, and then be prepared to engage in them.

Planning behavioural experiments: steps to discovery

First, we need to put the rule 'on the table' in everyday language; that is, to name it in a way that we know what we are dealing with. For argument's sake, let's work with a common rule in worry: *Worrying helps me to solve problems.* We should try to nest the rule within our everyday experience. As it stands, the rule is phrased in a very general way. What might this rule sound like when brought to the 'coalface' of our lives? For example:

> *If I worry about problems at home then I can find better ways of solving them.*

Second, although we have our rule in everyday language, it is still a little too vague and we need to tie it down to an everyday example. We also need to get a little more specific and find out what problems the worrier is trying to solve by worrying and what exactly might happen if they *did not* worry.

> *If I didn't worry about what to do with the kids over their summer break, then I'd have a nightmare on my hands; they'd be bored and get annoyed with me.*

The more specific we get the easier it is to find ways of challenging rules. More global or general rules are much harder because they don't give us clues about what we might be able to do to challenge them. The following questions can help to get down to the level of detail needed.

> Supposing you didn't worry about this; what would be so bad about that? Supposing you didn't worry about this; what would that say about you, or what would that mean to you?

Like all rules, the rule *worrying helps me to solve problems* is a prediction – it tells us what would happen if the worrier did not worry – and it also helps us to understand why the worrier is so keen to act upon the rule by worrying. Pause for a moment and see if this makes sense to you.

Third, there is a need to get a sense of how big an influence the rule has in our lives. To do this we rate how strongly the worrier believes the rule on a scale of 0–100 per cent, with 100 per cent corresponding to *I absolutely believe this to be true*. We can check this rating later to see if things have changed.

Fourth, we need to think of other ways of seeing things. Essentially, we are trying to find other information or evidence that suggests that this rule may not be wholly helpful. Remember the flat earth example. It's as if these two (or more) ways of thinking are placed on a set of weighing scales: which of these two ideas makes the most sense, when we consider all of the information available? There are several questions that the worrier can be asked to help bring this information to the surface. For example, is your worry actually solving the problem, or are you just going over and over the same concerns? When you worry, how does it leave you feeling and how do your feelings influence your ability to think of solutions? Is there a more helpful way of preparing for the summer break, rather than worrying? Even if you could think of nothing to keep your children occupied, what would be the worst thing that could happen, or what would it say about you as a person?

This fourth step is often a tricky one, since the worrier has been stuck in a particular way of seeing the world and thus stepping outside of this viewpoint can be difficult. Questions like *Is there another way of seeing this?* or *What ideas would you give to a friend who was struggling with the same problem?* might help. By posing these questions we are trying to soften the rule and enable a new rule to emerge. When it does, then rate this new idea on the same scale.

Emerging idea or prediction

Worrying doesn't seem to be the best way of solving problems. If I worry, I get anxious and can't think straight, so I need to do something instead of worrying.

Fifth, we need to think of a way of exploring the new understanding captured by these statements. We have to progress towards testing the emerging idea or prediction by doing something new. In this example, to start with we may decide to focus on finding ideas for a weekend rather than the whole summer break. By doing this we are testing things out in a small way first, where there is more chance of success, and so we will develop better ideas about how things work. The worrier could worry as usual for one weekend and then do something new the following weekend. So for the first weekend they would worry as usual and see what activities they come up with for the children. For the second weekend, we would ask them to write a list and ask the children what they might want to do and then decide together. Which of these two strategies work best?

Test 1
I'll worry about what I can do with the kids over the weekend. How many ideas can you come up with by worrying?

Test 2
This time, I'll write a list and ask the kids to do the same and then decide together what we can do.

Sixth, we need to consider the things that could get in the way of finding out something new. A useful question is, *If you did this, would it help you to think and feel that worrying is not the best way of finding solutions to problems?* If the answer is no, then we need to think again about how to test this rule out. By asking this we are trying to get the 'yes buts' out in the open before we embark on an experiment. It's like a dry run in your mind to see if the experiment will help. So be prepared to redesign the experiment if needed. Treat each step forward or back as an opportunity to learn something new.

The most important thing is to do something in a different way and break the pattern of your worry, so don't get too hung up on the details. Try it out and review, try again.

Looking for safety behaviours

With most rules, there are often subtle safety behaviours that coexist. These may become more obvious as you try to challenge and change your worry rules. These mostly small, inconspicuous actions are very powerful, and while they reduce our fear in the short term, they have a number of unfortunate side-effect like keeping the problem of worry going or eroding our self-confidence. So we simply need to drop the safety behaviours when doing our behavioural experiments. But not all at once: do so one at a time, dropping the easy ones first and then moving on to the ones held most strongly, moving finally to do something new without any safety behaviours at all.

If you believed the rules above, what might you end up doing to make you feel safe if your rules were threatened? What might your safety behaviours be? If the worrier was not worrying to solve problems then they might increase other actions to compensate, like seeking reassurance, or looking for subtle signs of disapproval, or being extra nice to the children, just in case.

Improving test 2
This time, I'll write a list and ask the kids to do the same and then decide together what we can do. I won't ask my partner for advice or help, or keep checking with the kids that they are happy with the plan.

Seventh, we need to do the experiment.

Eighth, we need to review what happened, what things you noticed and what you have learnt. With this rule, the worrier might notice a sense of relief as they hand over some responsibility to their children, or their relationship with their children might improve as they spend more time talking and discussing things rather than telling them. Often, people find that there are many more advantages to the new way of doing things than were first apparent when working through the test. At this stage we return to the rule or belief that we held and ask how this new experience has challenged this. We then re-rate the beliefs. Finally, we need to think about how we can push the idea much further. So, where else might this rule have an influence? What other situations, relationships or events might be influenced by this rule? What other experiments could help to challenge the rule?

There is a simple experiment planning sheet (see Exercise 7.3 overleaf) to help you plan your behavioural experiment on worry. In each of the following chapters we shall refer back to this sheet and the steps outlined above.

When trying new things out, expect the unexpected. This unexpected information helps develop our understanding of how things work. Whether things go to plan or otherwise, the new learning will add to your understanding.

Finally, while we have focused a lot on ideas, beliefs and rules, behavioural experiments are really about changing the way we feel. And this is the acid test: as a rule of thumb, if your feelings don't change, then think about what you are doing and ask if there are any safety behaviours that you have not spotted and dropped. Is the experiment real enough? Is it triggering some anxiety or is it too safe?

EXERCISE 7.3: CHALLENGING YOUR WORRY RULES – BEHAVIOURAL EXPERIMENTS

1. Spot the rule or idea to be tested
Use the safety behaviour list, the sentence completion tasks, the questionnaire information, your Worry Diary, etc., to spot an idea or rule.

2. Putting the rule 'on the table'
Name it, so that we know what we are dealing with. Frame it in *if-then* terms. Make it real by linking it to a real situation. What is your prediction about? What will happen if you break, bend or disregard the rule? Write it here . . .

3. Rate your prediction
Put a cross on the line below.

0%   50%   100%

A

I do not believe this   *I believe this completely*

4. Emerging idea or alternative prediction
Is there another way of seeing this? What ideas would you give to a friend who believed this? When you are less worried, do you see things any differently? What else might happen if you broke your rule? Write it here . . .

5. Rate your alternative prediction
Put a cross on the line below.

0%   50%   100%

B

I do not believe this   *I believe this completely*

6. Figuring out what to do
How could you test your prediction? Start simple, start small, and build towards more emotionally loaded experiments. What exactly will you do? What safety behaviours might you need to consider? Can you drop them one by one and see what happens? What else might stop you from learning?

My experiment is

7. Do it! (Guard against perfectionism and putting thing off.)

8. Review what happened
What things have you noticed? What have you learnt? How do you feel now? How does this new experience sit with your prediction? Re-rate both your predictions. What does it tell you about your rule?

    0%   50%   100%

A ——I——I——I——I——I——I——I——I——

B ——I——I——I——I——I——I——I——I——

I do not believe this   *I believe this completely*

What now? What other experiments can you do?

PIT STOP

Let's stop and think about what you have just been reading. Can you summarize the key ideas you have taken on board? What is sticking in your mind? Maybe write them down. If you have any questions, jot these down too. You can return to them once you have had a chance to digest the information.

What is sticking in my mind from my reading so far?

1.

2.

3.

8

Learning to tolerate uncertainty

In the traffic metaphor in Chapter 1 we suggested that there is a level of uncertainty in travel, with unforeseen delays, breakdowns and so on. We noted that when the flow of traffic was very heavy or if conditions were bad, as in heavy rain, then these other factors acted together to increase the level of uncertainty and made journey times especially unpredictable. Living with this kind of uncertainty is something we have to tolerate, if we are to get to our destinations without feeling exhausted and stressed. Uncertainty is the fuel for worry and it drives much of our worry; and so, like learning to tolerate the uncertainties in driving, we need to learn to tolerate life's uncertainties. The following chapters will help you do this.

Introducing uncertainty

Uncertainty is a state almost *all* of us find difficult at times and some of us find it unbearable. When we are uncertain we have less knowledge than we would like to have, nothing appears to be clear-cut, and it is often impossible to predict what exactly will happen next, although some things are more likely than others. It leads to feelings of unease, apprehension and sometimes a mental paralysis, as we rapidly oscillate between solutions, unsure of which path to follow. Some situations leave us all in a state of limbo, and, when relative certainty materializes, there seems to be a sense of relief as a degree of predictability and order returns. Take the example of a family waiting in an A&E department for news of a loved one involved in an accident; sometimes the uncertainty, or not knowing, is the hardest thing to bear. Once they know what the situation is, whether it is good news, bad news or somewhere in between, they can start to deal with it.

Uncertainty, like gravity, is a constant feature of our world, and it influences many aspects of it. A quick look at the world news tells us that uncertainty has influence at both government and individual levels. Stock markets and oil prices are influenced by uncertainty caused by conflict, climate change, politics and industry. With all the media, twenty-four-hour news coverage and of course social media, we are increasingly aware of events unfolding. When an event is unfolding, the little drips of information, the contradictions between them, and the reports that 'we are still waiting to hear . . .' will all fuel the uncertainty. Before the technological, information and, especially, digital revolution, we would not have found out about an event until well after it occurred. We probably didn't even know that something was going to happen, or something was happening, let alone had happened. When we did find out it was already after the event, it was no longer uncertain, at least in the headlines. But this is no longer the case. Constant coverage gives access to all the things that could happen before they do.

At an individual level, a person's mood and wellbeing might be influenced by the uncertainty found in their own relationships, health and work, or in the health, safety and important activities of close family and friends. Life, further, is full of novel experiences, many of them good, but these also come with a degree of uncertainty – indeed, uncertainty, like gravity, seems to be a part of the jigsaw of life.

As uncertainty is universal, it appears to be something we *all* have to learn to manage and tolerate. In order to explore the idea of uncertainty further, try the following exercise and read the analogy below.

EXERCISE 8.1: BEGINNING TO NOTICE UNCERTAINTY

Read a recent news article or a story in a magazine and see if you can spot the uncertainty within it. Or watch your favourite soap, pick one character and see if you can spot the uncertainty they experience (without some uncertainty, there is probably no storyline!). Think about someone you know well: what uncertainty do they have to deal with? Alternatively, look for 'uncertainty' or 'uncertain' in a news or current affairs website; what stories come up? Or enter it into an Internet search engine and see what images or topics come up.

For instance, in the classic film of the play *Twelve Angry Men*, the jury debated what at first appeared

---

to be a clear case of murder. Henry Fonda's character used uncertainty (reasonable doubt) as a motivation to explore the facts properly. This set in motion a sequence of discoveries that enabled him and the eleven other jurors to move from a finding of almost certain guilt to a finding of not guilty, and thus to set free an innocent man.

Choose a character from TV, a book or film, and use the following questions to help you to explore uncertainty:

- What makes this/their situation uncertain?
- What do they know? What don't they know? What are they unsure about?
- What might be the gaps in their knowledge?
- How does their uncertainty influence their actions?
- How do they try to manage their uncertainty?
- Would anyone feel uncertain in this situation? If not, then what other things make the situation uncertain for them?

Horror film analogy

Uncertainty is a feeling we all experience while watching horror films. Usually there is a sense of suspense, since we know that something frightening is about to happen. In the best films, we're not quite sure what will happen; where, when or how it will happen; or even whom it might happen to. In fact, we can't even be sure if it will happen at all, as numerous close shaves tend to build up the sense of suspense. There is, however, a sense of inevitability that something bad will take place, and the best directors push this to its limits. When people are in this state of suspense, it's not unusual for them to try to do something to take control of the situation. They may, for example, leave or turn the TV off, cover their eyes to stop seeing the film, or cover their ears to block out the music. Their actions are motivated by the real and uncomfortable feelings that go with this sense of terrible dread and uncertainty.

Worry and uncertainty?

Worry seems to be a natural reaction to uncertainty. In a state of uncertainty, because we do not know what, when, where, how or even if bad things will happen, it makes it much harder for us to do anything about them in any *real way*. Our minds and imagination step up their activity to try and solve the problem of uncertainty. From uncertainty emerges a spiral of thoughts about what might happen. The *what ifs* and the subsequent whirlwind of worry are an attempt to predict what will happen next, and what to do if it happens. It's almost as if worry is used as a bridge to span the unknowns (i.e. the uncertainty) so we can see a way to get to the other side. In uncertain situations, worry tends to spiral following well-worn paths about relationships, finances, family and so on, while at the same time rapidly following an infinite number of smaller tracks within these themes, as the worrier 'seeks' solutions. This frenetic mental activity unfortunately tends to reveal new problems, which in turn generate more worry. At these moments of uncertainty, because our worries feel real, we have a genuine desire to stop the bad things we worry about from happening and we then try to think of ways of avoiding the imagined horrors. The solutions we come up with start us thinking about other things that could happen, and we may begin to worry about those instead. Our worry quickly becomes a way of trying to wrestle certainty from the jaws of uncertainty, but, unfortunately, it has completely the opposite effect, making things feel more uncertain.

We can all experience this when faced with uncertain, big, life-changing events that are happening now or are known to be just around the corner, and most people if not everyone will worry about the big event. One of the problems for worriers is that worry and the types of things we do when we worry are used to try to solve all life's uncertainties and not just the life-changing ones, although some of these can actually be useful: thinking about the different things that could happen, what might be the options, what might happen within each option, which one may be best, etc. In GAD, *the solution of using worry to try to resolve uncertainty becomes a one-size-fits-all approach for trying to take control over the uncertainties in life.*

Worry and uncertainty are intimately linked: uncertainty is seen as the fuel for worry and because worrying generates more uncertainty, this in turn fuels more worry (see Figure 8.1 overleaf). While all of us want to decrease life's uncertainties and so worry less, we can never eradicate them entirely, and efforts to do so tend to result in more uncertainty (we will explore this in more detail later). So we cannot decrease the levels of uncertainty in the world, but we might be able to help you to adjust your reaction to uncertainty by gradually reintroducing it into your life. Remember that CBT is about your view, or your appraisals, of what is happening (see Chapter 4). This is also true with uncertainty. Your view or appraisal of uncertainty is critical in helping to understand your reaction to it. If we can offer you other ways of thinking about uncertain situations, then we will help you to tolerate the not knowing, to worry less and react in more helpful ways. We know from research that worriers have difficulty accepting uncertainty, they become upset by it, and then have difficulty acting in helpful ways when facing it. One of the things they do instead of acting is worry. As uncertainty fuels worry, our task in this chapter is to help you to manage and tolerate uncertainty, and, in doing so, to manage and reduce your worry.

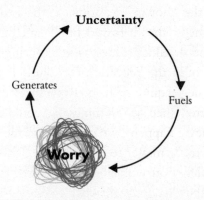

Figure 8.1: Worry and uncertainty

Insurance metaphor

If uncertainty feels like the suspense we experience in a horror film, then we can think of worry as being like an insurance policy covering the uncertainties of life. Insurance can't stop things from happening, it just reduces the financial losses if they do. Some insurance makes sense in many cases, but if the cost (premium) is too high, is it really worthwhile? If you are buying a toaster, is it worth paying half of the price again, just to have a three-year guarantee (there is a guarantee of one year anyway if the toaster is faulty)? If you believe all toasters break down within a short time frame, then it may be worthwhile. Otherwise, you may accept the uncertainty, decide you will deal with it if it happens, and keep your money in your pocket. Likewise, worry can't really stop bad things from happening; it just seems to offer the chance of reducing the losses.

However, the cost (premium) in hours of wasted worrying, the knot in the stomach, the loss of sleep and enjoyment, the furrowed brow and the tension between the shoulder blades, is just too high. Worry appears to offer the promise of a solution to uncertainty, but never quite delivers. If we spent a little less money on insurance against things that could go wrong (but may never happen), we could spend more on the things that really matter to us. Likewise, if we spent a little less energy on worrying about things that could go wrong (but may never happen), we could spend it on pursuing things that really matter right now, such as family, friends, fun and the things we really want from our future.

Remember, though, some insurance for big events is probably a good idea, such as life insurance if we have a family or responsibilities, building insurance for fire, flood, etc., car insurance for major damage, etc. Insurance companies will also try to sell you other add-ons for additional, usually less significant risks such as losing keys, or scratch and dent insurance, etc. Likewise, let's keep worry (or something like it) for the big event, and not buy the insurance, pay the premium, and worry for all of life's less significant uncertainties.

Why do worriers react to uncertainty?

It is not the situations themselves that are the problem, nor is it the presence of uncertainty. Rather, it appears that worriers seem on the whole to be much more sensitive to even tiny amounts of uncertainty in everyday situations. In their excellent book on cognitive behavioural treatment for GAD, Professor Michel Dugas and Dr Melisa Robichaud helpfully suggest that the intolerance of uncertainty can be thought of as an allergy. With something like hay fever, you only need a tiny amount of pollen to cause an allergic reaction. This is also true of worry; you only need a tiny amount of uncertainty to trigger excessive worry and anxiety. For many worriers, if there is a million-to-one chance that something bad could happen, then because there is this *splinter of doubt* that it could happen, they worry. The *splinter of doubt* then fuels the whirlwind of worry. Uncertainty can be obvious to us all – for example, being called in for an unexpected appointment with the bank manager, or a family member falling ill. It can also be subtle, and might be found in conversations – for example, someone saying, *I'll be in some time after nine.* Worriers may prefer certainty, which is, unfortunately, frequently impossible to have. Consider the following examples.

Ellie worried about whether her husband could find his way home following sales trips. He had done so nearly every working day for the past ten years from all parts of the country and he had *never* got lost. Despite knowing this, she also knew that there was a slim chance he *could* get lost, that his car *could* break down, that he *could* be delayed by an accident, stuck in traffic or that he *could* even have had an accident. It was these *splinters of doubt* that gave rise to uncertainty, which, in turn, fuelled her worry. She wanted to be 100 per cent sure, but even after ten years she could not be certain – even though he had never been more than two hours late and always phoned if he was stuck in traffic. Despite some misfortune being highly unlikely, it *was* possible and this was enough to start her worrying. Her worry had become such a habit that she was barely aware of it, though she did notice feeling exhausted and tense most of the time.

With Ellie, above, it was the tiny amount of uncertainty, or the *splinter of doubt*, that triggered her worry. Because of its very nature, once worry has started it generates its own uncertainty, which means that it will continue under its own steam until something interrupts the flow.

Following a routine check-up, a doctor gave Oscar, a worried man, some feedback. The doctor told him, 'There is only a very small chance that your pain is anything to worry about, but I think it's best we meet in three to four weeks to see how things are.' The considerate and careful doctor gave the man some reasonable advice, but, because of the way he approached the world, Oscar assumed the worst and started to worry even more. He began thinking, *If it was nothing, then my doctor wouldn't be concerned; what if he's not telling me something? What if he's saving the bad news for next time? This isn't fair. I can't handle this; I need to know now.* Before he drove home, he tried to telephone his doctor from the car park outside the surgery.

In this story there are three things to notice. First is Oscar's tendency to assume the worst. Second is his hypersensitivity to the uncertainty found in the situation. There are several sources of uncertainty: the language that the caring doctor uses – he says there is a *very small chance* and what Oscar wants to hear is that there is *no chance*; the apparent contradiction between 'nothing to worry about' and coming back in for another appointment; and, finally, the self-generated uncertainty found within Oscar's worry. Third is that he also found uncertainty nerve-racking and upsetting and could not tolerate it; put another way, he is *intolerant of uncertainty*. Research has shown that this is one of the most important influences on our tendency to worry: intolerance of uncertainty forms the cornerstone of the psychological ideas that explains GAD and the self-help treatments found in this book.

As we saw in the case stories at the beginning of the book, worriers often avoid facing uncertainty at all costs. Sometimes they would even prefer bad things to happen immediately rather than live with the sense of not knowing what will happen next. It's not that they want the bad thing to happen, but not knowing if, or when, something may happen feels terrible and intolerable. They find it hard to put plans into action because they can't be sure their plans will work out; or, at the slightest hint of things not going to plan, uncertainty may stop them in their tracks. This might be a good time to reread the case stories at the beginning of the book; compared to when you first started to read them, what do you notice now?

Learning to spot my reaction to uncertainty

Although worriers are sensitive to uncertainty, they do not often notice the experience, for many reasons. First, it is often embedded in life events (see Ellie's and Oscar's stories above). Second, worry is a habitual response to uncertainty, almost like a reflex, so we may not pay attention to what triggers the worry and it may feel as if it comes out of the blue. Third, worry is an overwhelming experience at the time, making it hard to think of other things. Fourth, worriers tend to need only tiny amounts of uncertainty to trigger worry and so we are by definition looking for something small or seemingly innocuous. Fifth, worry is everywhere, like gravity, and, like gravity, we may be blind to it unless we look for it.

EXERCISE 8.2: NOTICING MY EXPERIENCE OF UNCERTAINTY

By now you will have been keeping a diary of your worry and have become better at spotting the *what if* statements, the types of worry and the themes of worry. You can use your Worry Diary to help you to reflect on uncertainty in each bout of worry. The following questions may help you to do this:

- If you consider worry as a way of bridging uncertainty then what are the unknowns in that situation? What do you know and what don't you know?
- In this situation what were you unsure of?
- Was there something unknown to you? What was it?
- How did uncertainty influence your actions?
- How did you try to manage the uncertainty?
- Thinking of all the worry episodes, what did

---

you notice in your body, thoughts or behaviours that might act as an early warning sign for uncertainty?

Assessing your tolerance of uncertainty can help you to tune into the feeling of suspense described in the horror film analogy above (see page 165) and you can begin to become more aware of when the intolerance appears, noting what triggers it and what you did to handle this feeling. It's almost as if we have to tune into what tells us we are in an uncertain situation. Of course, worry is the most likely thing that you will notice, but there may be other things, such as physical sensation, a mood, a feeling, a sharp intake of breath, a statement or phrase you say, a thought that jumps into your mind or one you think habitually, a habit you fall into, an action you can't help doing, a mannerism, and so on. The list is endless, but for a moment stop to think: is there anything you do that might alert you to the fact that uncertainty is around – like a smoke detector? Think through your thoughts, feelings, actions and physical sensations when faced with uncertainty. What do you think, feel, sense or do?

What is intolerance of uncertainty?

This is an important idea, so it is vital that we spend some time thinking it through. People who are intolerant of uncertainty, like worriers, tend to experience uncertainty as stressful and upsetting; they feel that an uncertain future is unfair and intolerable, that surprises are threatening and unsettling, and that uncertainty interferes with their ability to live, they feel uncertainty in their body, often in their stomach. A very straightforward way of describing this is to say that *worriers hate not knowing*. It is the no man's land between the knowing and not knowing that they find so unbearable.

Since we wrote the first edition we have found out a lot more about intolerance of uncertainty – when we finished the first edition at the end of 2007, there were about 200 books and articles that used the Intolerance of Uncertainty Scale found on page 181. As we finish the second edition there are almost 600. So, based on research from around the world and on our own with colleagues and creative, hard-working students in Newcastle upon Tyne, here are a few of the things that we have found out about people who report being more intolerant of uncertainty:

- They worry more (OK, we already knew that, but it's worth restating).
- They perceive more situations as uncertain.
- The uncertainty in everyday situation bothers them more compared to people who are more tolerant of

uncertainty (perhaps obvious, but important to show it).

- Uncertainty bothers them in uncertain positive situations, even when they are *not* predicting that bad things will happen.
- They are more likely to predict negative outcomes.
- When they predict bad things happening, they imagine the worse possible scenarios and also believe that these are much more likely to happen (a double whammy).
- Uncertainty is felt in the body: they are aware of internal information (feelings and body states) and report this as more intense, upsetting, etc.
- They use a wide range of strategies to manage uncertainty.
- They are more likely to give up some of what they value to make things more certain.
- Intolerance of uncertainty is on a continuum, from not quite tolerant to very intolerant.
- There is a lot more evidence that people can change their intolerance of uncertainty and become less intolerant/more tolerant.
- When people become more tolerant of uncertainty, worry and anxiety goes down.
- Although intolerance of uncertainty is most present in worry and GAD, it is also present in a wide range of other anxiety-related psychological problems, although we know rather less about its specific role in these.

Rules that underpin the intolerance of uncertainty

Individuals with an intolerance of uncertainty have unwittingly developed a way of seeing the world, or an outlook, that is underpinned by a set of rules and beliefs about uncertainty. These 'silent' rules carry with them negative predictions about what might happen if they are exposed to uncertain situations or events, and motivate strong feelings of anxiety and dread. For example, a rule might sound like this: *If I'm not totally sure about something, then I'm asking for trouble*, or, *If I do something new, I cannot be sure I'll cope.* As you know, these rules influence our actions. In both these examples, a person holding these rules would understandably avoid situations that threatened to break them. For people who are intolerant of uncertainty, the whirling stream of ideas and doubts created by their worry also erodes their confidence in their ability to make good decisions. If we are less confident about our decisions, then we will worry about whether we have made good choices.

Let's look more closely at the first of these rules in the example below.

Peter's Rule: *If I'm not totally sure about something, then I'm asking for trouble.*

Peter is trying to buy a washing machine and he quickly realizes that there is an overwhelming number of brands and choices. His rule tells him to be careful and make the right decision. It also instructs him to be totally sure of his choice. Every time he comes close to making a decision, another type of machine pops up and he starts to worry that the washing machine he is about to choose may not live up to its five-year guarantee or that the model out next week may be better and he'll end up regretting the choice he's made. He walks in and out of the shop. He stares long and hard at the details of the machines on display without really taking much in. He leaves and heads into another store where the process starts all over again. Eventually he makes a snap decision, not based on the information he now has, but as a way of escaping the awful feelings of uncertainty. Although relieved to have made a decision, then he goes home and starts worrying about the decision he has made . . .

This type of experience might be common. For some worriers, their rules may paralyse them and they may never feel confident enough to make a decision. For others, any decision, even the wrong one, is better than being stuck with the horrible feeling of not being sure.

Assessing your tolerance to uncertainty – tuning in

On the following page is a questionnaire developed by a team of Canadian researchers. It is called the Intolerance of Uncertainty Scale, or the IUS for short, and just as it says on the tin, it tries to measure an individual's intolerance of uncertainty. This can be a useful questionnaire to repeat every week as you progress towards overcoming your worry. As we have suggested, the intolerance of uncertainty fuels worry. If we can reduce the fuel by enabling you to become more tolerant of uncertainty, then we can reduce worry.

To score the questionnaire, simply add up the numbers that you have circled. People who suffer with GAD or excessive worry tend to have higher scores, and on average will score about 87. Scores above 50 suggest some problems with uncertainty. So, as a rule of thumb, if your score is above 50 then it might be worth spending some time thinking about and then challenging how you react to uncertainty.

The questionnaire will also give you a feel for what intolerance of uncertainty is. When you complete it, focus on each item. Which items stand out for you? What are you surprised by? Does completing it give you any further insights into your worry? Does it raise any questions for you? Are you surprised at your score, and if so why?

EXERCISE 8.3: INTOLERANCE OF UNCERTAINTY SCALE

You will find in the scale below a series of statements that describe how people may react to the uncertainties of life. Please use the scale to describe to what extent each item is characteristic of you. Write the appropriate number in the box on the right.

Not at all characteristic of me		Somewhat characteristic of me		Entirely characteristic of me
1	2	3	4	5

1. Uncertainty stops me from having a firm opinion. ❏

2. Being uncertain means that a person is disorganized. ❏

3. Uncertainty makes life intolerable. ❏

4. It's unfair not having any guarantees in life. ❏

5. My mind can't be relaxed if I don't know what will happen tomorrow. ❏

6. Uncertainty makes me uneasy, anxious, or stressed. ❏

7. Unforeseen events upset me greatly. ❏

8. It frustrates me not having all the information I need. ❏

9. Uncertainty keeps me from living a full life. ❏

10. One should always look ahead so as to avoid surprises. ❏

11. A small unforeseen event can spoil everything, even with the best of planning. ❏

12. When it's time to act, uncertainty paralyses me. ❏

13. Being uncertain means that I'm not first rate. ❏

14. When I'm uncertain, I can't go forward. ❏

15. When I'm uncertain, I can't function very well. ❏

16. Unlike me, others always seem to know where they are going with their lives. ❏

17. Uncertainty makes me vulnerable, unhappy or sad. ❏

18. I always want to know what the future has in store for me. ❏

19. I can't stand being taken by surprise. ❏

20. The smallest doubt can stop me from acting. ❏

21. I should be able to organize everything in advance. ❏

22. Being uncertain means that I lack confidence. ❏

23. I think it's unfair that other people seem sure about their future. ❏

24. Uncertainty keeps me from sleeping soundly. ❏

25. I must get away from all uncertain situations. ❏

26. The ambiguities in life stress me. ❏

27. I can't stand being undecided about my future. ❏

Source: Buhr, K. and Dugas, M. J., 'The Intolerance of Uncertainty Scale: Psychometric Properties of the English Version', *Behavior Research and Therapy*, 40 (2002). With permission from Elsevier.

The intolerance of uncertainty is a driving force behind our understanding of worry. It also helps us to make sense of why there is such a variety of ways in which people manage their worry. For instance, one worrier may avoid committing to a social engagement for fear of the unknown. Another worrier will react in almost the opposite way, over-committing to social occasions for fear of what others might say if they do not attend. Both are motivated by a common thread: the intolerance of uncertainty.

How does the intolerance of uncertainty link to worry?

Worriers struggle to tolerate even small amounts of uncertainty and when things are a little unclear or when a situation can be read in many ways, they tend to be more distressed than most by it. Uncertainty fuels worry and, understandably, worriers try their best to reduce it, for example by planning ahead. The more they get ahead of themselves, the more things seem uncertain as there are more unknowns to take into account. If they decide to avoid the situation or issue, then things remain uncertain because they genuinely don't know what might be happening. If they try to find out more about the situation, they will then learn more about things that they didn't know; this cranks up uncertainty all the more, fuelling more worry. They also tend to assume the worst and predict that bad things are going to happen. Because they genuinely believe that these bad things will happen, this leads to further worry and anxiety, making these uncertain situations more threatening and disturbing than the situation objectively deserves. Furthermore, if these bad things do happen, worriers assume that they won't be able to cope with them, leading to further worry. It makes sense that what worriers really want is absolute certainty, certainty either that something bad will never happen, or, if it does, that it is guaranteed when it will happen, how it will happen, and that they will be able to cope with it.

As we have said, overcoming worry demands that we learn how to deal more effectively with our reactions to uncertainty. We know that worriers find uncertainty intolerable and they will do many things in addition to worrying to try to minimize it. Unfortunately, nearly everything they try has the tendency to make things more uncertain and so worry much worse. It's important that you know this in order to enable you to tolerate uncertainty: you need to start to find situations where you can expose yourself to it, starting with small amounts. There is simply no other way around this. Just thinking about uncertainty and worry (or reading about it) will not enable you to change; you have to *do* things differently.

A pattern for the interface between worry and uncertainty

On the following pages we outline one way of thinking about how worry and uncertainty fit together. Within this picture you will find elements of the diagram of worry that we have been following throughout this book:

Trigger → What if . . . → Worry → Anxiety → Demoralization and Exhaustion

Here we are adding to this the intolerance of uncertainty and its relationship to worry. It is important to understand how the intolerance of uncertainty influences your worry for a number of reasons: first, to map out your problems; second, to help you understand your worry; third, because this understanding also tells us what we need to do to help you change. Below are two diagrams (Figures 8.2 and 8.3): one is the bare bones, the second has some thoughts and statements added that worriers typically suggest. You may need to study these a few times, but we will pull out the key points later on. As always, read with a pen and paper to hand.

When faced with an everyday situation where the outcome is uncertain, worriers tend to *want things to be certain and try to reduce the uncertainty*. Then they *assume the worst, fall into worrying* and then believe that they *cannot cope* with the worst-case scenario they imagine through worrying. They may think, *What if I make the wrong decision?* or, *What if I can't cope with this?* These *what if* statements simultaneously trigger worry and a demand for certainty. As the worrier searches for certainty (*I must get this right, I must be certain*), another set of conflicting thoughts or questions appears that hints at how impossible certainty is (*I could get it wrong; How can I be certain?*), triggering yet more worry. The worrier is now caught in a trap between the futile pursuit of certainty and the avoidance of uncertainty. This generates a number of strong feelings, including anxiety coupled with an intense feeling of indecisiveness, which further erodes the worrier's confidence in their ability to make decisions. The feelings are often accompanied by strong bodily sensations.

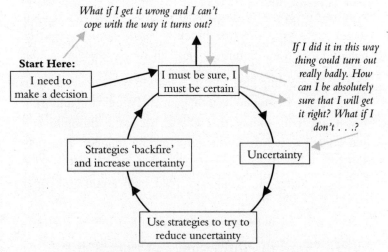

What if I get it wrong and I can't cope with the way it turns out?

Start Here:
I need to make a decision

I must be sure, I must be certain

If I did it in this way thing could turn out really badly. How can I be absolutely sure that I will get it right? What if I don't . . .?

Strategies 'backfire' and increase uncertainty

Uncertainty

Use strategies to try to reduce uncertainty

Figure 8.2: The uncertainty cycle

Understandably, the worrier then falls into habitual ways of acting to try to reduce the level of uncertainty. Unfortunately, many of the actions they take have the opposite impact: rather than reducing uncertainty they tend to increase it, triggering further worry. The worrier may avoid making a decision, for example, which increases the pressure on them to make a decision. With each cycle, the worrier feels less certain and more overwhelmed.

In the next diagram, to help you understand the cycle, we have added more detail, in particular concerning how worry interacts with each stage of the uncertainty cycle. We have also added worry, which sits at the centre of the diagram.

Worry is both *fuelled* by uncertainty and in turn *generates* uncertainty. Each stage of the uncertainty cycle produces more uncertainty and so more worry (see the pair of arrows pointing in opposite directions) between worry and each stage). Let's take the first block, *I must be sure, I must be certain*. Here these statements lead to worry – *What if I am wrong? What if I mess up?* – which then generates more *uncertainty*, both fuelling more worry (see the pair of arrows) and also leading on to the worrier using *strategies to try to reduce the uncertainty*. Unfortunately, these strategies tend to generate more uncertainty (see the pair of arrows), leading to more worry but also propelling the worrier back around the cycle to pursue certainty.

What drives the intolerance of uncertainty? Underlying rules

There appear to be three main sets of rules that underpin the intolerance of uncertainty. One group tries to work together to reduce the risk of bad things happening in uncertain situations, another tells us to value certainty and to act only when certain, and the third reminds us of the awfulness of uncertainty and why we should avoid it. The rules around certainty and uncertainty seem to be locked in an antagonistic embrace. From this conflict emerge jittery tension and feelings of being ill at ease. We will explore these rules in more detail below.

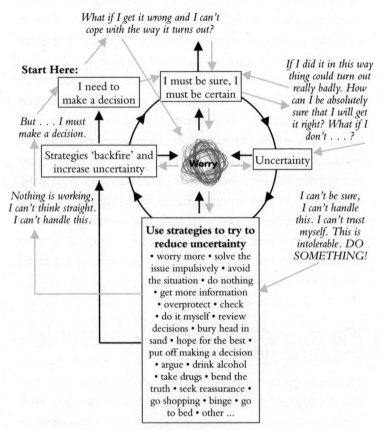

Figure 8.3: The relationship between the intolerance of uncertainty and worry

Let's look first at the rules that aim to reduce the risk. This makes good sense when the stakes are high, in life-changing events such as getting married or divorced, having children, buying a house, changing a job, and so on, but makes much less sense in everyday events such as taking your car to get its MOT, visiting the doctor for a routine check-up or going to meet your children's teachers. The focus is entirely on what could go wrong and how this could be stopped from happening, or at least on reducing the likelihood of it happening or reducing the possible effects. Despite their efforts at prevention, worriers also believe that they may not be able to cope if the worst did happen. It becomes much safer to assume the worst than to take the risk of assuming that everything will be fine – it is like preparing for a hurricane when only light rain has been forecast. In this way worriers reduce the uncertainty by convincing themselves of the nightmare version and acting, or being ready to act, as if this really were the case. Sometimes, even though the nightmare version is awful, it feels much more certain and safer than the alternative of uncertainty. For example, if there is some uncertainty about a relationship, then for the worrier it seems much safer to assume that the relationship will break down. Then, they might be able to do something to try to prevent this from happening. And they assume that, should the worst happen, they will *not* be able to cope. By doing this, they can prepare themselves for the worst-case scenario. Worry takes us on a tortuous journey around the hellish things that could go wrong, and because these experiences feel very real, we want to make sure that they don't happen. In short, the worrier believes that it is *always better to be safe than sorry*.

The other two groups of ideas thought to underpin the intolerance of uncertainty are about certainty and uncertainty themselves. With regards to certainty, worriers believe absolute certainty can and should be achieved, and, because of this, they should delay or put off acting until they are sure. But to be sure means to cover all the bases; and as we check out one detail we become more aware of even more possibilities and so become less certain. As we will discover, certainty is a belief and is rarely achievable and so the worrier's pursuit of certainty is often in vain. Beliefs about uncertainty suggest that being uncertain is very unpleasant and should be avoided at all costs. But to avoid uncertainty we have to hang on to what seems most certain – and then anything that might happen that does not fit the plan becomes very unsettling. This means that trying to avoid uncertainty gives rise to rigid plans that are then easily undermined as circumstances change. Flipping between trying to find certainty and avoiding uncertainty leads to a sense of disorientation and, paradoxically, to an increase in the levels of uncertainty. While experiencing this flip-flopping, the worrier is at the same time trying to be safe and certain, which is nearly impossible given how they are feeling and acting. This is an unbearable state for them and worry is used as an attempt to find certainty within uncertainty. In summary, *It's better to be safe than sorry, but how can I be safe when I can't be sure?* – which makes uncertainty intolerable.

These three sets of beliefs appear in the diagram below. They are related to one another, as you will see. The beliefs about it being better to be safe than sorry follow on from one another. The beliefs about certainty and uncertainty create a tension between them, which pushes us even harder towards being safe rather than sorry. The questions in Exercises 8.4 and 8.5, below, aim to bring this idea alive for you.

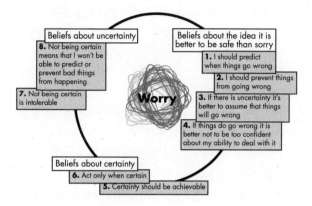

Figure 8.4: Beliefs that are thought to underpin the intolerance of uncertainty

EXERCISE 8.4: OUTLINING YOUR THINKING IN A WORRISOME SITUATION

This exercise helps you to outline your thinking in a worrisome situation. Think about the last few times you worried and then answer the following (note that only some may apply to you). Each question corresponds to a box on the diagram above.

1. Were you trying to predict that bad things might happen?

2. Once these were in mind, did you try to prevent them from happening in some way, either in thought or in deed?

3. Did you feel unsure or uncertain in this situation? If you did, did it feel safer to assume that something bad would happen?

4. If this bad thing did happen, did you doubt your ability to cope with it?

5. Do you believe that you should be absolutely sure or certain?

6. Did you need to feel certain before making a decision or taking action?

7. Was the sense of not knowing intolerable?

8. As you felt more uncertain, did this make it harder to prevent bad things from happening?

EXERCISE 8.5: EXPLORING YOUR RULES AND BELIEFS ABOUT UNCERTAINTY

The table below offers some rules and beliefs that are related to the intolerance of uncertainty. Complete the questionnaire. Rate each item then return to the items you scored most highly on. Which situations do the high-scoring items apply to? List them. How can you begin to challenge this rule by changing the way you act?

Assessing my rules or beliefs about uncertainty

Rules and Beliefs Questionnaire							
Review the list of statements below. Circle the number that best represents you.							
	Strongly disagree					Strongly agree	
Predict and prevent bad things							
I should always work out everything that could go wrong.	1	2	3	4	5	6	7
I am always responsible for stopping bad things from happening.	1	2	3	4	5	6	7
If things are uncertain then assume the worst							
If there is uncertainty, then something will go wrong.	1	2	3	4	5	6	7
I should avoid change.	1	2	3	4	5	6	7
If there is a chance bad things will happen, then they will.	1	2	3	4	5	6	7
If I make a mistake, then the repercussions are unknown.	1	2	3	4	5	6	7
If I feel uncertain, then something bad will happen.	1	2	3	4	5	6	7
If a situation is uncertain, then it is dangerous.	1	2	3	4	5	6	7
Doubt capacity to deal with the problem							
If I do something new, then I cannot be sure that I will cope.	1	2	3	4	5	6	7
If my life is uncertain, then I will not cope.	1	2	3	4	5	6	7
If I am surprised, then I will not know how to act.	1	2	3	4	5	6	7
If I can't see what's coming, then I will not cope.	1	2	3	4	5	6	7
If others help, then I can handle it.	1	2	3	4	5	6	7
If I ask for others' advice, then I will be more certain.	1	2	3	4	5	6	7
Certainty should be achievable/desirable							
I should always be certain.	1	2	3	4	5	6	7

If I am certain, then I feel safe.	1 2 3 4 5 6 7
If I am certain, then I will be prepared.	1 2 3 4 5 6 7
If I am certain, then I make good decisions.	1 2 3 4 5 6 7
If I do not ask others for their opinions, then I will doubt my judgement.	1 2 3 4 5 6 7
Everything people say should add up and make sense.	1 2 3 4 5 6 7
Uncertainty is distressing.	1 2 3 4 5 6 7
Only act when certain	
If I am sure, then I can act.	1 2 3 4 5 6 7
If I do it myself, then I can be certain that it is done right.	1 2 3 4 5 6 7
I must always ask others before acting.	1 2 3 4 5 6 7
A good decision is one I never question.	1 2 3 4 5 6 7
I must make careful choices.	1 2 3 4 5 6 7
If I keep a routine, then I will not worry.	1 2 3 4 5 6 7
If I keep a routine, then I will be more certain.	1 2 3 4 5 6 7
If I feel uncertain, then I will be stuck.	1 2 3 4 5 6 7
Not being certain means that I will not be able to predict or prevent bad things from happening	
If I open myself up to uncertainty, then I will not be able to cope.	1 2 3 4 5 6 7
If I open myself up to uncertainty, then I will be overwhelmed.	1 2 3 4 5 6 7
If I open myself up to uncertainty, I will worry uncontrollably.	1 2 3 4 5 6 7
If I am uncertain, then I must be wrong.	1 2 3 4 5 6 7

Unless I cover all the bases, then I can't proceed.	1 2 3 4 5 6 7
If I feel uncertain, then I will not act.	1 2 3 4 5 6 7
If I can't be certain about tomorrow then I will avoid going out.	1 2 3 4 5 6 7
If others do things, then I cannot be certain that they have done it right.	1 2 3 4 5 6 7
If I can't see the end of the road, then I will not start my journey.	1 2 3 4 5 6 7
If I am doubtful, then I will not act.	1 2 3 4 5 6 7
If I make a decision, then I should always question it.	1 2 3 4 5 6 7
If I make a quick decision, then it will come back to haunt me.	1 2 3 4 5 6 7
If I put it off, then I won't feel uncertain.	1 2 3 4 5 6 7
If I let others out of my sight, then I cannot manage the uncertainty.	1 2 3 4 5 6 7
I should trust my instincts and avoid anything uncertain.	1 2 3 4 5 6 7
I should avoid change.	1 2 3 4 5 6 7
If I make a mistake, then I will be overwhelmed with doubts.	1 2 3 4 5 6 7

Each set of rules can have dozens of variants and they will apply to many situations, or to only a few. If these rules are resonating with you, now is the time to act to break the rules on purpose (see the chapter on behavioural experiments).

EXERCISE 8.6: RECOGNIZING MY STRENGTHS

Finally, as a consequence of thinking these issues through, have you noticed situations in your life where uncertainty does not lead to worry?

- Are there situations in your life in which you can manage the uncertainty? How do you do this, and what makes these situations different?
- What does this tell you about how you react to uncertain situations?
- How do others cope with uncertainty? What can you learn from how they do this? Ask a friend or observe a colleague.

What have you learnt from the exercises above? Have they helped you to understand how uncertainty and worry are linked? What have you learnt about uncertainty or how you and others cope with it? Write down your responses.

PIT STOP

Let's pause again and think about what you have just been reading. Can you summarize the key ideas you have taken on board? Make a note of any new ideas that are sticking in your mind? What have you taken from this chapter so far? If you were to put your learning on a T-shirt, what would the slogan be? If you have any questions, jot these down too. You can return to them once you have had a chance to digest the information.

What is sticking in my mind from my reading so far?

1.

2.

3.

9

Certainty and uncertainty – the broader picture

We will now broaden the focus to consider uncertainty in a broader context. We suggest this, in part, to help you understand how the pursuit of certainty and the eradication of uncertainty are equally problematic.

Life is full of uncertainties and rarely are things clear-cut; but on the occasions where we do know where we stand, because things are fairly certain, we are less likely to worry. On the other hand, some life situations are both highly distressing and uncertain, and the lack of clarity can be disabling for us all. Almost all of us will worry in response to these highly stressful and uncertain situations (e.g. learning that a close relative has a serious and potentially life-threatening illness). Most of life, however, lies somewhere between these two extremes, and it is usually neither clear-cut nor highly distressing and uncertain. It is not their response to the highly uncertain or clear-cut situations that makes people who are intolerant of uncertainty stand out. Rather, what marks them out is their response to the normal, everyday and moderately uncertain situations. Those who worry less in these situations are aware of the uncertainty, and accept and/or expect it; although they probably would like things to be more clear-cut, they have learnt and developed ways of tolerating uncertainty.

Figure 9.1: Uncertainty as the fuel for worry

The impossibility of certainty

In our uncertain world we play the odds every day of our lives. For example, when a woman rides a bicycle to work she weighs up the probability of being in an accident against the benefits to her health, the environment and her purse. She takes reasonable precautions such as making sure the bicycle is well maintained (that brakes work, the tyres have tread), she chooses to wear reflective clothing and a helmet, she might figure out the safer routes and then she plays the now reasonable odds. Or, think about the road where you live. You may have crossed it several times in the last few days. While having an accident might be awful, the probability of having an accident is low, but it is not, nor ever can be, zero. Or, over your lifetime you may have eaten hundreds of sandwiches bought from supermarkets. While it would be terrible to get food poisoning, the probability of getting ill from eating a sandwich from a reputable supermarket is very low, but, again, it is not zero. We can never cover every eventuality because we live in a world characterized by novelty and uncertainty. As the ancient author and natural philosopher Pliny the Elder suggested in AD 79, 'the only certainty is that there is nothing certain'. Indeed, being certain about something locks you into a particular way of seeing the world, and prevents you from seeing other views. Consider Clayton:

> Clayton thought, *I'm certain that I won't like London.* He was so sure that he never went and never entertained the idea that London could offer him anything. His view locked him into a particular way of thinking, which influenced his actions and thoughts, and denied him the possibility of discovering something new and exciting. One day, his work took him to King's Cross Station in London. Having a few moments before his train arrived, he wandered up the Euston Road. Looking up he saw St Pancras Station and was captivated by the structure of the building. He wondered to himself how he could have been so foolish as not to have come sooner.

In Chapter 2 we talked about keeping an open mind: unfortunately, certainty has a way of closing our minds. Think about the last time you were convinced that you would not like a film, a book, a restaurant, a pub or an evening out, and were then pleasantly surprised. So, being certain can be unhelpful. Certainty is also an illusion. We cannot be certain about anything, because certainty is a belief, not a fact. If we are certain about something we tend to have to blur the edges of the world, since ambiguity and uncertainty are inherent within all things. Trying to iron out the uncertainty in life is like trying to squeeze a large octopus into a glass box. This is a very difficult thing to do, particularly if the octopus doesn't want to oblige. But if we succeed in containing it, we lose its rich shape and form; the octopus becomes little more than a colourful cube. What we mean here is that reality has to be distorted, cleansed and sanitized if uncertainty is to be excluded. If this were possible, then what kind of world would we be left with?

The idea that life can be certain also brings with it the suggestion that the future can be predicted in some precise way, which, at some level, is partly true – as day follows night – but usually life brings with it uncertainty. The near future is relatively more certain. Think of weather forecasting! Shorter-term forecasts are usually more accurate than longer-term forecasts. It is instructive to look at the predicted maps for hurricanes in the Atlantic. Even with hundreds or even thousands of storms that have been studied since the 1950s, the predicted track of the next storm is still uncertain, and is usually represented as a cone. That is, the predicted storm centre for the next few hours is usually quite predictable within a few miles but, even with the best models, one day away has about a hundred miles' prediction error, and five days about three hundred and fifty miles'.

Of course, let's not get carried away: we need relative certainty as much as we need to expect relative uncertainty and, as with most things, a healthy balance of both is best. The bottom line is that trying to protect ourselves against all uncertainty is an unattainable goal, like trying to walk on your shadow. Uncertainty is in everything, it's everywhere and is part of life. In this respect it's like gravity, death and taxes: we can't avoid it or will it away.

'To be absolutely certain about something, one must know everything or nothing about it.' Olin Miller, author, 1918–2002

A certain world

While you may argue that your life would be wonderful if all uncertainty were excluded, think this through for a moment. What would life be like without surprises, without unknowns, without mystery? As an exercise, why not try to imagine a world where uncertainty was excluded. The film *Groundhog Day* plays with this idea. Bill Murray's character experiences the same day over and over and over again, but even here the main character is able to learn new skills, like jazz piano and ice sculpture. And, while the events happen predictably, his reactions to them add a degree of uncertainty. So, even the world of *Groundhog Day* is not completely certain.

What would your uncertainty-free world be like? In your imagined world, it's not enough just to exclude worry and to impose certainty in all those situations that trigger worry: you need to exclude uncertainty completely. Here's one scenario: the Number 37 bus would always run to time and you would always get a seat, and Newcastle United would win the Premiership and the Champion's League every year. But your children would never surprise you with new ideas, each new film that was released would not have a twist or a surprise ending, none of the books you read would tell you anything new – in fact, there would be no new films, books, bands, CDs or DVDs. You would be passed by the same cars and people every day, you would have the same conversations, you would know it was the third Tuesday in the month because you would be eating meatloaf, you would never have the opportunity of tasting a new fruit or a new chocolate cake.

A newborn baby is a wonder, but babies bring uncertainty, as life itself is uncertain. So would there be any children if we excluded uncertainty? Would we ever take the risk of having them in our uncertainty-free world? We could go on. It would be a mechanistic, mechanical world, where nothing new ever happened. It would appear that uncertainty is a critical stimulant to life, and that without it our lives would be poorer, impoverished and empty. Erich Fromm, a German social psychologist and psychoanalyst, suggested that *creativity requires the courage to let go of certainties*. If Fromm was right, certainty might stifle free thinking, and, taking his idea a little further, reaching absolute certainty might destroy a fundamental characteristic of what it is to be human, namely free will or the ability to choose.

Would you want to live in this kind of world?

Routines and shrinking worlds

Life has patterns and routines and sometimes we feel stuck in a rut, as if all we do is sleep, eat and work. Routine and patterns are helpful as they give a sense of rhythm, they ground us, they give an idea of where we are in the world and a sense of purpose. But sometimes we run too tightly around these routines and patterns. At these moments we often crave novelty or uncertainty to help us get out of the rut. The second reason relates to one of the consequences of worry: worriers tend to reduce the circumference of their world in order to manage their worry. They try to run on safe and familiar tracks, within routines and patterns largely to avoid uncertainty, but this can also place *real* limits, taking away new opportunities, new beginnings, new relationships or keeping people stuck within unhelpful roles or relationships. Another possible consequence of this limited lifestyle is low mood and depression, especially when people are stuck in familiar but unrewarding situations, roles or relationships. This makes the worrier's life much worse because, with low mood, it is often much harder to motivate ourselves to do new things or in fact to do anything at all.

The reasons why worriers may have started to run on such tight rails are less clear. But for some worriers, if their early lives were typified by uncertainty and insecurity, these patterns and routines may have offered one way of establishing certainty or, put another way, of managing their exposure to uncertainty. Such patterns and routines become familiar and comforting, but later, as we grow, we may begin to realize how they might also limit us.

If there are parts of the uncertainty-free world that you recognize, do you like what you see? Is that a world you want to remain in? If the answer to this is yes, then fine. We suspect, however, that the answer will be no – because you are reading this book, which tells us that you want to change something. An implication from all this is that injecting a small amount of uncertainty into your life could be a way of making your life much more enjoyable, and this is what we aim to help you do in this chapter.

EXERCISE 9.1: FINDING THE EDGES OF MY WORLD

Take a moment to reflect on the following questions. Jot down the answers in your notebook. Are there any things you would like to do as a consequence of thinking these through? Make a list, choose one thing and do it! Do any new ambitions come to mind?

How has worry or uncertainty impacted on the circumference of your world?

Is there anything you avoid doing now?

What does worry stop you from doing?

What have you stopped doing since worry became a problem? When can you get back to it?

Are there things that you would like to start doing? What are they? When can you start?

What are the advantages of letting go of certainty and letting new experiences in?

Are there any disadvantages?

An uncertain world

Now back to our extremes. At the other end of the spectrum from complete certainty is complete uncertainty. So, as we approach complete uncertainty, we would expect to encounter a pretty awful experience. Professor David Wilkinson, who works at Cranfield University in the south of England, has investigated how leaders cope with high levels of uncertainty and ambiguity in business settings and in the aftermath of events like terrorist attacks. He views ambiguity on a sliding scale from total certainty to total ambiguity or chaos. At the certain end of the scale, cause and effect are linked and there is clarity and order; the world makes sense and day still follows night. But, with increasing uncertainty and ambiguity, the relationship between cause and effect becomes weakened and eventually breaks down; day no longer follows night, things fall apart, the centre cannot hold, order is lost and nothing makes sense. Despite the nightmarish vision at the highly ambiguous end of the scale, he sees chaos as a positive state and as a moment of creativity and new learning. He suggests that 'at the moments of the most intense fear, the moments when there appear to be huge threats all around, when ambiguity is at its highest, when we know little and understand less, these are the moments of most potential for moving into a new world and taking the advantage'. These uncertain moments offer 'the most degrees of freedom to act'; he means that highly uncertain situations offer us the most choices and opportunities for acting in different ways.

This reminds us that, even at the extreme end of the spectrum, uncertainty can still be seen by some as positive and useful. As we said earlier, the key is how each of us views uncertainty.

Whether we 'buy' this perspective or not, it also shows that there are always other ways of thinking about high levels of uncertainty. While we may all be in awe and a little envious of those individuals who are able to cope and act in these extreme situations, we need to bear in mind two things: first, in our everyday lives we rarely, if ever, meet chaos, as there is usually some degree of order; and, second, at this extreme end of the scale the difference between worriers and non-worriers disappears. The 'big events' that Professor Wilkinson refers to are extreme, rare and highly unusual, and so both worriers and non-worriers would cope similarly. As we know, worriers tend to worry about seemingly insignificant everyday events that then may spiral upwards, and it is this that marks them apart. We all worry about the big occasions, and there is nothing to indicate that someone who worries about everyday events would, in more pressing circumstances, be less able to cope. Indeed, in our clinical work we have heard many stories of worriers who have successfully coped with and overcome 'big occasion' or life-changing problems, only to seek help for managing the everyday small ones. Also, we believe that absolute chaos would be as awful as absolute certainty; as we have said before in this book, balance is the key.

The cost of intolerance of uncertainty

For people who worry, there is nearly *always a cost* associated with the strategies they use to manage uncertainty. Individuals can be motivated to act in many different ways in response to this and we have listed some common examples in Exercise 9.2 (page 209). If the ideas don't fit for you, flip the idea over and see if this works. For example, consider the first statement, about reassurance seeking, in the exercise. The cost of this is that we never learn to trust our own judgement and that, as we get different views, we become more uncertain, and so forth. If we flip this, rather than asking for reassurance, a worrier may *never* do so. The cost is different in this 'flipped' version as the worrier never gets feedback or learns how to use helpful feedback when making choices. In this case they are trying to manage uncertainty by reducing the amount of information coming in. Similarly, take the second statement in the exercise: rather than checking emails and getting behind, a worrier might send them without checking as they feel overwhelmed by choices. Again the cost is different; in this case they may have to then spend lots of time dealing with the fallout of their hastily put together communications. Can you see how the various points in the exercise below, and the flipped versions, are all driven by the intolerance of uncertainty? We will come back to this idea in more detail in the next chapter.

EXERCISE 9.2: ACTIONS AND COSTS RELATED TO THE INTOLERANCE OF UNCERTAINTY

Spend a moment reviewing each statement and then score the questionnaire, spotting those aspects that are closer to your experience of worry. As a rule of thumb, if you are scoring 5 or more on an item, you may want to consider setting a goal to change this or consider a behavioural experiment. Because not all the items will apply to you, if an item reminds you of another aspect of your life then write this down. As you read, think about what benefits might come your way if you learn to sit with uncertainty and tolerate it. Second, you can use this as another way of helping you to spot how the intolerance of uncertainty might influence the way you live your life. As uncertainty is everywhere, a huge amount of energy and effort is put into trying to eradicate it: imagine using this energy and effort for other things.

Using the scale below, read each statement, decide how closely each statement matches your actions and then circle the appropriate number.

Very unlike me					Very like me	
1	2	3	4	5	6	7

Asking for reassurance on a decision you have made, and then feeling stupid for having asked because you knew you were right in the first place.	1 2 3 4 5 6 7

Checking emails, letters or cheques several times before sending them, and then getting behind on other jobs.	1 2 3 4 5 6 7
Reading all the cinema reviews and then asking your friend to make a decision about what to see because you just can't be sure they will like the film; then feeling disappointed about missing the film you really wanted to see.	1 2 3 4 5 6 7
Telephoning home while shopping in the supermarket because you just can't decide on what to eat and then feeling indecisive and down on yourself.	1 2 3 4 5 6 7
Always going to the same shop and buying the same food in case you buy something you or others won't like, but then complaining about the lack of variety in your diet.	1 2 3 4 5 6 7
Finding excuses why you should not delegate jobs at work; consequently you end up doing everything yourself.	1 2 3 4 5 6 7
Not allowing your kids to do things for themselves in case they don't quite get it right. And then feeling annoyed that you have to do everything yourself.	1 2 3 4 5 6 7
Pacing the house if your partner is five minutes late home from work and then being stressed out when they arrive.	1 2 3 4 5 6 7
You've bought something you have always wanted, but now can't enjoy it because you keep questioning your decision.	1 2 3 4 5 6 7

Asking someone to check your work, even though at the back of your mind you know it's perfectly fine, and then criticizing yourself for lacking confidence.	1 2 3 4 5 6 7
Wanting to know where everything is, and feeling unsettled if things are out of place, even when you don't need to use them right now.	1 2 3 4 5 6 7
Wanting to know where important people are and feeling unsettled if they are not where you expect them to be.	1 2 3 4 5 6 7
Needing to have plans for an evening clearly laid out beforehand and getting upset when things don't go as planned, even though everyone except you is having fun.	1 2 3 4 5 6 7
Following a daily routine for fear of going off track and then complaining how boring life is.	1 2 3 4 5 6 7
Taking over driving from your partner because you're worried about them driving; then getting tired and not enjoying the trip.	1 2 3 4 5 6 7
Avoiding committing yourself to something just in case it might go wrong, and then realizing you have missed out on some or all of it.	1 2 3 4 5 6 7
Finding good but imaginary reasons for not doing things and then realizing that you have missed out on something you would have enjoyed if you had taken the chance.	1 2 3 4 5 6 7

Procrastinating until tasks become bigger and more problematic.	1 2 3 4 5 6 7
Finding other tasks to do rather than the one that needs your attention, and then letting other things mount up.	1 2 3 4 5 6 7
Avoiding (or keeping contact to a bare minimum) people who may act unpredictably, and then missing out on other aspects of their company.	1 2 3 4 5 6 7
Making snap decisions that you may regret later because, at the time, it feels better than being stuck with not knowing what to do.	1 2 3 4 5 6 7
Following the crowd and doing things you don't really like to do because it feels less difficult than making decisions.	1 2 3 4 5 6 7
Getting lots and lots of information to help you make a decision, and then not being able to make sense of it all.	1 2 3 4 5 6 7

Do your responses in the questionnaire above give you any ideas about what you could do differently in the face of uncertainty? Make a list and then start with the easiest one first.

EXERCISE 9.3: ADVANTAGES AND DISADVANTAGES

This exercise will help you think about all you have read so far.

What are the advantages of accepting a little more uncertainty into your life?	What are the advantages of letting go of a need for absolute certainty?
Are there any disadvantages?	Are there any disadvantages?

PIT STOP

Let's pause again and think about what you have just been reading. Can you summarize the key ideas you have taken on board? Make a note of any new ideas that are sticking in your mind? What have you taken from this chapter? If you were to put your learning on a T-shirt, what would the slogan be? If you have any questions, jot these down too. You can return to them once you have had a chance to digest the information.

What is sticking in my mind from my reading so far?

1.

2.

3.

10

Unhelpful strategies in reducing uncertainty

By now you will have looked at spotting uncertainty within worrisome situations (see Exercise 8.2, page 174) and looked at some of the rules that underpin the intolerance of uncertainty. Spending time working out how you react to uncertainty is important because it's another way of stepping out of our habitual patterns; it also means that we are *stepping under worry* to focus on what drives it. As you know, working out how the intolerance of uncertainty impacts on our lives requires some thought. One way of spotting this is to pay closer attention to what we do in worrisome situations. To help you do this, review the common strategies listed below and use the mini-questionnaire to help you evaluate each strategy. As you discover some that fit your own experience, then a key question to ask yourself is, *If I were less bothered by uncertainty, what might I do differently?* Or, to put it another way, *If I were more tolerant of uncertainty what might I do differently?*

Some strategies can be thought to exist on a line: at one end of this is extreme activity and at the other is the polar opposite: virtual inactivity. For example, when undertaking an everyday task some people check a great deal while others will not check at all – these polar positions can be motivated by the same thing, namely an intolerance of uncertainty. At one end, the worrier continues to check because they can't be sure that what they have done is right. At the opposite end, the worrier avoids checking because doing so might raise the possibility (uncertainty) that they have done something wrong. For some of the following strategies we have added the polar opposite or 'flip' version – you will need to decide which end of the pole is most representative of you.   Having two ways to manage a situation, sometimes the worrier can move back and forth between the strategies, one moment checking over and over, the next avoiding checking at all. This flip-flopping creates its own uncertainty, motivating further worry. As you read the following pages, we would like you to think about which strategies you recognize and make a note of them. You may also come up with ideas for change – write these down and try them out. We will offer you hints to help.

EXERCISE 10.1: EXPLORING HOW I MANAGE UNCERTAINTY

As you read this chapter, use the scale and questions below to rate each strategy and so help you to work out how you manage uncertainty.

Think about how your actions might influence uncertainty; does it reduce or increase it? Does doing this result in any unhelpful unintended consequences?

Try to figure out how the strategy interacts with your worry.

How typical or characteristic is this strategy for you?

Not like me at all	A little like me	Somewhat like me	Moderately like me	Mostly like me	Nearly like me	Completely like me
1	2	3	4	5	6	

Can you think of a personal example when you used this strategy? Write it down.

In this example, what impact did this strategy have on how certain or sure you felt? What impact did this have on the sense of uncertainty? What impact did it have on your worry? How much energy and effort do you put into managing uncertainty by using this strategy? Could your energy be used elsewhere? If you were less bothered by uncertainty what would you do differently? How would you like to act differently in the future?

Strategy 1: Dealing with information

Worriers can manage information in two unhelpful ways: either they collect overwhelming amounts of information or they bury their heads in the sand and avoid seeking out information. Consider the case of Alison outlined earlier in this book (page 14). Here is part of her story again:

Recently she wanted to buy a new digital camera to take pictures at her son's twenty-first birthday, but she couldn't decide which one to get. She visited nearly every shop and received conflicting advice. She worried: *What if I make a bad decision? If I do, I may not understand the instructions, and if I take the photos I could annoy everyone by being intrusive.* Her worries went on and on. Paralysed by them, in the end she gave up on buying the camera. She got a few photos from friends, but not the ones she really wanted. She regretted this and felt ashamed that her worry had got the better of her.

Unfortunately, Alison's search for more information to help her come to a decision just stoked up her uncertainty and triggered more worry. This can happen in a number of ways. Often, the additional information does not necessarily make things clearer, but just gives us more to consider and worry about. Alison also held the belief, *If I can just get enough information then I can be sure*, but this led to a number of unhelpful outcomes. She received too much information, which made the task unwieldy and impossible, leading to her feeling overwhelmed. She then became increasingly worried about making the right decision, and about whether she'd be able to use the camera even if she chose well. In addition, with each piece of new information it was more likely that she would find facts that contradicted one another, which again led to more uncertainty and worry, triggering the search for even more information to resolve the issue. Another thing that made this worse was Alison's feelings. She felt anxious, and the sense of vulnerability that came with her anxiety eroded her confidence still further and led her to doubt her ability to make good decisions. So, even if she had reached a decision, she would probably then have worried about whether she had made the right choice, again opening up uncertainty, fuelling worry. Even if she had gathered all the possible information together, she may still have worried about whether her decision was a wise one.

Worriers may also fall into elaborate preparations, and develop back-up plans and fall-back strategies. The impact is to delay or avoid engagement with the decisions or tasks in hand.

The flipside of this is also possible. Some worriers will minimize uncertainty by avoiding seeking any new (often helpful) information. If a worrier avoids information altogether then they create a knowledge gap, which in turn will lead to worry to bridge it. If they do act in the absence of helpful information, they may also have to deal with the fallout from the unhelpful decisions, impulsive or uninformed choices they make. Or if they then do nothing, they may have to cope with the irritation or low mood associated with falling behind, being out of touch with things, or things happening with no input from them. In all of these cases, life then becomes much more complicated than it needs to be, motivating further worry and anxiety.

Hint: What are the advantages and disadvantages of collecting lots of information before making a decision? How does this help or hinder decision making? Does doing this make you feel more certain? What would happen if you decided to limit the time or the amount of information you could look at? Could you perform a behavioural experiment to find out what might happen? Or, what would happen if you increased the amount of information you sought? How might doing this improve your confidence? To get started, what could be a small decision to try new things out on?

Hints for the flipside: What are the advantages and disadvantages of avoiding collecting information or looking into things before making a decision? How does making no preparations or plans influence the outcomes of your decisions? How does this help or hinder decision making? Does making quick decisions make you feel more certain?

Strategy 2: Scanning for uncertainty

Because worriers find uncertainty unbearable, understandably and without realizing it they are on the lookout for it nearly all the time. Think about someone who has a phobia of spiders: they tend to be on the alert, scanning for spiders because being surprised by them would be awful. As a consequence of living on high alert, even things that are not spiders, but look like them, can trigger their phobia – a knotted-up piece of wool blowing across a floor, for example. Psychologists call this hypervigilance. It functions to help us detect threats quickly (in this case uncertainty) in our environment; but it also turns things that are not threatening into threats. As a consequence of scanning, worriers are able to spot uncertainty quicker and pick up on it more often than others. It's almost as if their minds zoom in on uncertainty and then magnify it, until it 'fills the screen'. When this happens everything about a situation then feels uncertain. Let's return to our case stories:

> Alex was the twenty-three-year-old who was full of nervous energy. He listened to music on his MP3 player, but pulled the headphone off to make sure he had not missed anything. He checked his ticket for the number of the bus, even though he knew he was on the right one.

Alex worried on his journey into work, and this was partly responsible for his pulling off his headphones. But, at the same time, he was searching for uncertainty, scanning his environment looking for things that were uncertain. Alex looked out for possible problems. He looked at his bus ticket (*Am I on the right bus?*), he listened (*Have I missed something?*), he may have also looked out of the window to check the bus was taking the right route into town (*Does the bus driver know where he's going?*). By doing this he felt more tense and anxious, which made his worry worse. As with the spider phobia above, any vague sign of uncertainty will trigger anxiety. For example, if the engine of the bus made an unusual sound, or if the driver opened and closed the door a few times, this would be perceived as a sign of uncertainty, followed quickly by, *What if the bus breaks down?* Any *splinter of doubt* will fuel worry, and as we live in an uncertain world, Alex would always have found reason to doubt, and therefore something else to worry about. Without him realizing it, scanning also kept the threat of uncertainty at the front of his mind, leading him to feel apprehensive and edgy. Even if he 'failed' to spot anything uncertain, he would probably still have worried that the uncertainty was yet to 'arrive'. This process stopped him from enjoying his journey to work; his mind was constantly on 'red alert', which is tiring, meaning that he arrived at his destination exhausted, despite having only just started his day. Scanning for uncertainty is like scanning for gravity; we'll always find evidence for it. Scanning does not reduce uncertainty – quite the opposite, it 'cranks it up'.

There is a flip version to this in which the worrier does their level best to avoid noticing anything – rather than scanning they are blocking the airwaves so that no uncertainty can be noticed. In this case, the 'flipped' Alex might turn up his MP3 player to loud and keep his eyes fixed on the floor. Doing this might help him to avoid noticing external sources of uncertainty, but such a strategy might cause further worry-inducing problems, such as annoying other passengers through his loud music, missing his stop or not noticing the bus is stuck in traffic and so failing to warn others he will be late for work. *Do you try to 'jam' or block things out to stop you noticing uncertainty or worrisome things?*

Hint: Do you know when you are doing this? What are the tell-tale signs? What are the advantages and disadvantages of this? How does looking or avoiding looking for uncertainty or blocking it out make you feel better? What could you do instead? What could you tell yourself when you find yourself doing this? Where would be a place or situation to let your guard down a bit and just go with the flow?

Hints for the flipside: Can you start to notice things? Can you attend to the uncertainty and notice it? Do this for a brief period first and then increase the time. Does paying attention to the world have benefits – seeing the colour of the sky in the morning, the light on trees and so on.

Strategy 3: Commitment

Rather than choosing to commit themselves or not commit themselves, worriers avoid doing either, which leaves them hanging in uncertainty. This increases the sense of uncertainty rather than decreasing it. Worriers often avoid commitments because they can't be sure how things will turn out. This might include everyday interactions or intimate relationships, where love or fidelity can't be absolutely guaranteed. The latter may result in the worrier avoiding relationships completely or partially engaging, with one foot in and one foot out the door, just in case things go wrong. The worrier may find relationships unfulfilling, as they cannot give themselves to the relationship just in case it fails. Also their focus is on what could go wrong, which generates more uncertainty and more worry. The worry gets in the way of simply enjoying the time they have with their partner, which may put the relationship at more risk. Avoiding commitment also applies to social engagements or work commitments – for example, worriers might avoid a night out where plans are not sufficiently clear and they don't know when or where they will be going. Or worriers might avoid committing to a training event at work because they can't be sure that they will understand what they are taught and will then worry about not being able to give good enough feedback to their colleagues.

There is a flip version of this in which the worrier struggles to say no and ends up over-committing themselves. If they say no, they can't be sure what others will think of them so they agree to more and more engagements. Or they may commit too quickly before checking things out, or stay committed when it is really time to let go and move on. Individuals who over-commit themselves will become exhausted and irritable, which will lead them to worry about inflicting their mood on others (*What if I lose my temper?*). Struggling with over- or under-commitment is unlikely to bring satisfaction in the long run, and might be linked to low self-confidence.

Hint: What is helpful about doing this? What is less helpful? What's the worse thing that would happen if you just 'dived in'? To get started, what would be a 'time-limited' commitment where you could try this out (e.g. an evening out, attending a meeting or agreeing to go to a one-off talk or gym class)?

Hints for the flipside: Could you try to say no, to limit what you agree to? Start with something small and manageable and build to bigger things; try saying no and see what happens. What do you actually worry about if you say no? Write this down. Then, say no and see how close your written worry is to what actually happens. Did it happen in the way you imagined?

Strategy 4: People or social occasions

As we have mentioned, some worriers reduced the circumference of their world in order to reduce the uncertainties. They have tight routines, which they rely on to manage the uncertainty in the world. To do this, they may have decided to avoid certain people and social events – indiscreet people, for example, or 'colourful', spontaneous or impulsive people. Worriers may avoid these characters because they bring uncertainty with them: do you know anyone who fits this bill? Sometimes this avoidance comes with a sense of responsibility within the worrier for the actions and behaviour of others, which motivates further avoidance. Often these people, however, are unavoidable, because they are work colleagues or family members or part of the worrier's social circle. This makes the worrier feel much worse, since they must be 'on guard' or hypervigilant when there is a chance that they will meet them. They might worry, *What if she's there tonight? Oh no, I can't go tonight, but if I don't go, then what if they think I am rude? They may never ask me to come out with them again*, or, *What if I end up sitting next to him . . .?* This uncertainty can lead to more worry.

Avoiding people or social events can be another way of avoiding commitment, which leaves the worrier hanging; for example, by avoiding people who show a genuine interest in them because they ask meaningful or thoughtful questions. This may lead the worrier to think, *What if they get to know me and don't like me?* Or, *What if I say the wrong thing and they get the wrong end of the stick?*, which leads to strong feelings of anxiety that motivate avoidance. If the worrier can't avoid a situation, they sometimes revert to safety behaviours to manage it. A very common one is to have a few quick drinks at a wedding to 'oil' the wheels of conversation, and to take the edge off their worry.

Another side-effect of worry is irritability, so sometimes we end up avoiding people because we can't be sure we won't say something we might later regret. Or we notice that our hypothetical worry telescopes to major arguments, falling out with friends, or even violence. As a worrier is concerned that these might actually happen, they avoid social situations. Poor concentration can also pose difficulties; difficulty concentrating may lead worriers to struggle to follow conversations and they may worry that they will not remember what has been said. As you can see, both these side-effects load more uncertainty into the conversation and with it more worry, which makes the problem worse. Unsurprisingly, worriers tend to avoid situations where their difficulty in concentration or irritability might be exposed. Worriers may then avoid social situations because they worry about making the wrong impression or about what others might think of them.

The feeling of being unable to relax (restlessness) also impacts on social situations. Worriers may be skilful social butterflies, moving from one conversation to the next, keeping out of the limelight, never really talking about themselves, and finally moving on before, or just as, the focus turns on them. This activity is tiring and stressful; while worriers keep their distance and try to reduce the uncertainty associated with becoming involved, such constant flitting around just loads it all back on again. It's like being the host of every social gathering you've ever been to – exhausting.

The flipside of this might be attempts at controlling social situations or gatherings. For instance, constantly talking so that others can't ask questions (thus limiting uncertainty – *where will the conversation go?*), or over-using humour to keep the conversation away from anything too contentious and worrisome.

Hint:

People: *Is there anything about the people you avoid that you like or miss? What would your social/work/family circles be without them? Is this the only part of their character? What else do you know about them? Would you bump into them any more or less if you stopped trying to avoid them? How does being on the lookout for them affect how you feel? Are you responsible for the actions of others?*

Side-effects of worry: *Would your friends be that bothered if you lost the thread of a conversion or forgot something? If this happened to someone talking to you, what would you think? If a close friend told you that they worried about concentrating or worried that they were more irritable than usual, what would you tell them? What are the advantages and disadvantages of avoiding people or social events? How does this leave you feeling?*

Hints for the flipside: Can you let go of control, maybe just a little at first, and see what happens? If you controlled conversations less, would this be less stressful, and might it provide you with more interesting, two-way conversations?

Strategy 5: Avoiding situations

Some situations inevitably have a level of uncertainty built into them – for example, a check-up at the doctor's or dentist – because their purpose is to turn relative uncertainty into relative certainty by finding out if there is a problem (tooth decay, gum problems, etc.) and then deciding what to do about it. In some situations there are factors clearly beyond your control: a social event where you don't know who you will sit next to, or a train trip (delays, noisy passengers), or the exact contents of an exam paper, and so on. Worriers would like to avoid these situations, which usually makes the problems worse and increases the opportunity for worry. For example, they might avoid the dentist because they can't be sure they won't need dental work done, which only means they are putting themselves at more risk of needing more serious work further down the line, which then triggers more worry. A related problem is when the worrier focuses on one situation to the exclusion of others. Often the situation focused on is much less important than the one they're avoiding. For example, avoiding the dentist while booking other less important and even unnecessary appointments elsewhere.

Hint: What are the advantages and disadvantages of doing this? Getting started: *what upcoming situations have some likely benefits, even though the uncertainty may be a little uncomfortable?*

Strategy 6: Checking – avoiding making mistakes

This is very common. Worriers often feel uncertain about decisions or choices that they have made and consequently revisit them to see if they did the right thing (*I can't be sure it's right*). This can be actual checking behaviour – for example, going back to reread an email several times – or it can be mental checking, in which an event is replayed several times in thoughts. Sometimes the worrier will develop elaborate back-up plans, in the unlikely event that something might go wrong. The checking triggers more *what if* questions and anxiety and sows further doubt. The worrier is drawn back to check, to answer the doubts raised by their worry (not by the thing itself); however, their worry increases rather than decreases uncertainty. The flipside of this is avoiding checking at all (*I don't want to know it's wrong*); the worrier is concerned that they might discover an error, so they choose to avoid checking, but the gnawing doubt remains and triggers worry. Checking is exhausting and takes the worrier away from simply enjoying a job done. Not checking at all can mean missing out on what could be an important feedback loop.

Hint: What are the advantages and disadvantages of checking? Getting started: Is there something I routinely check where it would not be a complete disaster if for once I did not check as much? To learn how checking influences you, pick something you don't usually check, and now check this as frequently as you check when worried. What do you notice?

Hints for the flipside: Are there things you avoid checking where it might actually be useful to check? Check things once only! Get some feedback on the things you have done? It might even be good feedback!

Strategy 7: Procrastination – avoiding painful feelings

Another form of avoidance is procrastination. This is where worriers find every excuse under the sun to avoid dealing with an uncertain problem or issue. Examples of this include putting off a conversation with a friend or colleague because they can't be sure how it will turn out, or spending time cleaning the house because they know the bills need sorting, or putting off phoning their bank for an overdraft because they don't know if the bank will agree to it or not. Sometimes the worrier will go halfway to solving a problem before backing off, leaving the problem unsolved. As with the example of the bank above, not dealing with something straight away means that the problem or issue remains. And if left, it may get worse, bringing more uncertainty than the problem contained in the first place. In addition, by trying to ignore something, our minds have a wonderful way of reminding us of unfinished business by sporadically dropping the issue or problem into our thoughts. This can happen when we are least able to do anything about it (say at 3 a.m.), and so triggers more worry. Or, the person is caught up worrying about the implications of their failure to address the problem, which means they again fail to do anything about it.

There is a flipside to procrastination: impulsivity. Here the worrier makes quick or impulsive decisions in order to avoid the uncertainty generated by the choices they face. This can lead to poor choices as the decision is made without consideration of the issues at hand.

Hint: What are the advantages and disadvantages of doing this? Do not wait for certainty before you act; experiment with being certain enough. What happens to your worry when you put things off? Can you actually solve problems by putting them off? Getting started: Where could I make a start on something where even doing only a bit can have some benefit?

Hints for the flipside: Can you sit with the uncertainty and take more time to make a choice? Put off a decision for an hour or a day; sleep on one rather than making a snap judgement.

Strategy 8: Looking for reassurance – avoiding taking responsibility

This is a very common way of dealing with uncertainty. Reassurance seeking is helpful in the short term because we usually feel much better once someone has told us everything will be OK, but its effect is generally short lived. Uncertainty drives the worrier's thirst for reassurance and before long they need more. How does this happen? They may seek reassurance when feelings of uncertainty are triggered by a decision or when they have solved a problem and want to know that they did OK. Any certainty that may have emerged as a result of seeking reassurance is both short lived and undermined by *what if* questions as they take the reassurance to pieces. As they do this, the levels of uncertainty increase and the worrier is then driven to demand more reassurance to stave off the uncertainty, and the cycle starts again. Reassurance has another side-effect that triggers more uncertainty and worry: worriers will often ask the people closest to them for reassurance. Worriers can do this repetitively, which after a while may irritate the people they ask and lead them to respond in a dismissive and unconvincing way or perhaps even to say unintentionally hurtful things – this can trigger more worry.

Worriers can be either very direct or very subtle about how they seek reassurance. For example, when wanting to find out if their friends enjoyed an evening out at the cinema the worrier might ask a series of questions. The straightforward questions would be, *Did you enjoy yourself?* and, *How did you find the film?* The more clandestine questions might be, *Do you like that type of film?* Or, *Did you notice that X didn't seem to enjoy it?* Seeking reassurance means that we never learn to tolerate uncertainty or take responsibility for our actions. It undermines our confidence in dealing with uncertainty and erodes our confidence in our decision making. Worriers can also use a 'hanging statement'. This is a half-question, a question without an ending, and the worrier implies the ending – for example, *I wasn't so sure about that* . . . (the question is, *What do you really think?*), or, *It wasn't as good as the others he made* . . . (the question is, *Did you really like this one?*). Of course the big problem with these hanging statements is that the other person doesn't really know where the worrier is coming from. It's a sort of bear-trap, where the ambiguous or unexpected response may unknowingly trigger more worry.

Finally, reassurance seeking can have a corrosive effect on our mood, as we sometimes seek it despite knowing in our heart of hearts that all is well, and then give ourselves a hard time for seeking it in the first place.

The flipside of this is never asking for feedback or advice about our ideas or decisions. The worrier in this case wants to avoid the feelings generated by uncertainty, as feedback often gives us more to think about. The worrier may also be fearful of critical feedback or advice. They may miss out on helpful feedback. They may also stay in a state of high uncertainty and feel stuck when the act of seeking a little advice or feedback might add some welcome certainty and help move things on. Or, they may find out things that would encourage or empower them to move forward in the face of uncertainty.

Hint: What are the advantages and disadvantages of seeking reassurance? How will you develop your confidence if you continue to ask others for it? Getting started: *What could I do without asking for reassurance – something which I would normally seek reassurance for if someone were around?*

Hints for the flipside: Could you begin to ask for feedback, or get some idea about what others think about your decisions or choices? Choose something small to start with. While the feedback may provoke worry, does it also give you fresh perspectives or new ideas?

Strategy 9: Avoiding giving others responsibility – over-protecting and failing to delegate

Worriers tend to look out for others and at the same time worry about them. As a way of reducing uncertainty and worry they may prevent their children or other family members from doing everyday activities. They may take on tasks themselves, rather than putting other people at risk. We saw this in Abby's example on page 60: while pregnant she took on running errands for her husband so that *he* would not be put at risk when driving. She did this because she genuinely cared about him, but she also wanted to manage her uncertainty. Worriers genuinely care about their families and friends, but because of the nightmare scenarios they have when they worry, they are often motivated to protect others from these awful hypothetical experiences. This strategy is a 'just in case' strategy. If the awful thing really happened, then they also worry that they would not be able to cope, leading them to protect, irrespective of the costs to themselves or others. Being the subject of over-protection can be annoying: children and other family members may 'rebel' and their behaviour become much more uncertain and unpredictable, which leads to more worry. Furthermore, for parents there is a delicate balance between allowing children to grow up and become autonomous through taking age-appropriate risks, possibly making mistakes, versus trying to keep them completely safe from all possible harm.

The flip version is about giving too much responsibility to others inappropriately because we worry that we cannot manage the responsibility ourselves. For example, asking a junior member of the team to attend a difficult meeting in our place, knowing full well that they are inexperienced (and feeling bad about this). Or not having the courage of our convictions, not speaking up and influencing decisions when we have something valuable to say, so that others make the decision and we end up resenting it and beating ourselves up for letting it happen.

Hint: What are the advantages and disadvantages of this strategy? How do those who are the subject of your protection feel? If you continue to overprotect them, what might be the outcome? Are there better ways of protecting your loved ones, apart from stopping them from doing things or doing things for them? Getting started: *Is there something that I know others can do, but I still do it for them or instead of them? Can I let them do it this time and sit with the uncertainty?*

Hints for the flipside: Can you begin to take back some responsibility? What happens if you do? While you may worry more, do you notice other benefits? Do you feel empowered?

Strategy 10: Smokescreen

Sometimes we avoid uncertainty by putting up a smokescreen to 'distance' ourselves from the uncertainty. Often the smokescreen is made up of 'every idea under the sun' as to why we shouldn't deal with an uncertain situation or event; apart, that is, from the real reason, namely finding the feelings of uncertainty intolerable. For example:

An office worker was offered a promotion in which he would get much more money, work on the same floor of the same building, have a bigger office, a nicer desk and view, work with a lovely team, and so forth. The promotion was offered because he was more than qualified for the new role. But he declined because he said he preferred his desk in the office, felt settled in his job, knew his way around, had a nice routine and wanted to stay close to his friends. Each idea was reasonable but may have masked the real reason for declining the promotion, namely that the uncertainty it would bring would have been intolerable. The smokescreen meant the worker never really got to grips with the underlying ideas that motivated him to avoid the risks and new experiences that came with the promotion.

While we have used a work-related example, the pattern can be seen in relationships, in our financial dealings, in the way we think about our health or in our avoidance of social events. So how does the smokescreen keep us worrying? As we have mentioned, by not addressing the underlying issue the idea that we would be unable to cope with uncertainty is kept alive. We never find out that, if we blew away the smokescreen, we would probably be able to cope and thrive. The uncertainty turns an opportunity into a threat. The smokescreen also has a secondary impact: the worrier avoids opportunities for growth and development, which may in the longer term have a profound impact on how they feel about themselves.

Hint: What are the advantages and disadvantages of putting up a smokescreen? Getting started: *Is there a time-limited situation, or a small enough action (e.g. a purchase), in which I could drop the smokescreen and become a man/woman of action?*

Strategy 11: Post-mortem worry

Once worriers have made up their minds with regard to a decision or problem, they may then begin to doubt whether they have made the right choice. On their way to making a decision, they would have wrestled with uncertainty until they 'bit the bullet' and decided. Once the decision is made, then uncertainty opens up again. The worrier will ask, *What if I have made a bad decision?* and then worry about the implications of their decision. Their questioning stimulates uncertainty and breaks simple decisions into a thousand pieces, and the worrier becomes lost within the labyrinth of ideas and begins to doubt their decision and themselves. Imagine a parrot sitting on your shoulder asking you these questions: Why did you do that? What if it goes wrong? Why didn't you get more advice? How could you be sure? (And so on.) How would you feel towards the parrot? The questions are undermining and critical, based on the idea that you do not have the capacity to make good decisions or choices. Remember that we are referring to everyday decisions – a choice about where to go for lunch with a colleague, or what car seat to put your child on, or which account to put your money in. These everyday choices are taken apart and scrutinized and, not surprisingly, we feel much more uncertainty when this happens, leading to more worry. The story earlier about Peter buying a washing machine on page 178 also hints at a secondary problem that comes with post-mortem worry, namely that the worrier is denied the chance to feel enjoyment or contentment in their decision making. For example, a student was worried about which laptop to buy. She eventually chose one and took it home. Once connected to the Internet her post-mortem worry started and she searched the Internet for cheaper and better laptops and soon felt stupid for choosing the one she had. This kind of post-decision worrying is particularly problematic when coupled with impulsive decision making linked to escaping uncertainty.

Hint: What are the advantages and disadvantages of this strategy? How does pulling your decisions to pieces help?

Have you ever found that the decisions you made were good despite pulling them to pieces? If so, how often? When you recognize yourself doing this, what could you say? Would you do this if it were someone else making the decision? If not, why not? Getting started: *Is there a small decision you need to make which you know you will pull to pieces afterwards? Make your decision and then sit with the uncertainty. When you start to pull it to pieces ask,* Why am I doing this? *and tell yourself that your decision is good enough.*

Other strategies

Uncertainty makes those who are intolerant of it feel awful. They feel it in their body. It affects their mood. It affects the way they think. Some people use drugs or alcohol to relax their body, chill out their mood, or slow down their mind. If they don't feel as bad when they do use drugs or alcohol, they are likely to do it again. These strategies tend to make their problems worse, as they do not address the underlying issue or problem that triggered the worry in the first place. They also have the effect of increasing uncertainty, as we tend to be much less predictable and ordered when we are under the influence of drink or drugs. There are also long- and short-term costs. For example, in the short term there may be immediate emotional costs as we 'beat ourselves up' for using alcohol or drugs to cope and avoid our problems. In the longer term we may begin to become reliant on drink or drugs to help us cope, or the problems that we continue to avoid may become bigger and more problematic, leading us to drink more to manage them.

If you are worried about how much you are drinking or about the drugs you are taking, then please go and see your family doctor and discuss this with them.

Some worriers tend to comfort eat or binge to manage feelings of uncertainty. Of course these strategies do not address the real uncertainty, only the unpleasant feelings that come with it. A similar pattern of short- and long-term costs is associated with this strategy, too. The long and short of all the strategies we have mentioned is that their aim is to reduce uncertainty, but they have the opposite effect because we fail to engage enough with our problems to solve them.

We mentioned that worriers tend to reduce the circumference of their world because of uncertainty. Uncertainty will also keep worriers stuck in unhelpful relationships because the worrier believes that leaving or ending them will generate much more uncertainty than keeping things as they are. We have often heard the phrase 'better the devil you know than the devil you don't' when working with people in these situations. If you are struggling within a relationship, or being abused in some way, find the courage to tell your family doctor; they will know where to get help. No one has the right to hurt or abuse you. In the first instance, you may need to talk things through to get your mind around what is going on and help you to make a decision about what will happen next. In the UK, the website NHS Direct has information about violence or abuse within the home (see Appendix 6, Useful contacts and information).

EXERCISE 10.2: PULLING THINGS TOGETHER

This exercise summarizes the key points in this chapter.

What are the key strategies that you use to manage uncertainty?

Overall, how much energy and effort are you putting into managing the unmanageable, that is managing uncertainty?

What ideas did you come up with to help challenge your intolerance of uncertainty? What behavioural experiments can you think of to help you learn to tolerate uncertainty?

In all the above strategies, the common process is that of increasing your exposure to small doses of uncertainty rather than always trying to eliminate it. The simple message is that if we can learn to tolerate uncertainty by doing things differently we can stop fuelling worry in our day-to-day lives. By being willing to embrace uncertainty in our day-to-day life, living with any expected but temporary increases in anxiety and worry while doing new things, looking out for and noticing the benefits of new behaviours, we can have a richer life with more variety, more pleasant surprises and more confidence, such that we can deal with the uncertainties life will inevitably bring.

PIT STOP

Let's stop and think about what you have just been reading. Can you summarize the key ideas you have taken on board? What things are sticking in your mind about uncertainty? Maybe write them down. If you have any questions, jot these down too. You can return to them once you have had a chance to digest the information.

What is sticking in my mind from my reading so far?

1.

2.

3.

In the next chapter we will give you some examples of behavioural experiments to help you become more tolerant of uncertainty.

11

Behavioural experiments – dealing with uncertainty

Before reading this chapter, it may be helpful to review Chapter 7 to remind yourself of how to go about developing behavioural experiments.

Behavioural experiments are about finding out something new, by doing something differently. This means changing the way you react to uncertainty and, rather than avoiding it, beginning to seek it out on purpose to see what happens. We do not expect you to dive into the deep end of uncertainty; it's much better to begin thinking about small, manageable and realistic steps. Expect to feel anxious and to worry more when trying out new things – we all do. Remember, do not wait until you feel motivated: go out and seek motivation by doing. *Motivation does not come before action, it follows it*. Act first, and the motivation will arrive.

What would these steps look like?

Take a strategy that you now recognize and begin to think about all the situations where this strategy appears in your life (we have asked you to think about this in previous chapters). Don't get too hung up on trying to separate out the strategies, since they overlap a great deal. The important thing is that you have thought about what you do in the face of uncertainty and spotted some of the unhelpful patterns you fall into.

Let's take seeking reassurance as an example. Here is a list of situations that Abby wrote down in which she looked for reassurance:

- about the clothes she's wearing
- about which clothes to buy while shopping
- about what food to cook
- about her appearance
- about whether she's a good enough partner (parent, friend, etc.)
- about her financial dealings
- about whether she has upset others
- about other people's whereabouts
- about whether her partner still loves her.

Next we put this list in order, starting with the 'shallow end' stuff first. Imagine you are putting each of these on a ladder, with the toughest one on the top rung and the easiest on the first. Abby did this with her list: she found that the easiest step for her would be to stop asking her partner what she should cook for supper. For her, the hardest steps were about her relationships, and she left these until she had got some experience of tolerating uncertainty under her belt.

In our example, we would ask Abby, 'Supposing you did not ask for reassurance; what is the worst thing that could happen?' This question is very helpful for getting to the hidden consequences that often underpin our rules. In Abby's case, she feared upsetting her partner by not asking him. She developed the following prediction:

If I don't ask my partner about what food to cook for supper, then I won't know what he thinks (I'll be uncertain) and I'll feel awful and I will worry that he'll be upset with me for making something he doesn't want.

At this point is might be helpful to think about the other side-effects of seeking reassurance, such as the costs to you or how it maintains poor self-confidence or the impact it has on those around you. The cost in this case may simply be that Abby knows what she wants for supper, and does not actually want to eat what her partner suggests. The idea is to begin to rock the foundation of the rules, to help you understand why challenging them could be useful and to develop alternative ideas about what might happen. Abby came up with the following alternative:

If I don't ask my partner about what food to cook for supper, then I may feel awful for a while and I may worry, but if I do this, I'll learn to tolerate uncertainty and I will start to feel more confident. I can surprise my partner with something new and I can prepare something I want to eat, which are added bonuses.

Now that Abby has set up the experiment she needs to do it and see what happens. She may need to remind herself of her goals and why it is important that she remains engaged with them. She needs to guard against perfectionism and be mindful of stalling because of the fear of uncertainty, which is only natural. She also needs to be aware of her safety behaviours and ask herself: *Am I finding reassurance in another way? What am I doing to keep myself safe?* For example, she may realize that she is seeking reassurance by asking her friends for ideas about what she could cook for her partner's tea, or asking her partner indirect questions – such as whether he is still hungry or whether he has eaten enough – or talking about a recipe to see his reaction. In these instances, once she realized she was doing this, she had to stop doing so. Lastly, she had to watch that she was not compensating by engaging in more of the other strategies mentioned above. For example, she noticed that she was tempted to play things safe and always include one thing her partner really liked as part of each meal. She also started scanning her partner's conversations for any food-related cues.

Once Abby had successfully tackled the above challenge, she needed to think about keeping it going, while tackling another of the situations in which she sought reassurance. This is a little like plate spinning – keeping one thing on the go while introducing something new – but after a while it can become second nature. As with all plate spinning, there is a manageable number of plates to spin at one time, so Abby needed to get the balance: enough different plates to keep things going, but not too many that she couldn't pay attention to each. She moved on to the clothes she would wear. When developing your experiment review the examples found on page 249 to give you some ideas.

While this may feel like a trivial example, remember that worry and GAD are about the everyday masquerading as big event worry. They're not actually about big occasion worry, because in those situations we are all likely to worry and, as we have said before, some aspects of worry, or something like worry, can be helpful. In order to help you to worry less and keep it for the big occasion, we need to help you to tolerate uncertainty in the everyday, not in the spectacular and unusual. So keep this in mind.

How do I know it is working?

As you actively seek out uncertainty it is perfectly normal to notice uncomfortable feelings and worry. In the normal course of things (and according to your previous rules) this would be a signal to stop what you are doing and to try to decrease the uncertainty. If you are using your level of worry, your anxiety or your discomfort with uncertainty as an indicator of whether the new way of doing things is working, the logical conclusion would be: *This isn't working!* So, how worried, anxious or uncomfortable you are feeling at the time are not the right indicators. The *right indicators* are the outcomes (namely, what happened) and how you feel about them afterwards.

Looking for Signs of Change

Did disaster strike? Was the outcome at least OK? Was it any better than OK? Did anyone else notice anything? Did anyone else notice something good? Did you discover anything new? Did you experience something new? How did you feel about what actually happened? OK? A bit better than OK? Any positive feelings like pleasure, satisfaction, surprise? Are you proud of your attempt to do something differently? Are you motivated to try something else? Did you manage (even if it was uncomfortable) to tolerate uncertainty?

If your answers to at least some of these questions are in the right direction, then you are making progress. This is why the post-experiment review where you compare the outcome with your predictions is absolutely critical. Although a few people can experience 'Aha' moments from experiments, when a blinding flash of realization leads to a new way of looking at the world, for most people change comes from chipping away at everyday experiences. It is only when we look back after a few weeks that we can see how far we have come. Remember, also, that the intention is not to become carefree, spendthrift, lackadaisical, irresponsible, uncaring or so forth. The intention is to become flexible, responsive and capable of spontaneity, all according to the situation. Although certainty may remain attractive but elusive, pursuit of it is no longer the main guiding principle.

Table 11.1: Ideas for behavioural experiments that stimulate tolerance of uncertainty

Don't ask for reassurance on a decision you have made.	Stop checking emails, letters or small cheques before sending them.
Take a gamble, go and see a film you know nothing about.	Buy food you have never bought Before.
Arrive ten minutes later than you normally would at an informal social occasion.	Take responsibility for something small and time-limited. Go ahead, don't ask for reassurance.
Go to a different shop for your groceries.	Delegate small jobs at work or at Home.
Having something you have never tried in a restaurant.	Go to a restaurant you have never been to (and don't read the reviews beforehand).
Allow your kids to do age-appropriate things for themselves.	Once you have bought something new, use it and keep using it.
Stop asking others to check your work.	Make a smallish, impulsive buy.
Put a cap on the amount of time or information you need to make a decision.	Stay in the here and now; go with the flow when in familiar settings.
Take opportunities to meet new people.	Try out new activities; take a taster session for a club or a hobby.
Within your circle of acquaintances, let people get to know you.	Sit still in social occasions; lose the butterfly wings.

Book a visit to your GP, accountant, dentist or bank manager, or anyone else you are avoiding.	Move things around in the home; break your patterns and order.
Ask your loved ones to *not* tell you exactly where they are or exactly when they will be home.	Don't stick rigidly to a plan; act spontaneously if an opportunity presents itself.
Break your routines and go 'off track'.	Let others drive if you always drive yourself. Drive yourself if you always let others drive.
Make a minor commitment.	Find good reasons for doing things instead of not doing things – then do them.
Act while the problem is still small.	Do the task that needs your attention and not the thousands of others that get in the way.
Be generous and less critical of yourself.	If you make too many snap decisions, use the time it takes to have a coffee to think things through.
Find your own path; don't follow the crowd for the sake of it. Do your own thing.	Say yes more often to small invitations.

Now, time for action and to challenge your intolerance of uncertainty. As the inspirational poet and writer Susan Kennedy (aka Sark) suggests, it's time to 'make friends with freedom and uncertainty'.

PIT STOP

Let's stop and think about what you have just been reading. Can you summarize the key ideas you have taken on board? What is sticking in your mind? Maybe write them down. If you have any questions, jot these down too. You can return to them once you have had a chance to digest the information.

What is sticking in my mind from my reading so far?

1.

2.

3.

12

The cradle of worry

For a moment, let us return to the traffic metaphor. Remember that in order to try to manage traffic, we needed to understand and then challenge driver rules or beliefs that influenced the flow of traffic, (for instance, *I must always keep up with the flow of traffic*; *If I drive at the speed limit, then I could annoy the drivers behind me*). Both these rules motivate faster driving. There are a number of rules and beliefs that have a very strong influence on our propensity to worry. We shall explore these rules in this chapter.

The link with uncertainty

There are three broad groups of beliefs or rules that influence worry and they all tend to make us worry more. What is important is where they are thought to appear in the timeline of worry. They provide a framework for worry, which we have called the *worry cradle* (see Figure 11.1 on page 256). We can think of these rules as if they form a *cradle*, providing the 'space' wherein worry can form, develop and grow. Just as in the bus stop example in Chapter 7 (page 135), the rules provide a framework or cradle for the actions that follow them; remember, the whirlwind of worry can be thought of as an action or mental behaviour. A *what if* question can be thought of as a sign that uncertainty has been 'spotted' within a situation. The *what if* question triggers more *what if* questions and a stream of worry begins to develop. At the same time, the worry activates the cradle of worry, which, in a sense, instructs the worrier to worry more. Many of the rules that make up the worry cradle tell us that worrying is, by and large, a helpful or useful thing to do. For instance, *Worrying shows that I care*. Other rules tell us that worrying is an **un**helpful thing to do. For instance, *If I worry, bad things are more likely to happen*. The final group of rules are more general rules related to our thoughts; for instance, *All my thoughts are important* or, *I should always think things through properly*. All three types of rule 'set us up to worry' and we will explain how they do this in more detail below.

The cradle of worry is made of three groups of rules:

- positive worry-promoting rules
- negative worry-promoting rules
- general worry-promoting rules

The next sections of this chapter will take in turn each of these rules and provide more detail on what they are and how they might influence worry.

Positive worry-promoting rules

We now return to the example of Tom waiting at the train station (see page 82).

Tom has now got to the train station. His train is a few minutes late and he wonders, *What if I am late for work?* This thought opens up doubt and uncertainty and he starts to worry. He starts to think about the implications of being late for work and how this will impact on his job, his relationship and his life. His worry quickly turns into a nightmarish daydream. His worries feel very real, they arrive thick and fast and they generate more doubt and uncertainty, so he worries all the more. His worry feels out of control and he starts to feel very panicky. He is barely aware of his surroundings as his worry carries him further away. He starts to feel anxious, tense and restless and he looks about nervously. He gets snappy with his girlfriend. Lost in his worry, he nearly misses his train.

In this example, uncertainty appears when Tom's train is a few minutes late, and triggers the *what if* questions that create more uncertainty and more worry. There are other 'silent' influences on his worry. We might ask Tom the following questions:

1. Supposing you didn't worry *at all* about being late, what would that say about you as an employee or as a person?
2. What are the advantages of worrying about this *(compared to not worrying at all)*?
3. If you didn't worry *at all*, what might happen?

In response to the first question, he might tell us that worrying about his job shows that he cares about it, and that if he didn't worry he would be a bad employee. In response to the second question, he might say that worrying in this way prepares him for the awful day ahead and potentially helps him negotiate his way through it. If we asked him how worry helped him do this, he might tell us that it is almost as if he is steeling himself for events to come by worrying about them first, even though they are highly unlikely to happen. To the last question, he might add that worry helps him to find solutions to the problems and that if he doesn't worry things through, then he may miss important problems. There are several silent rules in operation here:

- If I worry it means I'm a good worker.
- If I worry it shows I care about my work.
- If I worry, I'll be more ready for what the day will throw my way.
- If I worry, I'm preparing myself for the worst.
- If I worry it helps me to find solutions to problems.
- Worry keeps me on my toes.

These rules are the silent partners in the development of worry; they support worry and enable it to develop and grow. Stop for a moment and ask if you can see how Tom's rules supported his propensity to worry. These rules 'instruct us to worry', they 'tell us' that if we worry we can be better prepared, or that we can show we care, or that we are better people for worrying. As you no doubt realize, there are much better ways of preparing, or bettering ourselves, or showing we care. For instance, if you were to write a list of all the things that make a good employee, father, partner, daughter, guest, host, colleague, friend and so on, would you include worry on your list?

The diagram below shows how a situation activates the *cradle of worry*, which both starts us worrying and keeps us worrying. The worry itself then opens up doubt and uncertainty and triggers more worry.

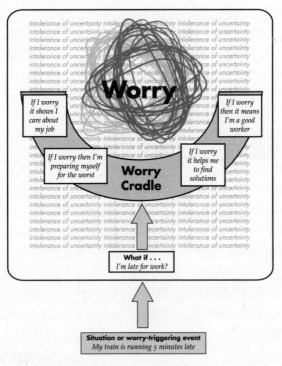

Figure 12.1: Building the picture: the cradle of worry

Discovering worry rules

In the bus stop example we could work out what rules were operating by looking more closely at what actions people took or noticed when strong feelings were triggered. This leaves us with a problem: with worry, worrying *is* the action and we can't see it! If we can't see it, then how can we work out what the worry rules are? We know that there are lots of actions motivated by worry and we can use these actions to help us spot worry rules; for example, when we check and recheck work, or when we struggle to act when faced with a problem. And we can use questions to help us discover worry rules. The series of questions below will help you work out your worry rulebook. It might be helpful to take a notebook and work through them to see if you can understand more about what rules may support your worry. Later in this book there are other ideas to help you develop a better understanding of the rules that might influence your worry. Research has found a number of different themes around which worry rules may circle, such as *worry motivates me*; *worry can protect me from awful feelings*; *worry helps me to find solutions*; *worry prevents bad things happening*; and *worry shows that we are good people*. There are others, and they will be explored in more detail later in this chapter, and we will also spend more time helping you to sketch out your own worry rules in Chapter 13.

EXERCISE 12.1: STARTING TO SPOT YOUR WORRY RULES

This exercise will help you work out and spot your worry rules. You will need your notebook to make a record of your answers. In the blank space insert the name of a loved one, child, family member, colleague or friend, or an event like an exam, a meeting at work, work or money. Think of what you worry about most and answer the questions focused on that. In Block 1, there are two versions of each question, a general version (a) and a more focused version (b). Think about two or three different things with which to fill in the blanks. It will feel a little repetitive, but that's OK; we are looking for themes and links to emerge and this will help.

Block 1

1a. Supposing you didn't worry, what would that say about you?

1b. Supposing you didn't worry about _____, what would that say about you?

2a. Supposing you worried less, what would that say about you?

2b. Supposing you worried less about _____, what would that say about you?

3a. Supposing you stopped worrying tomorrow, would you be bothered by this? If so, why?

3b. Supposing you stopped worrying tomorrow about _____, would you be bothered by this? If so, why?

4a. Supposing you worried less, would anything happen?

4b. Supposing you worried less about _____, would anything happen?

5a. What are the advantages of worrying?

5b. What are the advantages of worrying about _____?

6a. What are the disadvantages of worrying?

6b. What are the disadvantages of worrying about _____?

7a. Does worrying help you in any way? If so, how?

7b. Does worrying about _____ help you in any way? If so, how?

Block 2

1. If I didn't worry (about _____) so much, then ....

2.   If I didn't worry (about _____),
     then ....

3.   I should worry (about _____)
     because ....

4.   Worrying (about _____)
     helps ....

5.   Worrying (about _____)
     stops or prevents ....

6.   I ought to worry (about _____)
     because ....

7.   I should worry (about _____)
     or .... may happen.

8.   I worry (about _____)
     to ....

9.   I worry to stop or prevent ....

Review what you have discovered in this exercise.
Does it help you to understand why you worry in
certain situations? Or does it help you to understand
what motivates you to worry? What comes to mind?
Write it down and return to it once you have read
more. What rules have you discovered? Write them
down.

Remember these rules are like bad habits that we may not really want to admit to. Think about the last time someone pointed out one of your bad habits: how did you feel? Did you want to believe them or did you tell them where to go? You may think, *No way! I don't believe it; this can't be true*. This might be a sign, however, to stop and have a good think about whether a worry rule is influencing things. You may also want to check it out with someone you trust and who knows you well. As you read this, you may not be worrying or feeling anxious and the rules may feel remote and hazy; use a recent bout of worry to work with and then see if you can find the rules. Find a pen and paper and write the rule down as best you can. If it doesn't seem right, then play with the way it reads. Change the endings or the beginnings until it feels right to you. This is what we sometimes do in therapy sessions, 'playing' with the rules until they feel right. You could try swapping *I must* with *I must not*, or using *should* or *ought* instead. If your rule is an *if–then* rule, then change it around – for instance, *If I do this, then* . . . versus *If I don't do this, then* . . .; or, *If I worry about my decisions* versus *If I don't worry about my decisions*.

PIT STOP

Let's stop and think about what you have just been reading. Can you summarize the key ideas you have taken on board? What is sticking in your mind? Maybe write them down. If you have any questions, jot these down too. You can return to them once you have had a chance to digest the information.

What is sticking in my mind from my reading so far?

1.

2.

3.

Positive worry-promoting rules – the detail

Here we will look in more detail at the positive rules or beliefs that support worry. These rules suggest that worry is useful and that it leads to positive outcomes. These worry beliefs are common across the spectrum of worry, so people with GAD will have them, as will people who worry less. Positive beliefs, as we have seen, have been found to break down into five categories, namely that worry helps to

- find solutions
- motivate
- protect
- prevent bad things from happening
- show that we care.

As you go through this section, you will find it helpful to keep notes, as we will be asking you later to think in more detail about which of the following rules apply to you. Use the rating scales and questions on the next page to help you review and assess each section. This might be best done after you have read them. In addition, you may want to underline passages or statements, or if you have questions then write them down and you can come back to them once you have read further. We also want you to begin to think about how useful, all things considered, these rules are. And, as with uncertainty, we would like you to think about what you could do differently, using behavioural experiments for example.

The following groups of rules overlap to some extent. It's the central ideas we want you to take from them, since these will help you to think about your own rules and to develop personal versions of them.

GENERAL RATING SCALE FOR EACH GROUP OF POSITIVE WORRY-PROMOTING RULES

How typical or characteristic is this strategy for you?

None	A little	Some extent	Moderately	Somewhat	Mostly	Completely
0	1	2	3	4	5	6

How typical or characteristic is this group of rules for you?

None	A little	Some extent	Moderately	Somewhat	Mostly	Completely
0	1	2	3	4	5	6

How strongly do you agree with the idea that supports this strategy (e.g. that worry shows I care)?

None	A little	Some extent	Moderately	Somewhat	Mostly	Completely
0	1	2	3	4	5	6

Can you think of a personal example from this set of worry rules? Write it down here.

How strongly do you believe this to be true?

None	A little	Some extent	Moderately	Somewhat	Mostly	Completely
0	1	2	3	4	5	6

What impact does this rule have on your worry?

What could you do to challenge this rule?

Group 1: Worry finds solutions to problems

These rules are based on the idea that worry is a useful strategy that helps us to find solutions to problems. They suggest that worry enables us to look ahead and prepare for what might go wrong, or that worrying can help us to decide what we should do if this happens. Linked to this belief is a sense that if we worry we are more likely to produce well-thought-out and effective solutions. We might believe that if we worried less, then our chances of finding the best solution to a problem would decrease.

How this belief makes worry worse. This all sounds very reasonable, and to a certain extent this belief can be useful in life-changing or 'big occasion' events. But in these circumstances, muscle tension, restlessness, the loss of sleep and so on are 'accepted' as part of the deal. Unfortunately, worriers tend to use these rules to help them work with everyday events or issues, and worry here brings the same intense side-effects, which can make everyday problem solving much more difficult. If our worry is at a manageable level, it may well contribute towards developing better solutions, although there may be alternative or better ways. However, worriers can't regulate the flow of their worry, which usually comes at two levels of intensity: either high or none at all. If we worry a lot, our worry begins to interfere with our capacity to act and to solve problems. Also, by being overly alert to potential problems, each solution we come up with is 'shot full of holes'. Worse still, as we see each solution fail, this triggers the familiar spiral of worry – we're back to 'every silver lining has a cloud' again.

TYPICAL BELIEFS

If I worry then I will know what to do. If I worry this problem through, I will find the best way to deal with it.

Hint: Is this the best way to find the best solutions to your problems? What else could you do? Is there a less costly approach? What are the advantages and disadvantages of this approach? Does worrying actually solve your problems, or are you just going over and over the same stuff without moving forward? Does anxiety produced by worry help or hinder your ability to solve problems?

Group 2: Worry motivates

This is one of the commonest beliefs in people with excessive worry. In a recent tutorial a student said, *My worry motivates me to work; if I didn't worry then I wouldn't work.* This belief is only helpful if it does just enough to get us working; it then needs to 'leave us alone' to get on with the job in hand. With such a set of rules it's almost as if worrying somehow guarantees that things get done and that worrying increases the quality of whatever needs to be done.

How this belief makes worry worse. People who worry a lot tend to find that in general their worry is distracting and interferes with concentration; this stops them from working efficiently, leading to avoidance and procrastination, and it may even stop them completely rather than motivate them. In the example above, the student 'needed' to worry to start working, but if his worry increased to a significant level it would begin to interfere with his ability to concentrate and no doubt have a negative impact on the quality of his work, thus further increasing worry. It would be much better to be preparing an assignment without worrying, as there are other more important things to think about – inspiration, creativity, concentration and maybe even enjoyment! We know that the emotional consequences of worry such as anxiety and exhaustion will reduce motivation and can lead to a vicious cycle where worry produces anxiety and demoralization, which then make it harder to work, leading to more worry, and so on. The other important issue to mention with regards to this type of belief concerns yet another belief that silently sits within it; namely, that worrying about your work is the same as actually caring about it. If you worried less about your work or other life events, would it mean that you cared less about them? It seems clear that for most of us worry is thought to be useful at some level. It will be much harder to free ourselves from worry unless we challenge the idea that it is useful. So we need to be clear about the advantages and disadvantages of worrying and then ask where the balance lies: is it an overall advantage or disadvantage to worry?

TYPICAL BELIEFS

If I worry about it, it'll get done.

I should worry or else I'll never do things.

If I worry, I'll do a better job.

If I worry, it shows how much my job means to me.

Worry stimulates me and makes me more effective.

Hints: Is this the best way to motivate yourself? What else might your worry do as well as motivate you? What are the costs or side-effects? What could you do instead? Is there a less costly approach? What are the advantages and disadvantages of this approach? Does this way of approaching work make the quality of your work better? Does it mean that you care more about your work because you worry about it? Is there anyone at work who does not worry, but still cares about their work? What would be so bad about not worrying about work?

Group 3: Worry protects

In this group the worrier believes that to worry before a difficult event will somehow protect them against the onslaught of feelings when the event materializes. Of course, the assumption is that the event will actually happen and trigger overwhelming feelings. Some worriers think that if they worry beforehand this might somehow reduce the degree of awful emotions experienced *if* indeed the awful thing happens, which it very rarely does. It's almost like inoculating yourself against bad things by worrying first, or training yourself to cope with the overwhelming feelings by practising dealing with them first in your worries (a sort of mental gym), or, put another way, dosing yourself with medicine before you show any signs or symptoms.

How these beliefs make worry worse. It's as if the worrier is holding a heavy shield and a full suit of armour to protect themselves, even when there are no dragons to slay. Carrying the shield keeps the worrier on their toes, but it's exhausting to be on guard all the time. One of the key problems is that the worrier is nearly always expecting to experience really nasty feelings (which rarely happen), and this awful sense of apprehension can trigger more worry as we scan for danger. The other critical problem with this approach is that it really doesn't help us to cope with bad things when they do actually happen. None of us can completely prepare for unexpected really bad news such as a death, nor can we prepare for all of the possible awful but unlikely things that could happen. Further, our shield may be entirely useless against a foe that is not a dragon, such as a flood. Even though we would dearly like to know, it's impossible to know exactly what is around every corner.

TYPICAL BELIEFS

I should always worry because you never know what is around the corner.

If I worry about a situation now then it will not affect me so much later.

If I don't worry about it and it happens, I will feel guilty for not worrying about it (so I should worry).

Hint: Is there a better way to protect the ones you love? Is there a better way of dealing with strong emotions? How many times has this strategy worked for you? Has anything that you worried about ever happened? What else could you do? Is there a less costly approach? What are the advantages and disadvantages of this approach? What does it feel like to be waiting for some awful thing to happen? What will it feel like in a year when it still hasn't happened but you've been worrying and waiting all this time?

Group 4: Worry prevents

These beliefs hinge around the idea that the act of worrying alone can influence what actually happens, like a 'telepathic' hand reaching out from our minds and grappling with the world. In these kinds of beliefs, thoughts and actions appear to be fused together, and so worrying about something bad will make it less likely that the bad thing will happen. For example, Angelina, a seventeen-year-old, constantly worried about her health, but she never got ill. She started to believe that the reason for this was her worry, and so it made sense for her to keep worrying. But this way of thinking avoided considering all the other potential influences on her health, like her age, her diet, how unlikely serious illness is or the other things that she does to keep herself healthy. Her kind of worry also involves tunnel vision, where all

270

other explanations – in this case of her good health – are ignored. It's like focusing on one thing to the exclusion of all others.

On the other hand, some worriers believe that worrying about something good will make it more likely to happen. For example, Stan worried about whether his friends would enjoy a film they had gone to see. When they left the cinema Stan quietly asked them what they thought. To his relief, they all enjoyed the film. Without Stan realizing it, doing this reinforced the idea that if he worried about the film beforehand it would be more likely his friends would enjoy the film – so he would be more likely to worry about it again in the future. Asking his friends had the potential to go either way: Stan's friends could have hated the film! But a general and powerful psychological principle is at play called 'intermittent reinforcement'. This means that to reward what you do occasionally has a more powerful reinforcing effect than being rewarded every time. So if Stan only gets it right some of the time, this is still enough to make him believe that it works. Also, as we have said in the chapters on uncertainty, worriers tend to hold a set of beliefs that promote the idea that it is always better to be safe than sorry – Stan seemed to believe this as well.

How these beliefs make worry worse. This rule means we learn that worrying is the best way of preventing bad things from happening, which makes it more likely that we will worry. In another example, Kate worried that her relationship was doomed to fail, but it always seemed to just survive. She started to think that worrying stopped her relationship from folding, so in order to keep the status quo she needed to keep worrying. Acknowledging this was difficult for Kate as she felt ashamed by it. Worrying in this way fuses thoughts with actions, which tells us that worrying can have a real influence on the world. Worrying, rather than doing anything else, becomes the strategy of choice. The tunnel vision that comes with this type of worry ignores all other information, which means that it's very hard to stop and see what else other than worry might be influencing outcomes; in Kate's case, that meant things she could actually do to increase the chance of her relationship working.

TYPICAL BELIEFS

If I don't worry bad things will happen.

If I worry about it, it is more likely to happen.

If I worry about my work, it usually goes well.

If I worry about my children, they will be safe.

Worrying alone can reduce the risks.

Hints: Is worrying the best way to prevent bad things from happening? What else could you do? Is there a less costly approach? What are the advantages and disadvantages of this approach? Can you prove that worrying actually prevents bad things from happening? What else might be influencing the outcome? Are there aspects of the things you are worrying about which you are ignoring or failing to take into account? What about making good things happen: try thinking about winning the Lottery; would this work? If not, why not?

Group 5: Worry shows I care

This set of beliefs is very common. Here the beliefs circle around the idea that worrying means the worrier is a thoughtful, caring or loving person and, worse still, that if they didn't worry they would be inconsiderate, careless or unfeeling. Examples of this belief are, *If I worry about my kids, then I'm a good father* or, *If I worry about my friends, I'm a good person and they will like me all the more.*

How these beliefs make worry worse. The trouble with this set of worry beliefs is that the worrier believes that their self-worth is dependent on how much they worry. So these types of belief suggest that you really should worry because this is valued by others. But do you really need to worry to be approved of by your friends, family or work colleagues? If you told them that you were worrying about them in this way, what would they say? Might they tell you that you can show you care in lots of other ways? Might they value other things as more important than your worry (like your time, friendship, honesty, etc.)? Might they even tell you that when you get really worried about things, you are not much fun to be around, that you tend to nag or get too involved in things that you don't need to get involved in? Rather than feeling cared for, what may they be feeling? Supposing you didn't worry, what would be so bad about that? What would they like from you instead of worry? You may fear that this means you don't care, but why not ask and find out if this is true?

TYPICAL BELIEFS

Worry shows what a caring and good person I am.

If I worry, it shows I am thinking about my family.

If I didn't worry about my children, I would not care for them.

If I worry, it shows that I care.

If I don't worry I would be being negligent or irresponsible.

Worrying makes me a sensible person.

Hint: Is worrying the best way to show that you care? What else could you do? Is there a less costly approach? What are the advantages and disadvantages of this approach? If the person you were worrying about knew that you were worrying like this, what would they say? Has anyone ever reacted badly to your worry or complained about it? Do you consider that 'good people' are those who worry? What other traits might you value? Do you know anyone who is a good person who does not worry? What does this tell you? If worry really was a method of demonstrating that you were a good human being, why would anyone want to stop worrying? If you were running a workshop on how to be a caring, thoughtful, sensible person, would you teach people how to worry? If not, why not? What would you teach them instead?

Negative worry-promoting rules

So far we have focused on the positive rules that promote worry. These suggest that worrying is useful and leads to positive outcomes. Closely related to these are two main negative rules: *foreboding* and *raining on my parade*. We will outline each of these below. These worry rules state that worry tends to lead to unhelpful or negative outcomes. According to these rules, if I worry about bad things happening then they will happen (*foreboding*), and if I worry about good things happening, then they won't happen (*raining on my parade*). So I am damned both ways. Take Lela, who is going on holiday. She started to worry about losing her luggage. She worried that, because she was thinking about it, it was more likely to happen (*foreboding*), which left her more stressed and worried. In another example of the same, Jim was thinking about the money in his bank account when he started to worry about Internet fraud. Because he thought that worrying about something would make it more likely to happen, he started to believe that his money wasn't safe (*foreboding*). He worried all the more. Wendy, on the other hand, was looking forward to going to a music festival, but she started to worry about it. She believed that thinking about nice things meant that they wouldn't happen (*raining on my parade*). Every time a nice thought popped into her mind she thought, *It's not going to happen now*. She spent a lot of time talking herself out of enjoying things and couldn't look forward to anything. She started to worry about what other things she might think about and 'stop' from happening.

TYPICAL BELIEFS

If I think about it too much, it might happen.

If I think about good things, they won't happen.

If I think about bad things, they will happen.

Hints for Foreboding: What are the advantages and disadvantages of this approach? How often are your forecasts right? If you worried about your toaster blowing up, do you think you could make this happen, just by worrying?

Hints for raining on my parade: What are the advantages and disadvantages of this approach? How often have you worried in this way and got it wrong? What happens when you try to push any thought out of your mind?

General worry-promoting rules

So far we have discussed two types of thought that influence worry: the positive and negative rules or beliefs (*the cradle of worry*). In addition to these beliefs, there are other general rules that can have an influence. For instance, when something pops into our mind, we may believe that we should think it through to resolve it, or that it has popped into our mind because it's important. Here's an example:

Dawn was having a 'special' night out at the theatre with friends when an issue she had faced at work that day popped into her mind. Because she believed that *all her thoughts are important,* she could not dismiss it and began to wonder why the thought had appeared. She then began to think it through, trying to find a *quick* answer that was also *perfect*. However, the more she thought it through the more it unravelled and the more she worried. It did not help being in a theatre watching a play and therefore being unable to talk with her work colleagues about what she could do. To manage her uncertainty, she tried to *tie up the loose ends* in her mind, but she couldn't as there were just too many unanswered questions. She didn't remember much of the play nor the conversations with her friends at the interval. Unsurprisingly, she didn't enjoy her evening out.

In Dawn's example there are several beliefs or rules influencing worry. The first is that *all thoughts are important*; the second is that *if a thought comes to mind, I should think it through* (tying up loose ends); the third is that *I should resolve or solve the issue straight away and perfectly (instant and perfect answer)*, rather than 'parking it' for later and enjoying the play.

Use the rating scales and questions that you used for the other worry-promoting rules to assess the degree to which you agree with each of these rules.

Hints: All thoughts are important. *Is it true that all thoughts are important, or are you choosing some to pay attention to? What thoughts are not influenced by this rule? Would this thought be important to you if you knew the world were to end in an hour's time? Does it need all that attention? What's the worst thing that could happen if you didn't pay full attention to it right now? If it's that important, are you really likely to forget it? If you think you might forget it, write it down and come back to it later and see if it still seems important. What are the advantages and disadvantages of this rule?*

Hints: Tying up loose ends. *What's the worst thing that could happen if you didn't think a thought through? How successful has thinking every thought that comes to mind been for you? How often do you actually get to the end of thinking something through, or do you just go off in worry spirals? Are there better ways of doing this, such as writing stuff down, or talking it through with a colleague or friend? What are the advantages and disadvantages of this rule?*

Hints: Instant and perfect answers. *What are the advantages and disadvantages of this rule? What's the worst thing that could happen if you didn't come up with an instant and perfect answer? If it's really not that important, will 'good enough' be OK right now? If it is important, why not wait until you can sit down and spend some time working on it? What else could you do instead and what advantage might this have? What additional, unhelpful side-effects might come with this rule?*

If you challenged your specific rules, what do you think would happen to your worry? Or, put another way, what would happen if you weakened and undermined the cradle of worry? Without these rules to help worry grow and develop, you would worry less. Before we move on to how to achieve this, there is one last belief we should consider.

Starting to change my rules

In order to change your rules, it is important to uncover rules that are personal or specific to you. Trying to work on the broad categories, such as *worrying shows I care*, will not work. There are many reasons for this, but put most simply, 'off the peg' ideas are no substitute for those tailor-made for an individual. In addition, by trying to address these broad categories we might be overwhelmed by too much information; or, because it's not tied into a real experience, what we take from it might be woolly or hypothetical, making it hard to apply to day-to-day experiences. So, just as with setting goals (see Chapter 6) it is much better to have a specific rule to try to work with than a general one. For example, rather than the general *worrying shows I care*, your rule might be, *If I worry about my friends, then it shows that I care about them*. The way the second belief is written gives us many more avenues to explore: some of the ideas will result in concrete suggestions, like talking to your friends to find out if they agree with you. Finally, our rules tend to cross situations; for example, if we worry about our friends because we believe this shows we care, we will probably worry about our family, our work, our dog and so on, because we care about those too. So, once you have found a rule that seems to fit, ask yourself in what other situations this rule is active.

Try to uncover the specific rules that are active in a specific situation. If our efforts to work on our worry rules are tied into everyday detail, they are more likely to be effective. This is why we need a rule that fits closely to *your experiences*. Although many people can and will share a common set of rules, there are always *house rules* or *local rules* that are specific rules applied to a specific situation. For example, each local council has a different set of rules as to what can be recycled, when recycling happens and where.

Considering all the different ideas above, what specific rules are now standing out for you? Write them in the space provided below.

My positive beliefs about worry are:

My negative beliefs about worry are:

My general worry-promoting beliefs are:

Conflicting rules

These rules or beliefs about worry can conflict with one another, making for more uncertainty and therefore more worry. For example, if I believe that *worrying prepares me for things that could go wrong*, this belief tells me, or instructs me, to worry. However, I could also believe at the same time that *if I worry about something, it is more likely to happen*. So, because some beliefs instruct us to worry and others are telling us to not worry, we flip between worrying and trying not to worry, which has the overall effect of increasing tension, anxiety and worry. Sometimes we might feel that we should worry as it shows we care (instructing me to worry), but then this runs into another belief that suggests that worrying is bad for my health (tells me I should not worry). If you have two rules that get locked together like this, choose one to work on first and concentrate on this.

The turbo-charger – more negative beliefs about worry

We have been discussing positive, negative and more general rules that promote worry. We would now like to introduce another important family of negative beliefs. Professor Adrian Wells, a clinical psychologist and researcher working in Manchester, has written and studied worry for many years, and he termed this type of worry as *meta-worry*, or *worry about worry*. Typically, once worrying has started these negative beliefs kick in and 'turbo-charge' the worry. These beliefs tend to add an intense element of anxiety to the whirlwind of worry and in doing so they stimulate more worry.

A typical thought might be, *I'm losing my mind*. When thoughts like these appear they feel very real and so believable that they bring with them severe levels of anxiety or panic, which stoke up the worry all the more. These beliefs boost the intensity of the worry, turning the whirlwind of worry into a hurricane or tornado. The worry rules provide the framework for the worry to happen in, and these beliefs 'soup it up' once it appears. People with GAD tend to believe that once they have started worrying their excessive worry will lead to a number of unpleasant and distressing outcomes. These are listed below.

EXERCISE 12.2: BELIEFS THAT LEAD TO WORRY ABOUT WORRY

Stop for a moment and consider each belief in turn and ask which of them applies to you. You may want to rate them on the scale listed below. Reflect on these questions: which is the highest rated? Which beliefs fit most closely with your experience of worry?

Worrying excessively means that . . .   *Not at all.................Totally true*
Tick the boxes that apply to you   *0%————————100%*

❏ I am out of control   ....%
❏ I will be overwhelmed   ....%

❏ I will go crazy ....%
❏ I will be unable to focus or work or perform ....%
❏ I will be condemned to a life of anxiety ....%
❏ I am on the downward slide to depression ....%
❏ I will become ill ....%
❏ I lack confidence ....%
❏ I am weak ....%
❏ I will be stuck forever in worry ....%
❏ I am not in control ....%

You may wish to ask yourself the following questions to see if you can find out what thoughts might turbo-charge your worry:

Questions to help uncover the turbo-charge (negative thoughts about the activity of worrying)

What is the worst thing that could happen if you couldn't stop worrying?

What would it mean to you if you couldn't stop worrying?

If you continued to worry like this, what do you think would happen?

If you let yourself worry more and more, would anything bad happen?

In CBT the view that people have of their experiences is critical; the turbo-charger is an appraisal (or view) of the act of worrying and it is this view of worry that can be challenged. These negative beliefs are likely to develop and persist as worry takes hold of a person's life and will lead to counterproductive attempts to stop worrying. It is this that we turn our attention to in Chapter 13.

PIT STOP

Let's stop and think about what you have just been reading. Can you summarize the key ideas you have taken on board? What is sticking in your mind? Maybe write them down. If you have any questions, jot these down too. You can return to them once you have had a chance to digest the information.

What is sticking in my mind from my reading so far?

1.

2.

3.

13

Changing your worry rules

There are a number of ways of doing this. We hope that by becoming more aware of what leads you to worry, your worry will reduce. There are further exercises below to help you to think things through a little more. However, *thinking* is only one part of the learning cycle – we need to help you *do* things differently as well.

Helping you to think things through

If your mind works best with images then the pie chart on page 289 might be useful for you. In its simplest form, this pie chart is a graphical way of representing *all* the ideas and factors that may come to bear on a thought or rule, and by so doing it may help you to find other ways of seeing things or put things in perspective. This idea can be applied to most of the rules you will find in this book. Let's take this rule as an example: *If I worry about my children every day, this means that I am a good dad.* As we have suggested above, there may be better ways of showing that a father cares about his children than worrying. In the heat of the moment, however, when the whirlwind is intense, it is often hard to see this. So it's important to take time to think through these new ideas not when you are worrying but before. This kind of learning can help us develop a better awareness of our tendency to worry and of what motivates it, and provide us with a language that can help to check ourselves and turn down our worry dial.

The steps

Once we have our rule on the table, written in words that feel right and tied into our everyday lives, we then need to rate how strongly we believe it, on a scale from 0–100 with 100 per cent being *I believe this absolutely*. We do this partly to make sure that it's worth spending time focusing on this rule (a very low score would suggest that this is not an issue) and partly to enable the worrier to get a sense of how important or influential the rule might be in their lives. For example:

If I worry about my children every day this shows that I care: belief rating = 75 per cent.

Next we want to make a list of all the things that the father does to show that he cares. This may be a little tricky. It could help if he steps away from himself and considers other dads. We may ask him to bring a caring father or mother to mind, someone he knows, and then ask him to think of all the things that this father does to demonstrate caring. We may also ask how his own parents or carers showed that they cared. We may ask him to think of 'caring' in general – what do other people do to show they care? And so on. Here is our dad's example below:

What do you do for the kids to show that you care?

- Pick them up from school
- Make their breakfast and supper
- Wash their clothes
- Cuddle and kiss them
- Listen to them, pay them attention
- Give them my time
- Put them first
- Make sure they learn to look after themselves when I am not with them.

Next, we add 'worry about them' as the final item. Then we ask the worrier to draw a pie which represents caring as a father, and ask them to divide up the pie to show how much of each of these 'slices' contributes towards showing that they care (they can divide up the pie into portions that represent the relative importance of each slice). Sometimes it is helpful to give a rough percentage to each slice to help with this. So, for example, how much does cuddling and kissing them show that you care? This *is not* a mathematical task – it doesn't matter if things don't add up perfectly. What is important is that the worrier begins to think about how important all the other things are that they do, and also that they see that worry is often either not there or a tiny part of what they do to show they care, even if the worry take hours and hours of their day. Look at our pie on page 289. We have rated the example above, lumping three points together under 'practical stuff:

- Practical stuff   5%
    ° Pick them up from school
    ° Make their breakfast and supper
    ° Wash their clothes
- Cuddle and kiss them   15%
- Listen to them, pay them attention   22%
- Give them my time   24%
- Put them first   25%
- Make sure they learn to look after themselves   13%
- Worry   Less than 1%

Once the pie has been drawn, we ask the worrier to step back and think about what the pie chart is telling them. Finally, we ask them to re-rate their original belief and see what has happened to this. We can take it much further, and it is often helpful to follow up one example. For instance, if you spend hours and hours worrying, what does that take you away from? What could you do with that time if you had it? Maybe you could spend even more time with your children, or find something that you can enjoy together. What does worrying do to the quality of the time you do spend with them? How easily can 'worried dad' be really present? How easy is it to really listen, kiss, cuddle and play when worrying?

You may want to try this with one of your positive beliefs. For example, what else might motivate you other than worrying? And how influential might each of these strategies be to getting the *job done*? Could you try to do a little more of the others and a little less worrying? If you have found that worry shows that you care, then why not try this out with your rule?

Figure 13.1: Pie chart illustrating ways that I show I care about my kids

Surveys

In the flat world example in Chapter 7 (see page 139) we mentioned speaking to sailors to see if talking to others could provide more information to help us change our perspective. Thinking about what you have learnt so far about your worry, what would you like to ask others? You could, for example, ask other people if worry motivates them, and what other things they do besides that. Finding out how other people do things can give us ideas about what we might try ourselves instead of worrying, such as building in small rewards or using the support of our friends to help us achieve our goals. Or you may want to ask others what they do with the thoughts that just pop into their head about tasks or jobs that need their attention (see Dawn's example in the last chapter, page 276). Often, finding out that others have similar experiences can be helpful. Hearing that others have had the same thoughts about their worry makes us feel less lonely with it, and may help us feel less convinced by our worry – for example, through asking others if they ever thought that their worry would get out of control.

Getting active – behavioural experiments and other ideas

The worry rules you came up with in the previous chapters will suggest ideas for behavioural experiments. Please find a list below of some ideas you may wish to try. Remember that you will feel anxious and will worry, but the important thing is that you are also doing something new and different to challenge your rules and beliefs. It may be worth reading the called *How do I know it's working* in Chapter 11, section, which gives some helpful advice on what to do if you are feeling anxious about these new and uncertain experiences.

Table 13.1: Breaking the rules

Belief/ Rule	Ideas to help you challenge your rules and beliefs
Worry will drive me insane	When was the last time you thought this? How did you stop yourself from going insane? If you used a safety behaviour (e.g. counting, making sure you can still read, doing sums in your head, etc.), could you drop this and find out what happens? Then focus on a smaller worry to start with and see if you can actually drive yourself insane (we wouldn't be suggesting this if we thought it might work!). You may want to do this first with someone around, but then do it alone. Then pick a larger worry and do the same. And so on. Be aware of anything you are doing to keep yourself from going insane. You need to find out for yourself that there is nothing to be frightened of. What might happen? How will we know that you have gone insane? What would you be doing? What is your personal prediction?
I will lose control if I do not keep my worry in check	When was the last time you felt this? How did you stop yourself from losing control? If you used a safety behaviour (e.g. calming yourself, sitting alone or with someone, distraction, etc.), could you drop this and find out what happens? Then focus on your worries, concentrate on them and try to lose control. Again, like the example above, start small and work up to a significant worry. But you must *really try* to lose control, dropping all your safety behaviours. You may feel strong emotions, but this does not mean you are out of control. Stay with it and see. By the way, what would happen if you were close to losing control of your worry, and the doorbell rang and a friend dropped in? Would you stop worrying? How does this work, if you were truly heading towards losing control or going insane? If the doorbell did stop insanity, then psychologists and others would be out of work and working in hardware stores.

I have no control over my worries	Delay your worries by writing them down and promising yourself that you can return to them later. Give yourself a good twenty minutes later in the day to have a good worry. What do you find?
Worry makes bad things happen	Let's start simple. Worry for twenty minutes a day about how awful it would be to win the jackpot in a lottery. You could win, but it's unlikely. What does that tell you? Now, try the same, but this time think about your toaster breaking. Move it on to bigger and more difficult things. What do you find? While you may read this and say, *Yeah, yeah, I know,* you really need to do it to learn that this rule is unhelpful. So do it.
Worry helps me to solve problems	With a small problem, for twenty minutes a day, each day for a week, focus on the problem. Write the problem down and break it into small chunks. Spend at least as long as you would do worrying about the problem, but this time focus on finding a solution (see Chapter 16). What do you find? If you have solved it, have you done it any quicker than if you had just worried? If you have not solved it, did you feel less stressed or tense? Again, increase the 'size of the problem' slowly, but make sure you trigger some anxiety. Is there a less costly way of solving problems?
Worry helps to motivate me	Use the pie chart and see what else might motivate you (also see the section in Chapter 6 on approach goals). How did you feel when you used worry to motivate yourself? Would you be prepared to be a little less anxious and a little more positive through using helpful motivational ideas rather than worry? Next time use strategies to motivate yourself rather than scare yourself.
I worry to prepare myself for bad things happening	We cannot prepare ourselves for the unknown. Write down one or two specific examples of when you think this may have helped you. How effective was it – could it have been done any other way? Now think of all the times you have done this – would you prefer to follow the worry path or use one of the alternative ideas you have come up with?

I worry to prevent something bad from happening	The task here is to drop the worry and see what happens. Does the bad thing actually happen? Pick an easy situation first and slowly build up. Make a ladder of situations that are increasingly difficult. Sit with the uncertainty. Realistically, how could worrying stop something from happening? What else might be involved? (Design a pie chart.) What are the costs and benefits of doing this?
Worry shows I care	Is there a less costly way of showing this? What happened when you worried last – did it help or get in the way of you caring? Find other ways of caring and use these. (Pie chart?)
Rain on my parade: *If I worry about good things they won't happen*	Worry about a small nice thing that is going to happen (e.g. a cinema trip, meal out, meeting a friend for coffee) and see what happens. Do this again and again. What do you find? What other factors might influence good things happening or not (consider doing a pie chart to help you with this)? How important is worry compared to these other factors?
Foreboding: *If I worry about bad things happening, they will happen*	Think about a couple of specific examples of when this has happened in the past. Was your worry an accurate predictor of the future? How well did you predict the bad thing? Think about all the times this has happened and ask how good at forecasting the future is your worry. Let's test it out. Start by worrying about an inanimate object, your TV, car or MP3 player. What would happen if you thought about bad things happening to these? What do you find? Then move on to thinking about other things happening to you, and then to others. Make sure you write down clear predictions about what will happen, worry about it in detail and see if this works.

All thoughts are important: *If I think of something, then it must be important*	Write down all the little things you have worried about in the last hour. Now apply the following criteria: the end of the world is coming in half an hour. Which of these things do you want to spend your time thinking about? Any, none, some? What does this tell you?
Tying up loose ends: *If I think of something I should think it through*	Think about a couple of specific examples of when you could not stop yourself from thinking something through to the end, even though, deep down, you knew it was unhelpful. What were the costs of doing this? Did doing this make the outcome any better? Is this a strategy you would advise others to use? If not, why not? Pick a trivial worry that comes to mind, really push this, double-check that you tie up *all* the loose ends. What happens when you think things through so completely? Are things clearer or less clear? Are they more certain or less certain? What, if you just left it hanging, is the worst thing that could happen? Make a prediction, leave it hanging and see if your prediction comes true.
Instant and perfect answers: *I must resolve the issue, right now and perfectly*	What would happen if you did not try to resolve the worry and just waited? What's your prediction? In order to do this, we need a worry that has some kind of time limit so we know at the end of the day whether your prediction has come true – for example, worrying about missing a train, or worrying about meeting someone for lunch; something where you will know how things will turn out. When the issue appeared in your mind and you did not resolve it, what happened? Did your prediction come true? If it didn't, then what does that tell you? That you didn't need to find an instant and perfect answer? That you did need to worry? If it did happen, then what did you do? Did you come up with a 'good enough' solution? Did you muddle through? Would instant and perfect answers have made any real difference? So, try not to tie up the loose ends. Don't engage, don't worry, get on with what you are doing when the thought came to mind. Alternatively, you could pick a less than perfect or 'good enough' solution and see what happens if you go with this.

How does this worry rule work?

It is often helpful to sit with our beliefs and work out exactly how our worry might have an impact on events. Use diagrams to help you do this. For example, how exactly would worry about your finances stop them from getting out of control? How would worrying about something bad lead to it happening? Look at the diagram below.

Figure 13.2: Worry Stepping Stones

What steps need to happen in order to make this work?

Think about how your worry might operate. Split the rule and see how you would get from A to B? If you think you've found a way that it might work, then show it to someone else and see if they agree. Draw out your rules and see if you can make A link to B.

Closing comments

Doing something new to challenge your worry rules is a very important part of getting better. Thinking, reflecting and developing an understanding are critically important, but *actions speak louder than words* and you need to experience new things to really understand at a deep level how things can be different. You will be anxious about this and you will worry but that is to be expected. You can do this – you can 'turn down your worry dial' – but in order to do so you have to begin to do things differently.

PIT STOP

It may be helpful to stop here and think about what you have just been reading. Can you summarize the key ideas you have taken on board? What things are sticking in your mind about worry rules? Maybe write them down. If you have any questions, jot these down too. You can return to them once you have had a chance to digest the information.

What is sticking in my mind from my reading so far?

1.

2.

3.

14

Doing something instead of worrying

In April 2006 *Time* magazine ran a cover story on climate change with the headline 'Be worried, be very very worried'. What would you say if we proposed that the journalists at *Time* were suggesting that the best way to address the problem was through worrying? Do you think that if we *only simply* worried about climate change this would make any difference to the problem? Of course, this isn't sensible, but this slightly off-beat stance highlights one of the main issues for worriers – that worry is often used as the only strategy for dealing with life's problems. Unfortunately, it has a tendency to make them worse.

Needless to say, *Time* seemed to be suggesting that climate change is something we should be very concerned about, which many of us would agree with. So, if worry will not help us to address climate change, something else is needed to make a difference. Worry cannot be simply turned off like a tap; so what can we do instead of worrying? The simple answer is that we need to *act* in another way, replacing worry with something that can actually help us achieve our goal or solve a problem. Instead of continuing to worry about problems, we can try to solve them. In the example of climate change, actions might include 'topping up' our loft insulation, turning down the heating in our homes, cycling rather than driving, or lobbying our government for action. We need to learn to be active in the face of our worry rather than remain trapped by it. Worry should not be the only thing you do, but should become a signal or sign for you to do something else.

Instead of worrying about some types of problems, we should try to solve them.

Real Event and Hypothetical Event Worry

In Chapter 5 we discussed the idea that there are two broad types of worry. Some of the problems we worry about exist; these worries are called *Real Event Worry*. And there are worries about problems that *may* exist, otherwise known as *Hypothetical Event Worries*. This second type of worry may never exist in the way that we imagine it; even so, it is like a terrible daydream – a daydream, often set in the future, that includes all sorts of highly unlikely events. By comparison, *Real Event Worry* is about problems that exist, and so it is possible to do something about it by problem solving – even if you are not quite sure how to go about it, or not confident that you will succeed. In fact, worriers are rarely confident about their true abilities and this becomes another thing to worry about. On the other hand, *Hypothetical Event Worries* are, by their very nature, not yet real; they are about events or situations that are highly unlikely to happen, and are usually concerned with things so far into the future that problem solving them will *never* work. So, when faced with worry, we need to think carefully about what kind of worry it is we are trying to address.

Real Event Worry is about problems that exist, and so it is possible to do something about it by problem solving.

Another key issue is that worriers tend to confuse worrying with solving problems. Worry is exhausting; after a bout of worry we often feel tired and drained. Yet all the activity involved does not amount to change, since we are usually left with the problems that triggered the worry in the first place. While it sometimes feels as if we are doing something about our problems by worrying about them, in reality worry itself can never consistently solve the problems – *worrying is not problem solving*.

If we repeatedly fail to address problems, this can have a serious impact on how we feel about ourselves, leaving us feeling anxious, disheartened and less sure of ourselves. Failing to act might also lead to a sense of powerlessness and helplessness, and seriously undermine our confidence to cope. If we continue to worry rather than address our problems, then the problems usually get worse and we worry all the more. Finding another way to act rather than just worrying can help with these strong feelings. For example, a friend who was very concerned about the environment and very aware that it posed major problems, said that when he was active in doing something about them he felt empowered and hopeful rather than powerless and demoralized. Even though the environmental problems remained, he felt much better because he was doing some of the things that he could reasonably do to address them.

The next chapters will enable you to become better at solving problems and dealing with *Real Event Worry*. In the chapters on facing our fears (Chapters 17 and 18), we will turn our attention to dealing with the other type of worry, namely *Hypothetical Event Worry* – but one step at a time.

Approaching problems

With climate change, as with the traffic metaphor, in order to begin to solve the problems we have to engage with them. Research suggests that most worriers in fact have the skills to solve problems; unfortunately they tend to have unhelpful *attitudes* towards problems, which makes solving them harder. Typically, they see problems as threatening, they doubt their ability to cope with them, and even if they try to engage in problem solving they are pessimistic about the outcome. This means that overall they tend to have *an unhelpful approach to problems*, which has a dramatic effect on their capacity to solve them. Having this attitude is like trying to do everyday tasks while wearing boxing gloves; imagine trying to do up your buttons or zips in the morning. How would you use your phone, drive, write, type or prepare food? The boxing gloves would prevent you from using your hands efficiently, your dexterity would be lost and ultimately tasks would become frustrating. You would feel very demoralized and irritated, useless and pessimistic about things to come. But there is an important positive message within this metaphor, which is supported by research, namely that, although worriers might have an unhelpful approach to problem solving, once this has been addressed their problem-solving skills are found to be as good as those of non-worriers. In other words, once we take off the gloves we discover that, all along, we had the dexterity and skills to do these tasks; the boxing gloves kept us from finding this out.

We can break problem solving into two main parts. The *first* is improving our (unhelpful) approach to problems. This includes adjusting what we think when faced with problems, what we think of our skills in solving them (what are we like with the boxing gloves on) and our expectations about how well we might do (taking off the boxing gloves). Unhelpful approaches, together with an intolerance of uncertainty, drive the habitual and unhelpful ways that worriers manage problems. The first part is essentially about attitudes and bad habits. The *second* part involves the skills we possess for solving problems. It includes our ability to define problems, generate alternatives, choose solutions, put a plan into action and assess how well we did (or, exercising to improve our dexterity).

Before going on, stop for a moment and reflect on these two parts. Can you 'see' the distinction? One or both parts may require some attention. Think carefully about this – what do you struggle with? Is it your approach to problems (attitudes and habits) that stops you really

301

engaging, or is it your problem-solving skills that cause you to get stuck once you engage; or is it both that need your attention? We will return to these questions in the next chapter.

In order to help you overcome worry, you will need to learn to adjust your approach to problems, remind yourself that you have or can develop the capacity to solve problems successfully, and use these skills rather than engage in worry. Before looking into this further, the rest of this chapter will offer some reflections about problems and problem solving that you may find helpful.

What is a problem?

While this may be obvious, it is worth spending some time reminding ourselves of what exactly a problem is. This is because, without knowing it, we are dealing with problems virtually all the time, and this fact challenges the idea that we have difficulty solving them. When we think of problems our mind may naturally jump to serious issues or experiences such as unemployment, losing a job, depression, death, serious illnesses, and so on. Like most things, however, problems appear on a scale, from every-day events or situations, such as forgetting to charge your mobile phone or not having the right change for a parking meter, to major life events such as those mentioned above. Problems can also be repetitive or persistent, like those we face in relationships, or with health, or with our finances – for example, when the money going out of our bank account is always slightly more than the money coming in, or continuing to avoid talking about a difficult issue in your relationship. The diagram below helps us to consider all the possible problems we may encounter. It does not tell us about how much a particular problem should bother us – this will vary from person to person – but it reminds us that when we are referring to problems we mean all life's problems including the day-to-day and not just the 'heavy' or serious end of things. Remember, we know that worry tends to spiral from the day-to-day to the serious end of things, so we need to keep an eye on this.

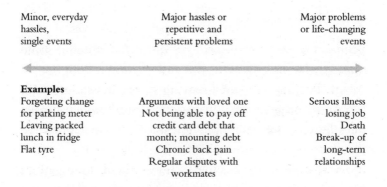

Minor, everyday hassles, single events	Major hassles or repetitive and persistent problems	Major problems or life-changing events
Examples		
Forgetting change for parking meter	Arguments with loved one	Serious illness
Leaving packed lunch in fridge	Not being able to pay off credit card debt that month; mounting debt	losing job
Flat tyre	Chronic back pain	Death
	Regular disputes with workmates	Break-up of long-term relationships

Figure 14.1: Problems on a scale of importance

What makes a problem serious depends on a number of things. Critically, cognitive therapy suggests that the issue is not *what* the problem is but *our view of it*. So what is a problem for one person may not be a problem for another, since their view may be different (remember the example of someone losing their job in Chapter 4). In other words, one person's mountain is another's molehill and vice versa. Expert worriers tend to start worrying about minor niggles and hassles and their worry often escalates or spirals into major hassles and even into major, life-changing events as their *worry moves* from left to right in Figure 14.1 (remember the express elevator). On the other hand, although major problems or life-changing events may feel highly likely, they do not occur on a day-to-day basis. They are much less common than events that underpin less serious worries; if you think about it, if they were as common as they seem then society would grind to a halt! None of us would have time for anything else, as we would all be dealing at the same time with hugely serious events! Most people and some worriers will distract themselves from major problems by focusing on and worrying about smaller things. For instance, they may clean the house, or spend too much time focused on peripheral stuff, which usually does little to solve the medium-sized or major problems they face.

So what ties all these different types of problem together? One way we can link them is to think of problems as a discrepancy or gap between where you are and where you want to be, or *what is* and *what you would like there to be*, or, put even more simply, a block to your goals. A problem could arise in any situation that demands we adapt and change our approach to finding a solution. In problematic situations, there is generally no obvious solution that jumps out. This might be because the obstacles are more noticeable than their solutions, which 'blocks' the solutions from view. When this happens our progress towards our goals is blocked and we have a problem.

A life full of problems

Problems are a normal part of life, and, like uncertainty, directing time and energy into avoiding them is pointless. It's like trying to live life without gravity having an impact on us. Think about this for a moment. How much time and energy do you put into trying to avoid the unavoidable (life's problems)? Remember, in life most people have to deal with hundreds or even thousands of minor hassles, tens to hundreds of major hassles and far fewer life-changing events. Unfortunately worriers don't keep worry for the big occasion, they use it for the hundreds to thousands of minor hassles.

As problems are everywhere, like gravity, then simply living means that we are overcoming them every day – we just may not notice that we are. We face and solve problems without even knowing it. For example, to get to a meeting on time I may need to plan my journey, take what I need for the meeting, get the right train and follow the directions I have been given. Each stage can be broken into a mini-goal, and within this example there are many, many more mini-goals that we have not outlined. My goals might be to pack my bag the night before; set my alarm; find the quickest way of getting to the city; take my laptop, phone and files; get the 7.45

train from platform 3; and then walk to the venue in fifteen minutes.

When moving from one place to another, there will be a number of things that might get in the way at any stage. Furthermore, things are much more likely to get in the way if we have not engaged with the problem and broken it down into practical steps. This is something we often do without thinking, and we may not even think of this as 'problem solving', but it is! We also may not think of this as goal setting, but again it is – *There is something I want to do tomorrow, my goal is to* . . . In the example above, obstacles could include no quick way of getting to the city, forgetting my laptop or not charging my phone, having no reception on my phone, cancellation of the 7.45, and inaccurate directions. So, now we have a series of problems that need to be dealt with. Each is an obstacle between the current situation and the desired situation, or each is an obstacle to my achieving my goals. As we have suggested, problems demand that we adapt and change to overcome them. So if my train has been cancelled, what do I do now? Get the bus? Phone ahead and warn my colleagues? Find out when the next train is and get on that one? Order a taxi or cab? Head for the waiting-room and get some work done? Go home? Buy a coffee and read the paper? There are many possible solutions, and the eventual solution will depend on many things, such as how important the meeting is, how central is my role in the meeting, how much money I have, how bothered I am about missing the meeting – and so forth. This everyday example shows that in order to get by in life we are solving problems all the time and we may not even realize it. Some things I can helpfully problem-solve in advance (e.g. charge the phone); others we have to wait until they happen and then solve them (e.g. decide what to do once I know the likely delay).

> *If you are encountering problems all the time without knowing it, you are successfully solving them. Can you think of a problem that you have already solved today or this week? Did you run out of milk this morning? Did you have the right change for the bus? Did you forget your mobile phone? Did you encounter traffic or delays? Did your children forget their packed lunch for school? Did you spill coffee on your work shirt or blouse? What problems have you already encountered and dealt with today?*

This presents an interesting question? Why might some everyday problems get solved and dealt with while others become the subject for worry? The answer to this is not clear, but we know that worry tends to run on themes, with each worrier worrying about a different set of concerns. So it might be worth asking this question: *Why do I worry about some problems and not others that I take in my stride?*

Intolerance of uncertainty and problem solving

As we discussed in Chapter 9, the situations that worriers tend to avoid usually contain some element of uncertainty.

Problems are typically 'dripping' with uncertainty; it is hard to predict what will become a problem; once the problems appear there are aspects of them that are still unpredictable; the worrier doubts their ability to solve or cope with them; and, as you would expect, the outcome is usually unclear or tricky to predict. So it will be no surprise that when facing problems worriers tend to worry and are tempted to avoid facing and dealing with them. Worriers find it hard to put plans into action because they can't be sure that their plans will work or the slightest hint of things not going to plan may stop them in their tracks. So it is also not surprising that people who suffer with excessive worry or GAD tend to have an unhelpful approach to problems. As you know, worriers tend to be acutely aware of even the merest hint of uncertainty – remember that all you need is a *splinter of doubt* to stoke up worry. So, when faced with a problem, worriers tend to 'examine' the problem from this perspective. It's almost as if they are looking for and amplify the uncertainty in any problem. When we defined what a problem is, we noted that a problem is something that does not have a clear or immediate solution; in other words, the outcome is uncertain. So as you learn to tolerate uncertainty you will be more able to tolerate the uncertainty found within problem solving. In fact, you can begin to treat problems as another way of overcoming your intolerance of uncertainty.

Learning to spot problems (sooner)

If problems are 'dripping' with uncertainty, then the same

things that trigger worry (remember the splinter of doubt) might also tell us that there is a problem to deal with. However, the whirlwind of worry often obscures the problems that caused it in the first place so we have to learn to tune in to detect problems when they arise. So what can you do to help you learn to spot problems sooner? We will outline some ideas below.

The first thing you can do is use your worry awareness diary to help you think about the type of problems that triggered your worry? If you have kept a Worry Diary, you will already have this information and reflecting on your diary while thinking about 'problems' might help. Again, a notebook and pen are essential.

SUGGESTION FOR YOUR WORRY DIARY

With each bout of worry, ask the following questions:
Was there a problem that triggered this worry? Was your worry a way of trying to deal with the problem? Apart from worrying what else can I do about this problem?

The second idea is for us to become more aware of our feelings when we face problems and learn to use them as an early warning signal that there is a problem we need to attend to. In their excellent book called *Solving Life's Problems: A 5-Stage Step Guide to Enhanced Wellbeing*, Arthur

Nezu, Christine Maguth Nezu and Thomas D'Zurilla remind us that feelings are a signal that a problem exists; but *the feelings, however, are not the problem.* Their book is well worth a read and many of the ideas that are found in this chapter are based on their work.

Our actions can also provide clues about when problems are afoot – this is the third idea to help us spot problems sooner. Is there anything you know that you generally do when you are struggling with a problem? Worry will no doubt be top of your list, but is there anything else that will help you to spot problems? Is there something you do habitually as a sign that there is something going on for you? This might be working longer hours, drinking more alcohol, smoking more cigarettes, avoiding work, people, places or things that remind you of the problem, sleeping badly, biting your nails, pacing the room, and so on. What are your signs that there is a problem? Remember that these actions are not the problem, but are a *sign* that there is a problem. For example, it might be that you know you have to have a difficult conversation with your partner, so rather than deal with this you stay later and later at work. Or you notice your bills are piling up in the hallway, but you decide to clean the house from top to bottom rather than opening the bills to find out what you owe. Do any of these sound familiar?

Fourth, we can use the experience of our body to tell us that there is a problem around. For some, feeling as if we need the loo, or headaches, or stomach upsets may be a sign that there is a problem. Often we trust our gut

310

instinct, which can be a good way of making a decision, but it must not be the only way, since solving problems in this fashion may lead us to avoid actually thinking it through.

Fifth, there may be tell-tale thoughts or statements that habitually fly through our minds or that we mutter under our breath. These are important because they may be the very first sign of a problem. For example, in the film *Four Weddings and a Funeral*, Hugh Grant's character would habitually swear when a problem appeared (see the first scene for example). You may know the sorts of words that appear for you – write them down. We can turn these habitual statements into early warning signs, and these may enable us to become more aware of the problems as they appear.

Stop and consider which of the ideas above fit with your experience of dealing with problems. Apart from worry, what might tell you that there is a problem to be solved?

Fitting this into the diagram of worry

Because problems don't get solved, the main outcome of poor problem solving is to increase the level of uncertainty and thus worry. We will now return to Tom, whose story we considered earlier (page 82). Track the example through: we have included all the details so far.

Remember poor old Tom. He has a really important meeting and again he is waiting for his train. His train is late and he wonders, *What if I am late for work?* This thought opens up doubt and uncertainty and he starts to worry. He starts to feel anxious, tense and restless and he looks about nervously.

Rather than worry, Tom could have done something else about his train being late. He could have tried to find another way of getting to work, or find out from the station attendant when his train would actually arrive, or remind himself that he was only five minutes late, or phoned work and explained what had happened. As he was standing at the platform these solutions flashed through his mind, but all they did was trigger more worry. With each solution arrived a whole new set of worries – we're back to every silver lining has a big black cloud! He worried that if he got a taxi he would get snarled up in traffic, and that if he asked the platform attendant (whom he knew well by now) he would get annoyed with him for asking the same questions again. He tried to calm himself down, saying quietly, *It's only five minutes, Tom; pull yourself together*, but when he looked at his watch, he realized he was now six minutes late. He started to feel irritated with himself. He put off contacting work because he wasn't sure how they would react. Tom believed that if he tried to solve his problems he would just make everything worse. Convinced that there was nothing he could do, and convinced that he was going to lose his job, he worried all the more. Lost in his worry, he nearly missed the announcement about the alternative

312

travel arrangements that would get him to work just a few minutes late!

Unfortunately, as well as having to cope with the train services in the UK, Tom has an unhelpful approach to problems; he thinks he's not good at solving them; he's fairly pessimistic about the outcome and is sure that anything he does will make things worse. Each time his train is late he faces a new problem, and he comes up with several potential solutions, but each solution arrives with more worry and uncertainty. He thinks about calling a taxi, but then worries that he might get caught up in traffic, but then he thinks that if he doesn't call a taxi his employers might be annoyed with him for not taking the initiative. However, if he takes the initiative, he might end up being disciplined for spending company money without authorization. If, though, he pays for the taxi himself, he might not have enough money to pay the household bills and his partner will be furious, and so on. He is paralysed by choices and the worry that comes with each new solution. At this moment, 'every silver lining has a cloud'; as he finds a potential way out, his worry interferes and brings to mind several new awful outcomes. Either he ties himself up in knots trying to figure a way through, or he avoids trying to do anything about the problem; it's almost as if it is much safer to sit perfectly still and hope that things work out.

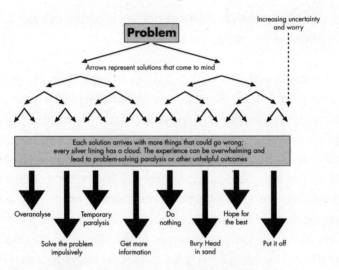

Figure 14.2: Every silver lining has a cloud

As Tom continues to sit with his problem, the problem slowly gets worse (it is getting later and later), confirming to him that he cannot solve problems. Then he starts to worry all the more with the arrival of more *what if* statements triggered by his failure to act, leading to more worry. His worry generates more anxiety including powerful physical sensations (stomach churning, tension, etc.) making it much harder for him to try to solve the problem he faces. He paces up and down the station platform and checks his watch over and over. The anxiety he feels focuses his mind on all the things that could go wrong, which leads him to worry more, pushing him further away from solving the problem. Each time he falls into this trap, he unwittingly reinforces and confirms the idea that he is no good at solving problems.

Doing something instead of worrying

Follow this through on the diagram below.

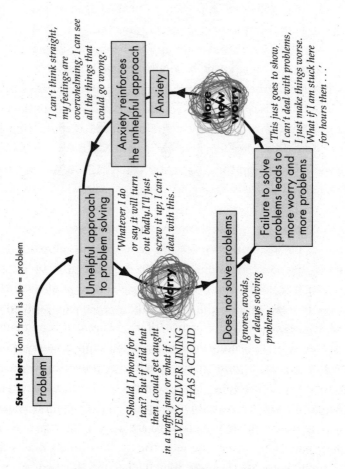

Figure 14.3: Unhelpful approaches to problem solving –
a typical vicious circle

The worrier's lack of success in dealing with their problem in the first place reinforces the *beliefs* that support their unhelpful approach to problems in at *least* two ways. First, the problem remains unsolved and, as a result, it may get bigger and more problematic: in Tom's case, not letting people know he might be late is probably more serious than being late but warning people in advance. Second, the lack of success erodes the worrier's confidence and leads them to deploy other unhelpful ways of trying to address the problem, which may also fail. Examples of these include ignoring; delaying; focusing on the wrong thing; and partially engaging with, or impulsively solving, the problem. These lead to poor solutions, or make the problem worse, which in turn serves to confirm the starting point, i.e. that the worrier has an unhelpful approach to problems. Both of these reinforce the idea that the worrier *can't solve problems* or that *attempts to solve problems never seem to work*, and so the unhelpful approach to problems is maintained.

Can you think of an example where your worry about a problem has meant that you did not solve it, so that it became a self-fulfilling prophecy such as, *I **think** I am no good at solving problems, my worry gets in the way of me solving them, and this confirms that I **must** be bad at solving problems*.

Walk yourself through the diagram above and see if it makes sense to you. It may be helpful to spend a few moments drawing out your problem-solving pattern. There is no right or wrong way of doing this and there are more ideas about how we get stuck with problem solving later in this chapter. But have a go – again, resist the urge to find the perfect solution. If worry interferes then wait for it to pass and ask yourself, *What was I doing before I started to worry?* and then return to it.

The following questions may help. They match up with Figure 14.3 above:

- Can you think of a recent problem you faced?
- What went through your mind when you faced this problem?
- How did it leave you feeling?
- What was it about the problem that might have led you to feel uncertain?
- Can you recognize the *what if* statements that appeared when you faced or tried to solve the problem?
- What did you do to deal with the problem (avoid, delay, put off, etc.)?
- What happened to the problem as a consequence?
- When this happened, how did it influence your worry?
- When you started to worry, how did it make you feel about your ability to solve problems?
- How might this influence your approach to problems in the future?

PIT STOP

Let's stop and think about what you have just been read-ing. Can you summarize the key ideas you have taken on board? What is sticking in your mind? Maybe write them down. If you have any questions, jot these down too. You can return to them once you have had a chance to digest the information.

What is sticking in my mind from my reading so far?

1.

2.

3.

15

Getting better at approaching problems

Typical unhelpful attitudes, thinking patterns and habits

We want to describe what happens when worriers are faced with problems because understanding how things work gives us better ideas about what to do to make things better. To become better at solving problems the first step is to really understand what you are doing now. For example, a garage mechanic will spend time trying to work out what the problem is before taking an engine to pieces. Working out what the problem is helps them to decide where to start and what to do. It would be a little disconcerting (and very expensive) to drive into a garage and for them to start to take your engine apart without working out what needs to be done. We should not do this with worry.

There are two sections to this chapter. The first will focus on how our thinking and attitudes can influence our approach to problems. The second section outlines some common and unhelpful patterns or habits that worriers can fall into when faced with problems. Both sections will include hints about how to address these thoughts and patterns. For each attitude, thinking style or habitual pattern use the scale below to work out if this pattern is character-istic of the way you deal with problems. This will help you to work out what you need to focus on.

How typical or characteristic is this for you?

None	A little	Some extent	Moderately	Somewhat	Mostly	Completely
0	1	2	3	4	5	6

For high-scoring patterns ask the following questions:

Can you think of a time where this influenced a problem you were trying to solve?

What impact did this have on the problem? What impact did this have on your worry?

What could you do to challenge this? Write a simple sentence to capture the essence of what you have to do.

We have offered some hints for each pattern, but there is nothing better than a solution that works with the problem pattern you bring.

SECTION 1

Thinking pattern 1: Seeing problems as threats

If every time a problem appears a worrier sees them as *entirely* threatening, it is not surprising that they find it hard to solve them. Worse still, this perspective allows them to see only the negative aspects of the problem, which offers only a restricted viewpoint. Indeed, because of this, it makes absolute sense to avoid problems at all costs. Seeing problems as threatening or menacing generally means that worriers fail to recognize that there are both positive and negative aspects to them. As we have mentioned above, problems appear on a scale, and to see them all as inhabiting either end of the pole is unhelpful and unrealistic. Rarely are problems entirely threatening or loaded with opportunities. One way of working towards challenging an unhelpful approach to problems is to turn your approach to them on its head. To do this we have to begin to think of problems as coming with both opportunities and threats. Consider what Lee Iacocca, former CEO of Ford and Chrysler in the US, said – 'we are continually faced by great opportunities brilliantly disguised as insoluble problems'.

We return in a new way to the saying 'every cloud has a silver lining'. Opportunities might include personal growth, improving relationships, learning new skills, developing existing skills or simply having new experiences. Personal growth and development usually takes place outside our comfort zone, so be ready to feel anxious, but look for the opportunity at the same time. We are not suggesting that you develop an overly optimistic rose-tinted view, but we are suggesting that when you recognize the threat then you might seek out the opportunity; look for both sides of the story before making up your mind.

Hint: Choosing a small problem, notice the threat and then ask yourself whether there are 'hidden' opportunities attached to the problem. What might you gain or learn from the experience? Are there opportunities for personal growth, developing new skills, improving relationships or simply having new experiences? How could facing this problem help me to grow? If I didn't see this problem as a threat how might I do things differently?

Thinking pattern 2: Taking problems personally

Sometimes worriers believe that they attract problems or that having problems is in some way abnormal and that the world is conspiring to single them out and load them up with countless hassles. This view of problems can be very disheartening and it makes it hard to find motivation to engage in solving problems or to feel hopeful about our efforts. Thus, problems remain unsolved and sooner or later this triggers more worry and feelings of demoralization. However, a viewpoint can change and once the worrier sees that they are not alone in their experience and that others have similar hassles, they can begin to feel less persecuted and engage with their problems.

Hint: Make a survey of your friends and family and make a list of the everyday problems that they have: see how many of them they share with you. You may also want to ask them if they believe that others are abnormal for having problems. If they say no, what does this tell you?

Thinking pattern 3: Prejudging the outcome of our efforts and doubting ourselves

Often, worriers will think that whatever they do the problem will turn out badly; they are in essence prejudging themselves. Understandably, having this view makes them less likely to engage with problems. This can be captured in the following statement: *If I try to solve it, it will go wrong and then I'll pay, so best do nothing*. This stance motivates worriers to stand back and avoid getting involved in solving the problem. This can apply even if they know that not doing anything will make the problem worse. If the idea that *any attempt at problem solving leads to catastrophe* is never challenged, then it makes perfect sense to avoid trying to solve problems. But if we avoid solving problems, they never go away, nor does the worry triggered by the problems. By using this strategy, the unhelpful approach to worry is strengthened since it supports the idea that problems are threatening and that we do not have the ability to cope; we thus remain defiantly pessimistic about the outcomes of our problem solving.

Hint: Before you start to solve the problem, write down what you think will happen – the full catastrophe version. Then have a go. Was your prediction accurate? Was it as bad as you thought or was it 'good enough'? How often have you doubted yourself and then found that things worked out 'OK', even if not perfectly? How does thinking like this help problem solving?

Other common patterns – thinking chutes

There are other thinking patterns that worriers may use without even realizing it. These 'help' us to make quick decisions about the problems we face. They are, in a sense, mental short cuts. However, they are unhelpful as they are used habitually without any real consideration of whether they are useful. Imagine these thinking styles are like a mental laundry chute or a slide: once in them it is very hard to change direction. This means that once our thoughts are taken down a particular chute we tend not to consider other information that lies outside the chute. If our thinking is boxed in or constrained in this way, it will have a very strong influence on *what* we are able to think about. So, spotting these thinking chutes is very important to problem solving, because if we are trying to solve problems based on unfair, wrong or misleading information generated by them, then problem solving will be much, much harder.

For example, if a worrier always blames himself for problems, then this quickly takes him down the self-blame chute, leaving him feeling distressed by his problem. The self-blame chute doesn't give him a chance to think about who else may be involved, or what other factors may be influencing the problem. The chute moves him quickly towards a conclusion, which is accepted because no other ideas or viewpoints are given a chance to influence the outcome. This is another reason why we have to *slow everything down* to look at the things that influence what we think and to begin to work out which thinking chutes we use habitually.

Our language gives us clues as to the presence of these

thinking chutes; words like *should*, *mustn't*, *always*, *never* are often used. Once we have identified them, we need to find ways of challenging them. In the table below is a list of thinking chutes with descriptions, and then questions to help you challenge them.

Table 15.1: Thinking chutes and other routes

Thinking chutes	Questions to help spot your thinking chute	Question to help challenge your conclusions
All or nothing	Am I seeing this problem in all-or-nothing terms?	Is it that clear-cut? Is there a way I can see it which is less all or nothing?
Mixing feelings and facts	Am I feeling strong emotions? What are they telling me? Do my strong emotions stop me from seeing the 'facts'?	What do I know to be true and what do I feel?
Sweeping statements (generalization)	Am I thinking that this problem is the same as many others? Or am I making a sweeping generalization on the basis of a single event or single piece of information about this problem?	Is it true that this problem is the same as others? What may be unique or different about this problem?
Focusing on the negatives	Am I overly focused on the negative or upsetting aspects of this problem?	What am I ignoring in this situation or event?

Destroying the positives	Am I 'shooting down' anything positive that I have contributed to solving this problem?	What have I 'shot down'? Make a list. Was I fair to myself?
Jumping to conclusions	With this problem in mind, am I jumping to conclusions without considering all the evidence?	What is *all* the evidence? What am I ignoring?
Mind-reading	Am I mind-reading? That is, am I thinking that I know what others are thinking about this problem, or do I feel like I know what is behind their actions?	Could I ask them to find out?
Fortune-telling	Am I predicting how this problem will turn out before even starting to solve it?	How often are my predictions right?
Magnifying or minimizing the problem?	Am I exaggerating any aspect of this problem? Am I minimizing any aspects?	If I am exaggerating, what am I playing down? If I am minimizing, what I am ignoring?
Putting others on a pedestal	Am I putting others on a pedestal (*they could solve this, but I can't*)? Am I putting myself down to put them there (*I can't solve this, but they could*)?	Do I have experience of solving other similar problems? Is it true that others are better at solving problems? *How does approaching* things in this way help me?

Snowballing or catastrophizing	Am I focused on the worst possible outcome for this problem?	How often have my worst possible outcomes come true? What other outcomes might there be? Do I need to adjust my imagined catastrophe?
Pressurizing	Am I focusing on what I think I should or ought to do with this problem, rather than on what I can actually do?	What actually can I do?
Personalizing	Am I always blaming myself for problems? Am I taking this personally?	Who else is involved? What other things are influencing this situation?

Focus on a recent problem – a real event that you worried about and that you needed to *do* something about. It may be helpful to think through this situation and your worry in the light of the above table. What thinking chutes might you have taken?

You will no doubt recognize catastrophizing as a pattern, but what other patterns are typical in how you think about problems? Highlight the thinking chutes you need to work on. If you can spot them you will be in a much better position to shift your perspective and find new ways of reacting to life's problems. Also, recognizing these patterns may help to interrupt the flow of worry.

SECTION 2

Typical unhelpful patterns or habits

In this section we have identified common patterns or habits. Like a dog chasing its tail, each pattern or strategy adds more uncertainty, worry and anxiety, which makes it much harder for us to solve problems. This in turn leads on to more worry, anxiety and uncertainty, strengthening the unhelpful approach to problems. It is important that you begin to recognize which strategies are typical for you and understand how this makes your problems worse.

Pattern 1: Confusing worrying with problem solving

Worriers tend to worry when faced with problems. This can give them the impression that they are thinking the problems through and developing action plans, but if all they do is worry, the problems never get solved. As the problem remains unsolved, it triggers more worry, and so on. Worry can feel like an activity, almost as if we are doing something about the problem, but we are not.

Hint: Recognize to separate worrying from problem solving. Am I doing something to solve this problem or am I only worrying? Apart from worrying, what else can I do?

Pattern 2: Avoiding or delaying the problem solving

Worriers tend to avoid or delay solving problems. As a result, what could be a minor problem can develop and spiral, leading to more (secondary) problems and to even more worry (e.g. avoiding paying credit card bills, leading to charges and increasing debt). In addition to the problems getting worse, this strategy then influences how we think about problems. If many of the problems we face 'snowball' and get worse, it is not surprising that when new problems appear we start to get nervous, making catastrophic predictions about what could happen. In this way this strategy maintains our unhelpful approach to problems.

Hint: By facing the problem now, things are likely to get better. Ask yourself, what is the worst thing that could happen if I faced my problems now? Write your worst-case answer down and then try to solve the problem. Does your worst-case answer fit with what happened?

Pattern 3: Trying not to think about it – putting it to the back of your mind

As we discovered in the chapter on positive beliefs about worry, trying not to think about something has the unfortunate effect of making it jump into our minds all the more often. These intrusive thoughts can be regarded as a sign of unfinished business, which our mind is trying hard to get us to deal with. So, as long as the problem is still a problem, it will butt in until we deal with it. This usually happens when we are reminded of the problem by something else, or it can just appear in the way other things might do (e.g. remembering to return a phone call). When the problem appears, it does so with a 'mental flinch' followed by a stream of worry, and because the problem appears frequently and regularly, it tends to trigger more worry – again ending up making us more concerned about problems when they appear in the future.

Hint: Trying to push a thought out of our minds never works – the problem only pops up all the more often. So, face the problem in your mind – doing so will not make it any worse. Write the problem down. It may help you see what you need to do to solve it. Make a list of things that need to be addressed.

Pattern 4: Asking others to solve the problem

If we continually ask others to solve problems for us, we are denying ourselves the opportunity of finding out that we could manage the problem for ourselves. This keeps the idea alive that we cannot deal with problems, or that if we try to solve them they will go wrong. In doing this we maintain our unhelpful approach to problems.

Hint: Start with smaller problems first. Deal with them without asking for reassurance and once you are starting to feel more confident move on to the bigger problems. Ask yourself, What is the worst thing that could happen if I make a decision without asking for reassurance?

Pattern 5: Solving the problem impulsively

Another way of dealing with problems is to respond impulsively to them, without thinking things through, jumping at the first possible solution that comes along. Attempts to solve problems in this way often lead to hurried or incomplete solutions, or solutions that make the problem worse. As you can imagine, these kinds of solutions can then lead to more problems and ultimately to more worry. While intolerance of uncertainty affects all problem solving, it has a big effect on this type of attempted problem solving. It is often this intolerance that motivates people to make decisions quickly so they can defuse the sense of uncertainty. As we have mentioned above, this kind of response will work well from time to time, and it is the irregular nature of the rewards (i.e. things working out once in a while) that encourages us to adopt this strategy. But this strategy is like rolling a dice to make decisions; if we did it continually we would never learn to trust our own judgement. We would also continue to doubt our ability to solve problems and might believe that luck was the most important factor in solving problems, which simply is not true.

Hint: If you jump in without thinking, you need to make sure you give yourself time to think. Give yourself at least ten minutes to come to a conclusion or even better sleep on it; this really helps. Ask yourself, What's the worse thing that could happen if I delayed solving the problem for fifteen minutes?

Pattern 6: Trying to solve everything at once

Worry has the tendency to multiply and expand, and this pattern has echoes in problem solving. Often worriers will partially engage in trying to solve one problem, and then start on another. This is like the entertainer who spins plates on sticks, adding more and more, rushing between them . . . or the juggler who adds more and more balls. At best this is exhilarating but exhausting; at worst, well we know what eventually happens in these acts as the 'spinner' is overwhelmed and the plates crash to the floor. In problem solving, this can mean that nothing gets completed and problems are left in a semi-unsolved state, and the person becomes exhausted and anxious about unfinished business. In this state their efforts can actually provoke more uncertainty and worry, making focusing and completing the tasks much harder. This confirms to the worrier that they are no good at solving problems and their multiple attempts produce poor, incomplete outcomes; this reinforces the belief that efforts to solve problems will only result in negative outcomes.

> *Hint: Remember, one thing at a time. Resist the urge to start a new problem. If there are several stacked up that need to be dealt with, choose the one that needs to be solved first. You can't land all the aircraft at Heathrow Airport at once; you have to bring them down one at a time. Ask yourself,* What might be the advantages of solving one problem at a time? If I solved one problem at a time on a regular basis how might this help me?

Pattern 7: Approach–avoiding flip-flop

This is another common kind of pattern that worriers unwittingly fall into. They approach a problem and then flip-flop between trying to solve the problem by doing something purposeful and avoiding the problem. With this strategy, worriers are partially engaged in trying to solve the problem – it's like trying to clean the loo while at the same time trying not to look into the bowl too closely, or smell, or think. To do the job well you need to look and see what needs to be cleaned. This 'avoidance' leads to a less than clean loo! This is closely related to the pattern above. Problems are solved poorly and take much longer, and the resultant uncertainty triggers more worry. The worrier may approach the bills on the kitchen table and organize them and then feel overwhelmed by the tasks and end up avoiding them. They might return to the problem and try to phone the telephone company or electricity company, but put the phone down once they have got as far as 'press 5 to discuss your bill'!

Hint: Keep focused on one problem at a time; solve this before moving on to deal with another. Learn to spot when you change from dealing with the problem to flipping or avoiding, then catch this early, and without beating yourself up bring your attention compassionately back to the problem (don't give yourself a hard time for flipping or avoiding; just say, 'back to it').

Pattern 8: Over-analysis

Since problems lead to anxiety, the worrier might be motivated to try to reduce their anxiety by trying to think of all the possible ways that the problem could be solved and of the outcomes of each solution: each solution then generates more problems, which require more solutions, which generate more problems, and so on. A worrier may think and rethink alternative solutions, and in doing so get lost within the labyrinth of alternatives, never solving the problems. Each solution brings more worry and uncertainty, which leads to more anxiety, making problem solving all the more difficult. By over-analysis our minds tend to turn molehills into mountains, or kittens into man-eating tigers, so that the idea that problems are threatening is maintained.

Hint: Give yourself a time limit. What's the worse thing that could happen if you made a less than perfect decision? Ask yourself, How long do I need to make the perfect decision (to infinity and beyond!)?

SUMMARY BOX

What ideas have you come up with to change the way you approach and deal with problems?

•

•

•

•

• Now Do It!

16

Problem-solving skills

Research tells us that people who worry excessively possess problem-solving skills; in fact, their skills are as good as anyone else's. Unfortunately, in the population as a whole, the general level of skill in problem solving is not always as good as it could be, and many people would benefit from tuning up these skills. Consequently, like most people, and depending on your problem-solving style, it will probably be beneficial to review this chapter and then decide whether the ideas are going to be useful to you. For example, some worriers are impulsive decision-makers (to avoid uncertainty), and this chapter will probably help them to slow down and think things through. Others over-analyse things, and want to explore every avenue and idea to the limit, and this chapter may help them to speed up. Whatever your approach, keep this in mind: *one size does not fit all*, and you have to tailor the information to suit you.

Consider the patterns of unhelpful problem solving described in the Chapter 15. So, think for a moment about how you generally solve problems. Do you need to slow down and consider each step because you usually rush through, or do you need to speed up and come to decisions more quickly?

How might this help me?

Reviewing your problem-solving skills will add structure, which will demand that you take new mental paths to come to solutions rather than the well-worn routes of worry. It will help to take your mind and thoughts away from worry and give them back to you. When we see the detail spelt out in black and white on the page it can help us to stand back and see things differently. Problem solving is a skill and skills can be a chore to learn, but once we have grasped them we can go through the steps much more quickly. Think about learning to drive, where each skill is introduced one by one – knowing where to look or which gear to use requires a great deal of thought, but after a few months of driving they become second nature. So keep at it and you will reap the rewards.

Developing your skills

Stages of problem-solving skills

The stages of problem solving are listed below. We will add more detail but these are the essentials.

Quick problem solving

What's the problem?

Refine and define the issues.

Choose a Real Event Worry problem.

Choose a problem that is not life-changing (i.e. relatively

---

simple and small) and not involving or depending on others. And one where you can see the result quickly.

Break it down into mini-steps.

What is the first step in the sequence? What is the first thing you need to do? Don't get ahead of yourself.

At this point, what are the options?

Out of all the possibilities, identify two or three that feel OK but are not perfect.

Spend a bit of time thinking about each of these solutions or options.

Choose the one that seems slightly better than the others.

Slightly better in this case means real, the simplest, most likely to succeed, with good return on cost (time, effort, money, etc.) and with a good enough result.

Act on it.

What happened?

Was the outcome at least OK? Under the circumstances, is it 'good enough'?

What happened to your worry about this problem?

How does it feel to be one small step closer?

Don't get ahead of yourself: spend time reflecting on what has been achieved. Yes, there is a lot left to do, but don't look up, look down. You have made some progress, that's great. Now what's the next step? . . . Back to the top.

Stage 1: Learning to define problems

What is the problem?

Working out what your problem is can take you a very long way to actually solving it. Problems often appear as statements: *I'm stressed*; *I hate my job*; *the children are doing my head in*; *I never have enough money*. We talked about defining goals in Chapter 6: these are like those 'headline' goals that tell us very little about what we need to do to improve things. So we first need to break down large unwieldy problems into smaller, well-defined and manageable chunks. A really helpful way to do this is to ask this question repeatedly: 'What problems does that cause me?' This questioning helps us to understand the impact of problems, and to further define them.

Arthur's example

Let's use the following example: Arthur was worried, worried about everything, and that's about all he can say. He didn't know where to start. To help him sift more detail he drew the following diagram, his problem porcupine. He first added in the areas of his life where he thought stress might be having an impact. He then asked himself, *What problems does my worry cause me in this part of my life?* Look at the diagram on page 340 (Figure 16.1).

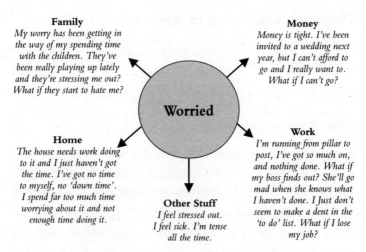

Family
*My worry has been getting in
the way of my spending time
with the children. They've
been really playing up lately
and they're stressing me out?
What if they start to hate me?*

Money
*Money is tight. I've been
invited to a wedding next
year, but I can't afford to
go and I really want to.
What if I can't go?*

Worried

Home
*The house needs work doing
to it and I just haven't got
the time. I've got no time
to myself, no 'down time'.
I spend far too much time
worrying about it and not
enough time doing it.*

Work
*I'm running from pillar to
post, I've got so much on,
and nothing done. What if
my boss finds out? She'll go
mad when she knows what
I haven't done. I Just don't
seem to make a dent in the
'to do' list. What if I lose
my job?*

Other Stuff
*I feel stressed out.
I feel sick. I'm tense
all the time.*

Figure 16.1: Arthur's problem porcupine

This is Arthur's first attempt at defining his problems and it
needs more work, but, critically, he is beginning to *put pen
to paper* to try to address his problems rather than avoiding
thinking about them or repeatedly circling around *all* of them
without doing something about *one* of them. Even on its own
it's better than the starting point he had of just feeling generally worried. He's even begun to see the relationships between
some of his problems – for instance, he wonders if his absence
from home is contributing towards his children being difficult.
This has enabled him to stand back and feel less upset by them.
As a rule of thumb, writing things down is a useful thing to
do: among other things, it puts the problems 'out there' so
that you can step back from them and think them through.

*In which areas of your life do you have problems? Draw out your
problem porcupine? Are there relationships between problem areas?*

Choosing a problem to work on

So what might Arthur need to do to sift his problems out further? The first thing that he needs to do is to work out which problem he would like to work on. This can be a difficult decision, but choosing something over which he has the most potential influence and that does not depend on others will set him up for some early success. This also means choosing a *real event* rather than a *hypothetical event*. If we review Arthur's problems we can see that there is a mix of *Hypothetical* and *Real Events* – for example, his worry about his kids hating him (*Hypothetical*) coupled with not spending enough time with them (*Real*); or, his worry about his finances (*Real*) linked with his worry about being unable to afford to go to the wedding (*Hypothetical*). Both the *Hypothetical* events are 'downstream' and set in the future – they are not things Arthur can do something about immediately – so he would be wise to choose something at the *Real* end of the spectrum. Some problems can be a combination of both real and hypothetical problems; but, crucially, in these cases we need the problem to be *real enough* to be able to *actually* do something about it. In Arthur's case he could choose working on his finances or finding time to spend with the kids.

Our problems are often linked and we may have to work on one problem before another. Arthur can see that his children's difficult behaviour and his worry about their rejecting him might be because he's not spending very much time with them, so figuring out how to free up some spare time could help. Also, some problems are more central, and focusing on these can improve other areas. Arthur might realize that work is the main problem for him, so he might try to focus on this first. If he chooses work, he would still be wise to choose an area over which he has the most potential influence, which does not involve other people and which is a *Real Event*. Within the *work group* there are several problems within this category. Review Arthur's worries about work; which ones are about a real event? For example, he is becoming unhappy at work, he worries that he has too much to do, he is worried about talking with his boss, and he is struggling to focus. Whatever problem he chooses, the important thing is that he starts to actually do something about his problems, working through them one at a time.

Of the problems you have looked at, choose one that is real, is relatively small and simple, is within your control and not dependent on others. Once you have one, see if you can break this down further into smaller chunks.

Write out your problem in clear and concrete language

In order to take his problem further, Arthur needs to *slow down* to get to the detail of the situation and then focus on the *facts*. When we are feeling upset or worried, the language we use reflects this. Arthur has said he is 'running from pillar to post' and we get a sense of what the problem is for him. But here we have an example of language that tells us very little about the specifics of Arthur's situation.

So we have to explore this further by asking him to tell us more about what this means. He might mean that he is having to juggle lots of different tasks from the same desk, or it might literally mean that he is driving from one meeting to the other across great distances. In order to get to clear language we have to find a way of describing what is going on that leaves nothing to the imagination. This means that we make no assumptions about what we think is going on, we only report what we actually know to be true. It's a bit like being a scientist and reporting only the facts without speculating or assuming. As a general rule of thumb, facts are what others would agree on, assumptions are more our personal viewpoint, opinion or beliefs. This is critically true of worriers, as worries can often feel very real and so are accepted as fact without question. Can you spot any assumptions or thinking chutes in Arthur's description? It seems as if he is assuming (worrying) that his boss will 'go mad' at him (*What if my boss goes mad?*). There is an assumption about what his boss will do; also, he is using vague language – what does 'go mad' actually mean? There are other silent assumptions that Arthur is making; he is ignoring other important facts, for example the work he has *actually* done. He is also taking the problem very personally and blaming himself, without considering all the other things that may be influencing his problem (please see the thinking chutes section in the last chapter).

Can you describe one problem only using facts? Are you making assumptions? Once you have discovered your assumptions – use the hints and questions in the last chapter to help you investigate them and start to look for evidence that might help you re-evaluate them. Can you separate out the assumptions from the facts in your problem? Does this change the problem in any way?

What is your goal with regards to this problem?

In Arthur's example, we considered where he is and where he wanted to be, or what his goal was with regard to this problem. So, remember it is helpful if our goals follow the SMART guidelines (see page 122). Arthur's goal was *I want to focus on these projects and finish them*; his new goal, using the SMART guidelines, is *I want to complete one project by the end of the week.*

What are your goals in trying to solve this problem? (Use the SMART criteria to help you.) Once you have a goal then turn this problem into a How can I *question; for Arthur it becomes,* How can I complete one project by the end of the week?

Spotting the roadblocks

Now that we have a goal in mind, it may help to ask what obstacles or roadblocks are stopping us from reaching our goal? What makes this a problem for us? Look at the exercise below.

What is getting in the way of my solving this problem right now?	
Roadblock	Finding solutions
Are there strong feelings blocking my way?	What problems does this cause me? How can I manage them?
Are others' expectations conflicting with my own?	Who can I talk to? How can I work this out?
Do I have the skills or resources?	Where can I learn them? Where can I get them?
Is uncertainty or perfectionism stopping me in my tracks?	If so, then act. All problems are uncertain, do not expect to feel certain. No solution is perfect; expect both advantages and disadvantages.
Is the situation currently too complex and knotty?	Do I need to break things down further? How can I break things down into smaller and more manageable chunks?

Exercise 16.1 spotting roadblocks

Note of caution – finding the perfect solution

The intolerance of uncertainty will also influence how you work on your problem-solving skills. How will it do so? As we have said, problems are 'dripping with uncertainty', each stage of the problem-solving process will trigger feelings of uncertainty and you may want to feel certain about one stage before moving on to the next. Don't try to wrestle certainty from the jaws of uncertainty. *Resist the urge to find the perfect solution* as this is probably a way of trying to attain the impossible. Perfect solutions simply do not exist and all solutions are trade-offs between competing demands. Things that are on average good enough will work, and if we manage a bit better than that from time to time then we will probably be successful. The only certainty in life is uncertainty. This problem-solving chapter is another opportunity to move ahead in the face of uncertainty by taking reasonable risks. If uncertainty is drawing you into playing it safe, into avoiding something, or is keeping you stuck at one stage, then ask, *What am I afraid might happen if I go ahead? If I put this solution into place right now, what am I afraid of happening?* Or, *What is the worst thing that could happen?* Write your prediction down and then see if this comes true in the way you imagined.

General helpful tips

- Write the problem down.
- Separate facts from assumptions.
- Use diagrams and pictures to help you.
- Notice habitual patterns of thinking or problem solving.
- You may need to take your time and slow down or speed up and limit analysis (depending on your approach to problems).
- Break big problems into smaller more manageable chunks.
- Set a clear goal – turn this into a how question.

Stage 2: Generating enough solutions

During this stage you should aim to free up your mind to think about different types of solutions to your problems. To do this, there are three things to bear in mind. First, you must try to *suspend judgement* about the usefulness or otherwise of each solution you come up with. Second, by being non-judgemental about your solutions you will increase the *quantity* of solutions available. Third, you need to come up with a *variety* of solutions and not the same solution masquerading in different guises. So, for example, the goal of getting fitter may lead to solutions such as running, weight training, cycling, Zumba, boxing, rowing . . . These are all similar solutions that live within the same family of solutions – doing exercise to get fitter. You can use the variety idea to trigger the discovery of more solutions. In this case, these might be thinking about eating healthy foods, going out for a coffee rather than a beer, taking the stairs and not the lift, getting more restful sleep, and so on. The three ideas we've outlined offer some variety. Research tells us that, if we use them to guide us when looking for solutions, we are more likely to come up with more effective solutions. The greater the range of solutions you have to choose from, the better chance you have of picking a good one.

Generating lots of different ideas is both a creative exercise and a skill, and like all skills it needs practice. Every new idea or solution you come up with should be thought of as a positive step, even if it seems a little 'off the wall'. Often we 'shoot the idea down' even before we finish thinking it (see the unhelpful thinking patterns in the previous chapter). If you notice your mind thinking *That will never work*, or *That's silly* or *That's stupid* then remind yourself that all ideas are valid *at this stage*. We need you to put your ideas on the table and leave them there. The ideas that you come up with will probably be coated in doubt, but that's OK, so long as you leave them on the table. Write down all the ideas: take a sheet of paper and write *Solutions* at the top and numbers one to ten down the page.

For each problem find at least ten solutions. Remember not to judge; think broadly or 'outside the box'. Use humour if that helps – turn the problem on its head. If you were solving this for some-one else, what would you suggest? How would someone else solve the problem? How would Gandhi, Nelson Mandela or the Dalai Lama solve it? Or, if a ten-year-old were solving this problem, how would they do it? If Marg Simpson, Dr Spock or Bob Marley were solving it, how would they do so? What ideas might they suggest? Or think about people you know – what ideas might they come up with?

Review your list

Once you have a list of ten solutions it's time to review them. You may want to do this using the ideas found in Chapter 6 on setting goals. For example, if I am feeling stressed by work then going for a relaxing sauna is a great solution – it's very clear, concrete and practical; it's obvious what will happen (but you still need to plan when and where!).

But what about things like improving my time-keeping? This needs specifying. How could you improve your time-keeping? What do you need to do to achieve this? These kinds of questions will look for more concrete, practical solutions. I may come up with several more mini-solutions to add to my list, such as 'Buy a good alarm clock', 'Get a diary', 'Teach the kids to make their own sandwiches', etc. If you combined some of these mini-solutions, would that make a better solution?

Have you noticed any patterns in your problem solving? Are there solutions you use regularly or habitually, apart from worrying? These regular solutions can often help, but sometimes we go straight to them, even when the problem doesn't fit.

Stage 3: Decision making

Now that you have ten solutions to your problem it's time to decide which one will be the best solution. As you know all too well, trying to make decisions can trigger worry, as they are a step into the unknown and into uncertainty. So here is another opportunity to challenge uncertainty. Be on the alert for perfectionism – for trying too hard to make the perfect rather than good enough solution. Remember to take one step at a time. If your worry gets the better of you, once it has passed return to the task, and if it happens again, then again bring your mind back when you can. But do so compassionately and without *beating yourself up* – this only adds to the problem and doesn't help in any way. Making decisions for yourself will develop your self-confidence and challenge the idea of uncertainty.

In this stage it's time to lift the ban on suspending judgement and bring your critical mind to bear on each solution.

Throw out the lame ducks

In the first sweep of the ten solutions we need to see if there are any real 'lame ducks'. Are there solutions that would be impossible to put into action? Are there solutions that are just too complicated, may backfire or have a low chance of working? Review your solutions and decide which of them you should put aside. Draw a line through these. Are there two or three that look like possible solutions? Try to order these with the most preferable solution first. If you feel like acting on a solution now, then do so; in coming this far you have already 'sifted and panned' for your solution. If you see 'gold' then go for it, but remember to stop and review how things went. If later you find out that your solution didn't quite work out, first congratulate yourself on actually doing something about the problem rather than just worrying, and then return to your list of solutions and try the next one.

Evaluating solutions

If you are struggling to decide which solution to use of the solutions you have come up with and reviewed, choose three and spend a bit of time thinking about each of them. Which one feels slightly better than the others? You could try to rate the three solutions on a scale from 0–10 to help you sort them (where 0 = worst solution ever and 10 = best solution ever). Or you may want to consider the advantages and disadvantages of each solution and then choose the one that is slightly better than the rest. Remember, slightly better means some combination of the simplest, most likely to succeed, with good return on cost (time, effort, money, etc.) and with a good enough result. You will never find the *perfect* solution. So choose the one that fits best at the moment. When you look at the solutions, is there one that needs to happen first? Can you arrange them like stepping stones?

Stage 4: Putting your solution into practice

One of the central messages so far is the need to keep a realistic idea of how things will turn out. No solution is perfect!

Now is the time to remind yourself of why you are trying to overcome your worry. In the chapter on goals we asked you to write down on a postcard why you wanted to overcome your worry and also to list the ideas that will keep you engaged with your goals. Think about how life will be when you are keeping worry for the big occasions and not for every situation or event.

Newcastle upon Tyne is on the east coast of the UK. The North Sea, even in summer, can be a chilly place, to say the least. Change is like going swimming in the North Sea. When you first get in, the cold and shivering tells you to get out. But after a while your body adapts and you can swim and enjoy yourself for a little while – really! Some people get so used to it and enjoy it so much that they swim every day of the year! So, in putting your solutions into action, we have to expect some uncomfortable feelings, but these will pass as you get more accustomed to the new experience.

Once you start acting on your solutions you will quickly find out much more about the roadblocks that lie in the way of your goal. This is to be expected; we are now in the world of experience and doing, and we will get much better information about how things really are when we are active in this way – there is simply no substitute for real-life experience. Just return to the earlier stages and add this new information: it is now 'grist for the mill'. As in other stages, if you are feeling uncertain and worried, then sit with it. Problem solving is a challenge to the intolerance of uncertainty, which, like a school bully, will want to 'up the ante' before leaving you alone. As far as you can, stay with the feelings and keep on track.

Questions and prompts to help you develop your plan

- What is my goal?
- What is my solution?
- How can I put my solution into place?
- What steps do I need to take?
- Make a list of the things you may need to do.
- Draw out a series of steps leading to your goal. What needs to happen to get you to your goal using this solution?
- What will tell you that you are on track to reach your goal using this particular solution?

- What could tell you that the solution isn't working? Again, we should not be dependent on our feelings as a guide, but need to focus on the facts.

Stage 5: So how did you do?

It is important after all this hard work to sit down and think about how you have done. What did you do well? What did you learn? What could you do differently next time? Were your fears confirmed? Were your predictions about how things will turn out accurate? Are you feeling better since you put your plans into action? What have you noticed as a side-effect of doing so? Were there any unexpected benefits or otherwise? You may want to walk back through the steps you have taken to define your solution and see if there are new ideas that come to mind.

What next?

We are drawing to the end of the problem-solving chapters. Now that you have the idea in mind about what you need to do, the next stage is to solve more of your problems rather than worrying about them. Return to your Worry Diary: what other problems do you need to take though this process? *Practise, practise, practise.* There are no short cuts or magic cures; the more you do, the better you will become at problem solving and the more you will internalize the processes we have discussed. And you will develop new mental pathways when faced with problems other than worrying.

PIT STOP

Let's stop and think about what you have just been reading. Can you summarize the key ideas you have taken on
board? What is sticking in your mind? Maybe write them
down. If you have any questions, jot these down too. You
can return to them once you have had a chance to digest
the information.

What is sticking in my mind from my reading so far?

1.

2.

3.

17

Understanding *Hypothetical Event Worry*

As you have learnt, there are broadly speaking two different types of worry. Some of the things we worry about actually exist: these we have called *Real Event Worries*. We learnt that we can deal with this type of worry by facing and dealing with the thing that caused the worry through problem solving. But other worries are about things that haven't happened yet, otherwise known as *Hypothetical Event Worries*. The things we 'see' in this kind of worry may never exist in the way that they are imagined but at the time they feel very real, just as a nightmare feels real. This type of worry is often set in the distant future and is usually about things that are very unlikely to happen. Trying to problem-solve this kind of worry is impossible as the problem doesn't exist yet, so we have to work with this worry in a different way – this chapter and the following one will help you to do this.

Worry often telescopes; thus *Real Event Worry* about everyday, minor hassles can telescope into *Hypothetical Event Worry*, which is almost always about potentially life-changing events at some point in the future. The following example illustrates the tendency of worry to telescope. A worrier may start to worry about the knocking noise in their washing machine, which then leads on to worrying about whether the machine is about to break down and needs fixing. The worry about the noise can telescope into thoughts (or 'flashes') of the house flooding, leaks damaging the electrics and great damage occurring to their home; or of how the worrier will not be able to do the 'mountains of washing' when the washing machine finally dies completely and they cannot fix it or buy a new one; or of how others might judge them for not being able to send the kids to school in clean clothes; and so on. Notice how the content of the worry is not static; it telescopes and spirals, moving into the near then distant future, shifting rapidly from a knocking noise to a sense of being harshly judged by others for things that could possibly (but are unlikely to) happen at some point in the future. While there are no limits on where your worry will take you, usually there are key themes or tracks that the worry takes, and the worry 'improvises' on and around these themes, much like a guitar solo that improvises around a chord or scale of notes.

So *Hypothetical Event Worry* almost always turns into 'horror stories', with images that are vivid, upsetting and seem very real at the time (remember the mirage analogy in Chapter 1). Were these scenarios to happen, they would indeed be upsetting and probably very difficult to deal with. But they are *not happening yet* and may never happen; our emotional reactions to them, however, are *as if* they were happening right now.

A critical message is that *Hypothetical Event Worry* is a stream of thoughts. These thoughts do not describe real events: they are not facts, premonitions or predictions; they are simply thoughts. Even though they are only the products of your imagination, they can be powerful and influential, because of the very real feelings they generate as they whirl around and seem to threaten things that are important to you. So, *Hypothetical Event Worry* ends up being about potentially life-changing events (that have not happened yet and may never happen in the way they are imagined) and can involve themes of loss of loved ones, rejection by others, breakdown of important relationships, loss of financial security, illness and suffering, and an inability to face or cope with any of these. Worrying like this understandably generates overwhelming levels of anxiety and feelings of uncertainty.

There are occasions when people worry about real events that are life-changing, like when a loved one has been taken to hospital and the doctors are trying to figure out what is wrong and what the treatment and prognosis might be, or if there is a rising flood and it is not yet known how high the waters will rise and if the flood defences will hold (a concern very salient for many people in the UK as we worked on this second edition in the winter of 2013–14). On these occasions everyone will worry, not just worriers; for want of a better word, worry is normal under these circumstances.

PIT STOP

For a moment return to your Worry Diary and think about the things that you worry about. Do you recognize what we are describing? Is it familiar to you? Make a note of some of the *Hypothetical Event Worries* that you have had. What themes have been emerging within your hypothetical worry? What things are sticking in your mind from the above? Write them down here.

1.

2.

3.

Developing our understanding of worry – what lies at the heart of worry?

At the heart of worry lie our dreams and aspirations, our ambitions and goals. All of us are afraid when the things we value are threatened. In the example above of waiting for news of a loved one at hospital, threat arrives in many ways. The threat could be about losing someone we love, or the threat of pain and loss to others, or a threat to our ability to cope and manage alone. In the second example, a rising flood involves not just a threat to the physical structure of houses, together with the mess that might result, and even the loss of possessions or lives; it's also a threat to our home and the life that we have there. For worriers, what threatens the things they value most arrives in the form of everyday events that trigger *Hypothetical Event Worry*. Because our goals and ambitions are set in the future, and the future is uncertain, there is always uncertainty as to whether our ambitions and goals will be realized. Everyday events contain *splinters of doubt* that trigger worry and which then act to threaten our hopes and aspirations. In the diagram below we have added this extra aspect, which now sits at the heart of worry: the *beating heart* of worry and its emotional core. The heart of worry may contain our goals and ambitions and at the same time contain strong visual images or powerful ideas about threats to our heart's desires.

Figure 17.1: The emotional core of worry

Let's take a 'concrete' example. Many of us will have the ambition of wanting a safe and secure home to live in. Think about the last time you sat looking at the wall. With the idea of a safe and secure home in mind, what's the first *what if* that goes through your mind when you first notice a small crack in the plaster? *What if . . .?* Where does your worry take you both in time and in place? If the first crack is connected to others, then the worry could telescope first to the need for more redecoration and then spiral to thoughts of major and costly repairs – and a house that's impossible to sell. And *what if* the minor cosmetic cracks were a sign of major structural problems and the eventual collapse of the house, leading to our loved ones being trapped in the rubble with serious injuries. To reiterate, this would of course be terrible if it happened, but can you see how the emotional experience of the nightmare vision spirals from that tiny crack, and how, as the worry plays out, it generates an increasingly terrible and highly uncertain future? The doubts, like cracks, trigger worry. *Hypothetical Event Worry* is wholly out of proportion to the starting point. However, as it telescopes into the nightmare scenario as you sit looking at your wall, you may experience some of the powerful feelings that you would almost certainly have if indeed the house were at the point of falling down around you. These feelings are accompanied by increasing levels of uncertainty as the worry continues to twist around and threatens your goals and aspirations.

Worry as a sign of hope and resilience?

It may seem an odd thing to say, but it can be very helpful for worriers to understand that worry is a sign of hope. For most worriers the problem is not that they believe they are inherently weak or that their families, homes, health or finances are ruined, but that they *fear* this *may* come true. These fears threaten the things that they would like to be able to do for themselves and others, leading them to feel anxious. In fact, worriers are in a strange way inherently optimistic in that they continue to aspire, they want to achieve things for themselves and the important people in their world and to better their situation. As bizarre as it may seem, they have hope; their worry tells us this. Put simply, if they did not have hope they would be very unlikely to worry. They would be defeated and depressed and not anxious. Most worriers have not *given up* and they continue to strive to achieve their goals and aspirations while at the same time worrying that they may fail; they may lack confidence, but they have not reached the conclusion that they *are* a failure. Worry is a burden, and worriers tend to get on and try to cope with life, worrying all the time but rarely giving in. Worriers often work terrifically hard to keep juggling the important things in their lives and this shows strength and resilience as they continuously fight against a *sea of troubles*. It is easy to see how worry might be accepted as part of just getting on with things. It is only when it gets too much or we enter a lull in the storm that we notice the energy and effort expended to maintain the status quo and start to recognize the true cost of worrying. This continual struggle might ring a bell for you when you think about your past, either your childhood or the period of your life before you started to notice that your worry was getting out of hand. Were you pursuing something important or

361

trying to meet multiple demands, and, although fearful that you might not succeed, did you continue your efforts and striving (and worrying)?

To clarify another related point, the low mood that comes from worrying is linked to exhaustion and an erosion of self-efficacy. It has been described as demoralization; rather than being about a stable and fundamental sense that the worrier is a failure and the world is hopeless, it tends to reflect the fact that the worrier is concerned that something *may happen* and they *may feel helpless* about this. They experience this as a *threat* to the core sense of who they are, who they would like to be and the corner of the world that they want to live in with the people who are important to them. However, it also requires strength and resilience to live with near-constant threat.

Why worry jumps from topic to topic and why it feels real

When we think about the experience of worry, we know that worry rapidly spreads out and hops around from one worry to the next. As our thoughts race and 'streak' across our minds, we may start off by worrying about one thing and in a flash end up worrying about something completely different. It's important to ask why this happens, and why we move between worries so easily. The answer may lie, in part, with the sheer speed of worry, and how it rapidly multiplies and connects with the network of our aspirations and our fears that these may not be realized. More importantly, however, it appears that worriers don't tend to settle on a worry for long enough to actually deal with it, either as a problem that can be solved in a practical way or as an upsetting emotional experience that can also be dealt with. Thus, with *Real Event Worry*, worriers find it difficult to get on and solve the problems (see Chapter 14), and with *Hypothetical Event Worry* they find it difficult to deal with both the thoughts and feelings about terrible events that haven't happened yet (and probably never will happen) and the uncertainty generated by these worries. So *Hypothetical Event Worry* is about dealing with *the thought* of such things happening. Even though it is just a thought, let's not forget that these worries can make us feel awful and be terribly upsetting, such as worrying about the possible death of a loved one or about failing to achieve something seen as essential to one's aspirations. Worriers will experience an emotional rollercoaster as their worry plays out, and the feelings that the worry generates are very real. But, at the same time as their worry plays out, they are often doing their level best to avoid *really seeing* the nightmares. It's a little like watching a film through your hands, or watching *Dr Who* from behind a sofa. It makes it much more frightening than if we simply watched from *on* the sofa or without our hands in front of our faces.

How this keeps our worry going

Worriers 'allow' themselves to experience only some of the nightmare. They protect themselves from the worst moments of their worry by avoiding the painful parts through focusing instead on something less bothersome, or trying not to think about it, or substituting worries for pleasant thoughts or images. The overall effect is to see the worry out of focus, which means avoiding the painful and upsetting details. It is also a largely unsuccessful attempt to reduce the uncertainty and anxiety that the worry generates. Therapists call this cognitive avoidance.

It is no surprise that worriers want to move on and away from these difficult emotional ideas as quickly as possible. As they do this, the worrier discovers a way of reducing the emotions generated by their *Hypothetical Event Worry*. The next time this happens they will be more likely to use this 'helpful' strategy of avoidance. In this way their avoidance is reinforced. Consequently, they never learn that they may be able to cope or deal with the emotions or experiences that appear in their worry (the out-of-focus stuff mentioned above). They also never learn to tolerate the uncertainty generated by them. By not inspecting them in detail, they never get the opportunity to see if the nightmare is really likely to happen – the glimpse of a nightmare scenario feels real, so it seems likely. Another important thing that happens when we use avoidance is that we are left with unfinished business; this might be a problem we have not resolved, or an idea about ourselves that we cannot face. Unfinished business tends to stick in our minds and demand attention; our minds are built this way. Problems that have been solved or faced do not demand our attention: they get filed away and do not pop up out of the blue in the way that unfinished business does.

Dealing with *Hypothetical Event Worry* means slowing it down and bringing it into sharp focus to *see* what it contains. By doing this we can learn that we can handle it, and that we have nothing to fear from it. The idea that worry is used as a way of avoiding dealing with or facing painful emotional material was first developed from the 1980s onwards by Professor Tom Borkovec of Pennsylvania State University in the United States. Professor Borkovec was a pioneer in the exploration of worry; his ideas have influenced many other researchers and the treatment programme that we are outlining was also strongly influenced by his ideas.

Expanding our understanding of the emotional core

As we explained earlier, worry seems to revolve around the 'emotional core'. This is made up of the things that are fundamentally important to us, the things that we value in our lives. In a sense it is how you want your bit of the world to be – for example, wanting to be a good parent to your children, having good health so you will be around to care for them, being a valued colleague at work, being liked by others, being a thoughtful and caring person, providing for and protecting your loved ones, and wanting the corner of the world you live in to be safe, predictable and certain.

The bad things that worriers tend to worry about in *Hypothetical Event Worry* are things that threaten all that is important to them (such as being a good parent, financial security, their health, their relationships, their family, and so on).

In our washing machine example above, the important things might have been to have a safe and secure home and to be seen as a competent parent, an accepted member of the community, and have happy children who fit in at school. These are ambitions that many of us would share. But when the washing machine started to make knocking noises, the worrier's sensitivity to uncertainty triggered worry: *What if the machine breaks? Then the things that I value may be taken away from me.* Their worry paints a picture and shows how their ambitions and goals might be thwarted. For example, their goal of a safe home is threatened by the worry that telescopes into thoughts and 'flashes' of the house flooding, the leaks damaging the electrics and so on. Can you see how this hypothetical worry threatens their ambition of a safe home? Their other ambition – to be seen as a competent parent by their neighbours – is threatened by the worry that *the washing machine has completely died and I cannot fix it or buy a new one, and then others will judge me for not being able to send the kids to school in clean clothes and my kids will be bullied because of it.* Can you see how this worry threatens the ambition of being a competent parent?

This is how an everyday happening that is a minor event in the great scheme of things, with a tiny amount of uncertainty, can trigger powerful worries, especially among those who are particularly sensitive or intolerant of uncertainty. This starts a process of worrying, which then telescopes, creating worries about threats to important ambitions or aspirations that the worrier holds.

Worry is triggered by mundane, commonplace and everyday things. Our minds turn the uncertainty we find in everyday things into nightmares, which then threaten all that we hold dear. Can you think about other examples where fairly innocuous things have triggered you to worry in this way? Think about noises you hear in the home, or comments people have made, or unusual smells that blow into the car while driving, or as yet unexplained pains in your body, or the slowness of a cashpoint, or someone not responding quickly to a text, or juddering on a train, or the frown on a teacher's face, or loved ones who are late or who are feeling unwell. What kind of *hypothetical worry* do you have? How might this be related to something you hold dear, or to an ambition or goal you may have? Later we will use an exercise to help you to 'chase the rabbit' and follow this idea up. It is called the 'downward arrow technique'.

Worry in words and pictures

Another aspect of worry that hints at its role in avoiding painful emotional material is the relative lack of visual images found in worry. Worry is often experienced in words and tends not to have many clear pictures, although we may experiences flashes or images throughout our worry. Mental pictures or images are thought to make a much bigger emotional impact than those thoughts that are expressed in words. Mental images are known to trigger strong bodily sensations and experiences and lead to immediate behavioural reactions such as fight, flight or freeze. Because these mental pictures are so upsetting, the worrier has learnt to use word-based worry as a way of getting away from them.

Worry almost becomes a 'getaway car' from the terrible images of what could happen to important people, goals or projects that lie within the emotional core of worry. We will come back to this idea in the next chapter.

There may also be other reasons why this switch away from images to thoughts occurs. As we mentioned in Chapter 3 regarding the evolutionary perspective on worry, when we worry there is an increase in brain activity in that area of the brain associated with planning-type activities. If we do get scary glimpses of what could go wrong in the future, it would be helpful in evolutionary terms (to the extent that this thing is likely to happen) to try to do something to counter this, such as planning and problem solving. There would be no value in having part of our brain (the limbic system) over-activated and staying in fear mode, trying to react with the immediate responses of fight, flight or freeze, for something that could possibly happen in the future but is definitely not happening now. So, having some images and glimpses of things going wrong in the future could have some value if they are realistic enough to trigger planning or problem solving.

This is all about keeping worry for the big occasion rather than using it dozens of times a day for everyday hassles that telescope and then masquerade as life-changing events of great potential threat but low probability of occurring.

Discovering the themes of *Hypothetical Event Worry* that make up the emotional core

For many reasons it may be helpful to be able to spot the

themes that underpin your worry. By recognizing the themes, you may be able to interrupt the flow much more readily by spotting these well-worn paths. It will also help to remind you that, while your worry moves and shifts, it does so around themes: usually there are between one and three of these. This means your worry is not random or unpredictable. It also helps to understand more about who you are and what's important to you, or what you value. This last issue is important, because knowing this will help you to understand more about why you worry about the things you do. For instance, in *Hypothetical Event Worry* a worrier may see images of their children being abducted, or being seriously injured in car crashes, or ending up on the streets and on drugs, and so on. It's *not* that the worrier wants these things to happen at some unconscious level; rather, it tells us categorically that one of their main goals is to look after and protect their children. Their worry spirals because of the possible threats to their goal, triggered by uncertainty in everyday situations such as the children walking home from school, a school bus trip or an argument at home.

Spotting underlying themes

There is a powerful technique that we can use to help you to find out what are the central themes of your worry: this is called the *downward arrow* technique. This is a method of chaining worries together and following the links to the core of our worry. The key questions that are repeated are, *Supposing that were true, what would happen next?* and, *Supposing that were true, what would be so bad about that?*

The first step is to find a hypothetical worry to work on. In the example above this might be, *What if my finances get out of control?* We then link the worry by asking the 'supposing' questions to see where they take us. In order to help you to spot the themes that underpin your worry we will first provide you with some examples to get a sense of how we track worry back to its core. Once you have a sense of this you will need to pick one of your own worries and see if you can do the same.

In the examples below, what might you think were the core values and aspirations for this person? The first two worries suggest that they valued their family above all, and that their goal might be to be a good parent and so have a happy family. Can you see how their worry developed around this theme? For the third column, a new theme is starting to emerge related to the importance of friends. We would need to chain a few more worries down to see whether or not this emerged as a theme. With our worries, all roads lead to the core, so it doesn't really matter which *Hypothetical Event Worry* you choose. Also, we may get to the core quite quickly or it may take us some time. Do not expect the themes to fall out in three steps like the examples above. As a rule of thumb, when you get to the bottom of the chain you will notice that the answers you come up with start to get repetitive, and then you have probably gone far enough. If you come up with a feeling as an answer, such as *I would feel terrible* or *I would feel bad*, then try to expand this by asking, *And if I felt this, what might this mean or what problems might that cause me?*

Table 17.1 Downward Arrow

What if my plane crashes?	What if my children grow up to be criminals?	What if my health deteriorates?
Supposing that were true, what would happen next?	Supposing that were true, what would be so bad about that?	Supposing that were true, what would happen next?
↓	↓	↓
I would be dead.	*I would struggle to feel close to them.*	*I wouldn't be able to get out and do the things I love to do.*
↓	↓	↓
Supposing that were true, what would be so bad about that?	Supposing that were true, what would be so bad about that?	Supposing that were true, what would be so bad about that?
↓	↓	↓
My family wouldn't cope.	*I might reject them.*	*I would lose contact with my friends.*
↓	↓	↓
Supposing that were true, what would happen next?	Supposing that were true, what would be so bad about that?	Supposing that were true, what would happen next?
↓	↓	↓
They would go off the rails and end up on the streets.	*I would be a terrible parent.*	*I would spend more time alone.*
What might be the theme?	What might be the theme?	What might be the theme?
What might this person value?	What might this person value?	What might this person value?
What is their goal in worrying?	What is their goal in worrying?	What is their goal in worrying?

EXERCISE 17.1: GETTING TO THE CORE OF OUR WORRY – WORRY THEMES

Choose a recent *Hypothetical Event Worry*. Use the downward arrow questions and see if you can track or chain your worry back to the core ideas. Once you have done one worry, what do you notice?

Now choose another and do the same again. How are they similar? What is different about them? What themes might be emerging? What are you learning about what you value and your goals and ambitions? Step back from the exercise, take a few minutes and come back to what you have written: do you see any patterns? Do the answers seem as if they are striking a chord? Do they seem too far-fetched?

And now take a third worry: do the same and review it, and so on. Once you have two themes, use them as a way of thinking about other worries. Can you see how these themes help you to make sense of these other worries? Can you see how your *Hypothetical Event Worry* is revolving around these themes?

This is a first step in understanding your *Hypothetical Event Worry*. The next chapter will help you to face what you see in your worry.

PIT STOP

Let's stop and think about what you have just been reading. What have you learnt about your emotional core? What is important to you? Can you summarize the key ideas you have taken on board? Make a note of any new ideas that are sticking in your mind. What have you taken from this chapter? If you were to print your learning on a T-shirt, what would the slogan be? If you have any questions, jot these down too. You can return to them once you have had a chance to digest the information.

1.

2.

3.

18

Learning to face your *Hypothetical Event Worry*

Learning about fear and avoidance

We now turn our attention to how you can face your fears. For a moment, let's think about when we were children. Like us, you may have believed that there were 'monsters' or other terrible things under the bed. If this is familiar to you, think about what you remember, using the following questions.

What things did you do to keep yourself safe from the monster? What things went through your mind as you lay in bed? Did pictures flash into your mind, which then kicked off worry – for instance, *What if it gets me? What if no one hears? What if I'm taken off to a faraway place?* And when these worries arrived, how did they leave you feeling? Did you try to push the thoughts of the monster away? Did you try to think about nice things instead? Did you count sheep, or focus on the wallpaper, rather than think about the monster? And did you ever flatly refuse to go to bed or make other excuses like, *Just a few more minutes and then I'll go to bed, promise!*? Did you ever ask someone to check under the bed or did you run from the door and leap into bed? If you were like us, you may have made sure that you slept with your arms and legs tucked in, 'just in case'. You might have scanned the room for noises, holding your breath so you could hear better, hearing your heart thumping and analysing every scratch, creak and knock, asking yourself, *What was that? What's happening? Who's there?* Your mind may have turned the noises into pictures, which flashed through your mind only to disappear into the pea soup. The images triggered thoughts and worries as in your imagination you 'saw' what was going on under the bed – big, sharp teeth, dripping jaws, a menacing face, which pushed you further under the duvet and triggered much more worry. You may have tried listening out for the things that lurked there, but heard nothing, or started singing to yourself to block out the 'terrible presence', but kept stopping just in case you had missed something. You may have tried to block the monster out of your mind by thinking nice thoughts, but the thought of the monster kept returning, more and more often, or the monster appeared in your daydreams, popping up unexpectedly. You may have held a teddy much more tightly, because you hoped that the teddy would keep you safe. You may have avoided looking under the bed for fear of discovering the awful things that lurked there. From time to time, you may have worked up the courage to look but done so very quickly, and by only snatching a glance you never really got a good look at what was there. You might have seen shadows or strange forms, which your mind then built into signs of the monster, which kicked off more worry. *What if he's moved? He might be crawling up the leg of the bed* . . .

Does this sound familiar? There are two main things we would like to draw your attention to. The first is that the overriding pattern within this story is avoidance of anything to do with the horrible thing that lies at the heart of the fear (the monster). The second is the way that our avoidance actually makes the problem much worse. Later we will spell out the ways the different layers of avoidance keep the fear alive. But this is like the layers on an onion; each layer keeps us from the awful things that lie at the heart of our fear. Helping a child or an adult to overcome their fear usually involves getting them to face whatever lies at the heart of their fear. Facing the fear doesn't mean we have to like the thing we fear, but we do need to front up and find out about it. People who fear dogs don't need to become dog lovers; they do need to be able to encounter dogs without fear and trepidation. This is usually best done in a stepwise way, starting off with the easier thing and moving towards the most fearful. In our clinical experience, the mind seems to always make things much worse than they actually are; the mind is both our greatest asset and our greatest foe when it comes to fearful situations.

With your notebook and pen, review the monster under the bed example and see if you can begin to work out what might keep the fear alive (see Exercise 18.1). If this proves tricky then read the next section on avoidance strategies and come back to it.

EXERCISE 18.1: MONSTER

- What things keep the fear of the monster alive (i.e. listening for noises, jumping into bed)?
- How might worry act as an avoidance strategy?
- Are there strategies that we have discussed in previous chapters that appear here as well? How might these keep the fear alive?
- What needs to happen to overcome the fear of monsters?

Avoidance strategies

In the next few pages there are descriptions of common strategies used to avoid focusing on hypothetical worry. Use the scale below to score each strategy to work out which of them is most important for you. We follow each strategy with some hints about how you can change things.

How typical or characteristic is this strategy for you?

Not like me at all	A little like me	Somewhat like me	Moderately like me	Mostly like me	Nearly like me	Completely like me
0	1	2	3	4	5	6

Can you think of a specific worry or image where you used this strategy? In this example, what impact did doing this have on your worry?

Strategy 1: Suppression

Worriers tend to avoid difficult images or powerful feelings by trying to push them to the back of their minds
or by trying not to think about them. Unfortunately, this
rarely works for long and there are good reasons why this
approach fails. Before we go on, try the following exercise.

EXERCISE 18.2: PINK ELEPHANT

Take a blank piece of paper with a pencil. For the
next minute or so, choose a subject that you want
to think about and let your mind roam around this
subject. As you are doing so, we would like you
to do one thing; *do not think about a pink elephant.*
Do not think about the pink elephant in words,
thoughts, pictures or images. Now put the book
down, close your eyes and spend a few moments
thinking about whatever you want to. With your
pencil make a mark every time the elephant comes
to mind.

Before you read on just reflect for a moment on what happens when you try *not* to think about the pink elephant.
For most people, the act of trying not to think about the
elephant means that they end up thinking about it even
more. The thought, *I must not think about a pink elephant*
reminds us about the pink elephant. Even if we are successful at blocking the elephant out, it often appears in another

way, peeking out from behind whatever it is we have used to push it out of our minds with. The colour pink may appear in our thoughts, or the fact that our mind is full of something else we have purposely put in the way of the elephant means that once this leaves our mind the elephant will pop up again. Or we may know that there is something behind the thoughts we are trying to ignore; it's like pushing a balloon under the water – it always wants to resurface. *So, trying not to think about something seems to make us think about it all the more.* Can you see how this might apply to your worry or the pictures that might flash into your mind? What happens when you try to push worrying thoughts or images out of your mind?

With worry it takes a lot of effort and energy to hold our thoughts 'under the surface', but unfortunately this does nothing to make them go away and, like the balloon, they eventually resurface. How much energy and effort do you put into trying to push your worries out? Is the amount of effort you put in worthwhile? Often, the worries resurface at the worst times, when we can do very little about them, such as in the early hours of the morning or when our attention is demanded by something else.

With the pink elephant experiment you may find the pink elephant popping up in your mind later or in your dreams in the coming days. This is called the *rebound effect*, where things we have tried to ignore pop up spontaneously even when we have given up trying not to think about them. Again, can you see how this might apply to your worry or to the images that flash through your mind?

So what should we do instead? The simple answer is that we should try not to push our thoughts below the surface. While this may not make our worries any less worrying or stop them from happening, it may have at least three important influences. First, you will spend less energy and effort trying to push these thoughts out of your mind. Second, you may in this way reduce the amount of worry by breaking a vicious cycle where trying to push the worries out makes you think about them all the more. Third, you will start to face the fear that is at the heart of worry and learn to tolerate it. Together, these reduce the amount of worry.

Hint: Rather than trying to push the images or your worry away, allow them to surface. Hold them in your mind and focus on them. If you find yourself pushing the worry away, then notice what is happening and allow it to come back to the front of your mind.

Strategy 2: Distraction

This is another way of avoiding facing an issue, but rather than trying to push a thought out we choose to try to think of or do something else instead. This means that we throw ourselves into tasks so that we don't have the 'space' to worry – for example, you might choose to watch TV, read, clean the house or put things in order (grocery cupboards, tool-boxes, the sock draw, and so on). Sometimes worriers do two or three of these at once as a 'belts and braces' approach to ensure that they do not have the mental space to worry. Distraction can also take the form of mental activity, such as doing sums in your head or imagining some beautiful deserted beach with palm trees and so forth. Unfortunately, however, distraction rarely works: slowly the worry will creep back in since it is more than likely linked to some unfinished business that will keep demanding your attention until we deal with it. Another of the problems worriers face is that the product of worry, namely anxiety, is accompanied by strong bodily sensations. While the worrier's mind might be able to focus on something other than their worry, the butterflies in their stomach or the muscular tension act to remind them of their worry. For example, if a worrier was using a daydream to distract themselves, at the back of their mind they might notice the feeling of butterflies and incorporate this into their daydream. Slowly this will be followed by other thoughts and worries, which dissolve the daydream and bring them back to the 'reality' of their worry. Try as we might, it is impossible to run away from the things in our minds. While the thought of doing so might be scary, the critical message is that, rather than avoiding these painful and difficult worries, we need to face them.

Hint: Rather than trying to find other things to do, bring your worry to mind on purpose. Notice what happens when you face your worry rather than distract yourself from it.

Strategy 3: Avoidance of mental pictures in worry

As we have mentioned above, worry is interesting because of the relative lack of pictures or images that make up the whirlwind of worry. Research has found that worry is a predominantly word-based experience, meaning that we mostly worry in words, not pictures. Stop for a moment and think about this. How do you experience the whirlwind? Is it mostly in pictures or mostly in thoughts or words?

When images do appear in worry, they tend to 'pop up' or flash into our minds, appearing and disappearing very quickly. Worrying predominantly in words seems to help us to avoid the sharp and painful experiences that come with these images. Strangely enough, worry can have a kind of soothing quality, since it transports the worrier away from the painful images that might flash through their mind. Images or mental pictures provoke stronger reactions in our bodies and trigger stronger emotions, and so if we worry in words we are less likely to be upset or physiologically stirred up. Thus we can understand why worry is used as the getaway car from these often apocalyptic images.

To demonstrate the power of images try the following exercise:

EXERCISE 18.3: CHOCOLATE CAKE

Imagine a thick slice of chocolate cake (or another of your favourite treats). Picture it in your mind's eye: think of the texture of the icing, the soft, moist

---

sponge and the way the light is caught by the icing.
Imagine the smell, the weight of it in your hand.
Then see yourself taking a bite, see the crumbs falling,
and 'picture' the taste exploding in your mouth. See
yourself licking your lips as you taste the chocolate.
What happens? What sensation do you notice?

Images are packed with information and you may have
noticed that using your 'mind's eye' to imagine the
chocolate-cake-triggered salivation may have also triggered
a desire for chocolate cake!

*Hint: Rather than moving away from the image, move
towards it. Describe it: close you eyes and picture it. What
do you see? Write it down, draw it. Try to see it for what it
is – it is only a thought.*

Strategy 4: Mental gymnastics – changing the detail of our worry

There are many seemingly small and insignificant things
that people do to manage the images and thoughts found
in their hypothetical worry. As the term mental gymnastics
suggests, these are ways of twisting and turning around the
images in our worry to avoid them. For example, we may
try to neutralize the anxiety we experience by thinking
of something else, talking to ourselves, replacing negative
images or thoughts with positive ones, or we may avoid
the worst parts by 'fast forwarding' the worry. We may also

keep our mind focused on the past so as not to think about the future. The overall impact of all these gymnastic movements is that the worrier fails to face their fear head on, which, as you will now understand, maintains their fear.

In the monsters under the bed metaphor above, in order to overcome the fear, the bottom line was that the child needed to face the fear to learn that there was nothing under the bed. This would also mean stopping mental gymnastics, like counting sheep or thinking nice thoughts or singing aloud to 'drown out' the thoughts. Of course, these are easier said than done, as the feelings of fear are very real. In order to overcome their fear, the child needed to challenge the underlying idea that there was a monster under their bed. This is also true for facing the fearful images that appear in *Hypothetical Event Worry*. In the case of the distressing images and streams of worry, we need to turn our attention towards them 'square on' without twisting and turning away from them using mental gymnastics.

Hint: Which mental gymnastics do you perform? What would happen if, rather than trying to avoid the worst moments, you faced them? What if you slowed things down, or focused on the images? What would happen if you did not try to think of nice things to counter the negative? Can you experiment with dropping your mental gymnastics to see what happens?

Strategy 5: How we act to avoid triggering our worry

As we have mentioned in previous chapters, worriers may

avoid situations, people, places or objects that they know are likely to trigger worry.

In some instances the worrier attempts to avoid situations or events that match in some way with what they imagine in their *Hypothetical Event Worry*. In these cases the worrier doesn't have to telescope their worry; the material is already there and because it's familiar they are already primed to feel terrible. So, if a worrier had awful images of a loved one being involved in a car crash, they may avoid watching TV programmes where car accidents may feature because they know that they will feel terrible if their worry is triggered. The boundary between what is real and what is worry becomes blurred.

If there is any agreement between the things they 'see' in their *Hypothetical Event Worry* and the things they experience in the real world, then this is taken by the worrier as a sign that they are right to be worried, because what they fear actually happens. It is worth considering where the worrier might find this 'evidence' of bad things happening. Often the evidence is found in television dramas or movies, which need things to happen in order to create the tension and the gripping yet perfect finale. The evidence might also be found in the news, which is almost uniformly 'bad news', with reports of multiple pile-ups, train and plane crashes or near misses, horrific crimes, or major financial scandals. Increasingly it may be found on the web, on social networking sites, or on blogs. None of this represents a true picture of life – its millions of safe journeys by cars, planes, trains and other modes of transport; its millions of evenings out that did not end in murder; and its billions of financial transactions that have been fairly and honestly conducted are never reported. The 'bad news' stories are indeed terrible – this is why they are reported – but this does not mean that they are likely or imminent in most people's lives on a day-to-day basis. But their upsetting nature, coupled with the feelings they generate, does make them feel more real and closer to home.

For others, the links between real situations and *Hypothetical Event Worry* can spread. For instance, if a worrier's goals and ambitions were about staying healthy and well for their children, then a film or book about a person who suddenly succumbs to illness and dies might well go to the heart of their worry. This could lead to an avoidance of all books or films on a health theme, or of visiting a friend in hospital.

Worriers may avoid objects that will trigger worry, and what they avoid is very idiosyncratic. It might be bicycles, beer or balloons, cats, cherries or candles, or dogs, diapers or doughnuts! Each object will be associated with a *splinter of doubt* and launch a stream of hypothetical worry that then motivates avoiding these objects. For example, *What if the cat I am thinking of getting for the kids causes an accident? I'll be sued, I'll lose my house, the kids will fail at school*, leading to, *My grandkids will not have a good start to life.* This hypothetical worry motivates the worrier to avoid buying a kitten, despite the fact that their children are only five and six years old and a long way from having kids themselves! Stop for a moment and work out some other *what if* statements that could be triggered by the things mentioned above?

What do you avoid to reduce or prevent worry? What do you shy away from because of worry? Does your avoidance influence your choices in life? If so, how?

We rarely if ever talk about our hypothetical worry, we may talk in general terms but never talk about the detail. We may fear telling others about our experiences because, if we did, we might fear that the worry was more likely to be realized, or that the person we tell might think us odd. Many worry rules (see Chapter 12) might be active at this level, such as, *If I think – and worse, if I talk – about it, it is more likely to happen.*

> *Hint: Make a list of the situations, people, places of objects that you avoid because they are linked with what you 'see' or think in your* Hypothetical Event Worry. *Choose an easier one to work on first, and expose yourself to it. You will worry and feel anxious, but notice what else you get from doing this. The new experiences, the new learning or the chance for growth.*

Learning to face our fears

As we mentioned above, this chapter is focused on helping you to deal with *Hypothetical Event Worry*. We have highlighted the ultimately unhelpful role of suppressing our thoughts, distracting ourselves, avoiding situations, places or people that trigger worry, and the subtle mental gymnastics that we use to help us manage these awful experiences. In the monster under the bed example, we learnt that we need to face our fears, and this is no different for our worry. So what does this mean? It means confronting the thing that frightens us. It means focusing on our *Hypothetical Event Worry*, slowing it down and exploring in detail the images that flash through our minds.

Avoiding getting to grips with *Hypothetical Event Worry* means that these worries can continue to dominate and influence our lives. Worry is an awful, fatiguing, exhausting preoccupation, and the cost of worrying is very high. Learning to face your worry and deal with it might in the short term make you feel more anxious and upset, but in the longer term you will move towards overcoming it.

Writing down your *Hypothetical Event Worry*

You may feel a little daunted by this, which is entirely understandable. You may say to yourself, *This will make my worry much worse!* Or you may think, *I won't be able to handle facing my worry.* But how do you know this? What evidence do you have to support it? How might thinking this keep you locked into a vicious cycle?

Remember that you probably experience parts of these nightmarish daydreams at least every day and often for prolonged periods of time where you catch glimpses of them before pushing them away. If you are trying to avoid them or not think about them but you still worry, then all these efforts have made no difference. As one client said, 'I've tried not talking and thinking about this and that didn't work.' So you have probably been trying one strategy (avoidance) to manage your worry for a very long time. Has using avoidance helped to reduce the impact of your worry?

Let's return to the monsters under the bed example. Glancing under the bed is no good because it doesn't let us get to see what is *really* under there. And because we don't ever get a good look, rather than making us feel better our efforts trigger doubt and uncertainty, leading to more worry. In order to put the fear behind you, you need to have a good look – into the corners, behind whatever is under there, shaking out hidden things, using a light to see clearly, maybe even moving the bed, checking it out under different conditions, all depending on what you specifically fear.

How do we have a good look at our worry? Well, we don't have to do this all at once; we can gradually build up. Actually, we have to do it this way, because each time you write out an account of your *Hypothetical Event Worry* you will discover new corners that you have not looked into. So this is a series of steps, eventually ending up with all of the fears at the heart of worry exposed.

The bottom line is that we know that writing down the things that concern us is by and large a helpful thing to do. It is a very useful thing to do for all sorts of reasons and all sorts of problems, which we will go into below.

How will writing things down help?

Writing things down is helpful for a number of reasons. First, seeing things written down helps us to stand away from the fears at the heart of our worries, rather than being in them. It might also begin to change the way we think about our worry. We might be able to see how realistic our worries actually are and to find out what really bothers us about them, rather than guessing based on glimpses and flashes. Research has found that writing can be a powerful therapeutic intervention. It can help us to process emotions: since we feel the experience as we write it, writing can help us to explore the themes within our words, so adding understanding and structure, which again can be very helpful. Writing also forces us to organize our thoughts; it stands in the opposite corner to avoidance. As someone said, *When I hear myself speak, I know what I think*. This is also true for writing.

As a first writing attempt, choose a *Hypothetical Event Worry*. You may want to use one of those from your downward arrow exercise earlier in the chapter. Take a notebook and pen and write down your worry. Imagine that you had to help someone to make a movie of your worry – think of all the *details* they would need to know. Use the prompts below to help you add the detail.

Tips: What to include in my writing

Setting the scene: Who is involved in your worry? What happens in your worry? Where and when is the worry happening? What do you see? Describe exactly what you see in detail. Is there anything that would help someone to understand the context of the worry? Again, imagine the film crew trying to capture your worry; what else do they need?

Actions: What do you or others do in your worry? If the answer is nothing, then what motivates you or others to do nothing?

Your emotional reactions: Keep asking yourself, *How am I feeling now?* Add this into the account. How do you feel?

Body sensations: What bodily sensations are you experiencing? How does your body feel right now? Where in your body are you feeling these sensations?

Sensory information: What can you smell, hear, touch, feel and see?

The meaning: What goes through your mind as you see your worry unfolding? What does your worry say or mean to you? What do the actions of others in your worry mean? What do the picture or images tell you? What is the worst thing about this? What does this say about you as a person?

Time information: Is it day or night? Is it morning, afternoon or evening, summer, winter?

Images: Focus on these, describe them in detail: what do you see? Draw a sketch of what you see. Who is in the image? Where are they? What is happening to them? What goes through your mind when you see this picture?

Themes: You will probably have a few worst-case scenario worries. Recent research has suggested that it is more beneficial to stick to the same theme within the worry. For instance, theme might be harm to a loved one: work on this until you notice an improvement before moving on to another theme.

Hypothetical Event Worry is a stream of thoughts. These thoughts do not describe real events; they are not facts, they are thoughts; they are products of your imagination, spinning around things that are important to you.

More tips: How to write

Choose a quiet moment, a time when you know you will not be disturbed – perhaps also a time when you know you are less likely to worry. So you may want to avoid doing this late at night to start with. Remind yourself that you have control over this process; no one can force you to do this. If you need reminding about why you are doing this, then reread the sections above.

When you start to write, do so in the first person and in the present tense. That is, write it in the moment, as if it is happening right now – for instance, *I am thinking that my seventeen-year-old son is in a car accident; I can see his face contorted in pain and crying out for me saying . . .* – rather than as an after-the-fact news report version – *My seventeen-year-old son was in a car accident and he cried out for me.* Can you see how the first version brings you much closer to the experience, which reduces the avoidance?

The key message is about wholly engaging with your worry and the fears that are at its heart; this means we also have to keep an eye out for avoidance in the form of suppression, distraction and mental gymnastics. Notice too avoidance of the details of the images you see in your worry. As you are writing you may be trying to think of nice things to neutralize the bad things that are being written on the page. This is based on the assumption that there is something to fear by writing things down. But on the first few attempts it's OK to use mental gymnastics or other avoidance tactics, so long as you are moving towards the goal of writing a full account of your worry, without using them.

Sometimes it might feel as if the worry has no ending: just keep writing until you have passed what might be the worst moment for you; or, if you notice that you are going around in a circle, it might be time to stop. Remember that we are also trying to help you sit with uncertainty: the aim is not about finding a good ending. In fact, for many worriers it is the not knowing that is worst, so it might be better if the ending were left hanging, as this will trigger more uncertainty, which you need to learn to tolerate. Remember that *Hypothetical Event Worry* is about things that could theoretically happen (and many different things could theoretically happen) in an imaginary scary future and not about what will happen.

It is normal to feel upset when doing this – the ideas and images may indeed be terrible. The reason why you find them upsetting is because *you really care* and they are the last things that you want to happen. Being able to tolerate upsetting thoughts and images will not make you insensitive or uncaring. It will mean that you can in fact tell the difference between thoughts and reality, treat thoughts as thoughts that don't need to be managed or controlled or avoided, and then get on with dealing with reality, which is the pursuit of things that are important to you in the present. So, tolerating the upset now while learning to treat upsetting thoughts as thoughts will move you towards the things that really matter. Imagine not being hijacked and terrified by your worry; imagine being able to just be, participating in and enjoying the moment – living now, not worrying about a possible scary future.

Review the above, take a notebook and pen, and start to write.

The second draft

Once you have your first draft it's time to review it to see if you have included all the details. Are there sections that you know you have skipped through? What were the worst moments? Have you written all that you could about these worries? Were you using mental gymnastics to help?

Once you have a detailed account of your worry, you are ready to move into the final stage. This requires you to expose yourself in a structured way to what you have written. Before we do this, we will spend a few moments talking about how we work with fear.

The same principles underpin the approach to worry, the approach to monsters under the bed or, say, the approach to a phobia about dogs. To help someone overcome the latter we would enable them to spend time with dogs, so that they can *learn* to face their fear. For the exposure to be helpful, they have to stay with the dogs until their fear naturally comes down – which it will. With the monsters, it's about working out what is a discarded sock or dust bunny and what is one's imagination. With dogs it's also about learning how dogs behave and how to behave with dogs, and to find out the difference between real dogs and those of our nightmares and dreams. We wouldn't want to start out with massive dogs, or excitable or unpredictable dogs – a small to medium, calm, well-tempered dog that is used to other people would be a good place to start.

There is a concern that anxiety, once started, will go on and on; this just isn't the case. Our anxiety will come down, even without our doing anything to make it come down. We have to learn to allow the wave of fear to wash over us, letting go of all our attempts to avoid or control it so that we can find out that nothing bad will happen. Indeed, on the other side of the wave of fear we find relative calm. As we mentioned above, anxiety is a very useful emotion, and in an evolutionary sense it tells us when we need to fight, run away or freeze, but in the case of phobias, worry or fears of monsters it has ceased to be of help because it is out of proportion to the real danger. The content of our *Hypothetical Event Worry* produces anxiety because it poses theoretically possible future threats to those things we value and hold dear, and it is this threat that we need to expose ourselves to.

The worrier is also learning about and exposing themselves to the absolute certainty of uncertainty, and that their aspirations and goals may always feel threatened because they are important to them. At some times and for some people, goals are indeed thwarted and ambitions not realized. Life is about adjustment, adapting and coping and then finding new goals in the event that these things do happen.

The possibility that things could go wrong is in an absolute sense true, since nothing is impossible. Arguing that it might be highly unlikely is not really going to wash – the, *Yes, but what if it did happen* will always be there. The worrier has to learn to live with this uncertainty and divert their energy from trying to manage it through worry and all its consequences to living with it in the present.

Finally

So, in order to work with your *Hypothetical Event Worry*, it is important to sit with your feelings without doing anything to make them better. The initial reaction drives us away from the thing we fear, that is, facing the detail of your worry square on. Ask yourself, *What is the worst thing that could happen?* Yes, you will feel anxious, but as you learn to face you fears, your anxiety will decrease. Your fears will, over time, come down on their own, but you need to find this out for yourself.

Take the final and detailed version of your *Hypothetical Event Worry* and read and reread it for thirty minutes a day. Use the 'Facing your Fear' exercise below to record the experience. Note that the form asks you to rate your anxiety before, during and after using the scale provided. Once you have done this with one worry, choose another. Probably you will need to do this two to three times so that you have got to the different parts of the fears at the heart of worry.

It is important to record your reflections and thoughts as you are doing this. For example, has doing this exercise taught you anything new about your worry? Has your relationship with the *Hypothetical Event Worries* changed in any way and, if so, how? Do you see your *Hypothetical Event Worries* any differently? Can you recognize them sooner now? Are you able to interrupt them, or have you found things that you can say to help you to 'put the brakes on'?

EXERCISE 18.4: FACING YOUR FEAR

Aim to fill out a form each time you face your *Hypothetical Event Worry*. Use the scale below to rate your anxiety or discomfort. Remember you need to work with your worry for long enough for the feelings to reduce.

Anxiety/Discomfort Scale

None		Slight		Moderate		High		Extreme
0	1	2	3	4	5	6	8	9

Session No._____

Day or date_____ Start time____:__ Finish time____:__

Place_____ Worry_____

Anxiety/Discomfort   Before ____ During (max) ____ After ____

(please use scale)

Did you use mental gymnastics?   No____ A little____ A lot____

How did you do this?_____

None		Slight		Moderate		High		Extreme
0	1	2	3	4	5	6	8	9

Session No._____

Day or date_____ Start time____:__ Finish time____:__

Place_____ Worry_____

Anxiety/Discomfort   Before ____ During (max) ____ After ____

(*please use scale*)

Did you use mental gymnastics?   No____ A little____ A lot____

How did you do this?_____

Session No._____

Day or date_____ Start time____:__ Finish time____:__

Place_____ Worry_____

Anxiety/Discomfort   Before ____ During (max) ____ After ____

(*please use scale*)

Did you use mental gymnastics?   No____ A little____ A lot____

How did you do this?_____

Session No._____

Day or date_____ Start time____:__ Finish time____:__

Place_____ Worry_____

Anxiety/Discomfort   Before ____ During (max) ____ After ____

(*please use scale*)

Did you use mental gymnastics?   No____ A little____ A lot____

How did you do this?_____

Breaking down avoidance

Now you have faced your fear, it's time to review the situations, people, places or objects that you avoided because they triggered or closely matched your *Hypothetical Event Worry* in some way. It might be that you have already started to do this, but ask yourself if there is anywhere or anything that you are still avoiding because you know that it triggers worry. It might be useful to go to the list of behavioural experiments on uncertainty in Chapter 11 and see if any of these examples stand out. You may notice that you worry a little more when you face these situations; this is normal and tells us that you are approaching situations that match closely with your *Hypothetical Event Worry*. The more you engage with these situations, the more opportunity you will have to trigger your *Hypothetical Event Worry*. Without wishing to sound mean, this is actually good because it will give you more opportunity to challenge your worry. This chapter is about facing the things that frighten us; we hope it is getting clearer now that, while it's often difficult to face your fears, doing so will help you to overcome them.

Where have we got to?

As you will see from the diagram below, we have now added the emotional heart of worry to the picture. We have also added cognitive avoidance and some arrows linking worry to this. We will talk through the additional parts that have been added.

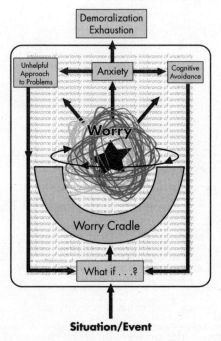

Figure 18.1: Building the picture: the emotional heart of worry and cognitive avoidance

At the heart of worry lie our dreams and aspirations, our ambitions and goals. All of us are afraid when the things we value are threatened. For worriers, the thing that threatens these ambitions and goals arrives in the form of worry, and usually in the form of *Hypothetical Event Worry*. The bad things in *Hypothetical Event Worry* tend to threaten all those things that are important. These bad things usually come in the form of images or flashes. Understandably, we want to avoid seeing these awful things, but the strategies we use to manage them make us worry all the more (see the arrow heading down from cognitive avoidance, in the figure above, to the 'What if . . .?' box). The simple message in this chapter is about learning to face our fears, and find out that we can survive.

Cognitive avoidance is made up of avoiding the following: mental imagery in our worry; attempts at suppression, distraction and mental gymnastics; and situations that trigger worrisome thoughts. As you now understand, the avoidance of the detail of your *Hypothetical Event Worry* means that you never fully face the fears that are bounded within them, and this means that the worry lives on. In this chapter you have learnt about the importance of breaking patterns of avoidance and about the themes that lie at the heart of your worry. You have also learnt that worry is a sign of hope because the things that are threatened in worry are the things that are really important to you, the things you want to happen, the person you want to be, the world you would like to live in. Dealing with your *Hypothetical Event Worry* means moving away from living in the scary imaginary future of worry with all its costs. It means moving towards living in the moment, actively pursuing your goals and enjoying the life you have now while learning to live with the inevitable uncertainty.

Our journey together is nearly over: you have now reached the last big block of treatment. You have come a long way and this might be a good time to sit and reflect on what you have learnt and what has happened to your understanding of worry. The diagram above might have been daunting for you to start with, but we hope that this 'central heating diagram' is now making sense to you. You may want to go back to the stories at the beginning of the book and see if you can make sense of them using the ideas you have discovered here. Or, take a piece of paper and have a go at drawing your worry patterns using the diagram.

The next chapter is about how you can stay well – there is some advice on sleep problems, for example – and there are also some loose ends that we need to tie up.

PIT STOP

Let's pause again and think about what you have just been reading. What new ideas or thoughts are coming into play now? Are you thinking any differently about your *Hypothetical Event Worry*? What things are sticking in your mind?

1.

2.

3.

19

Tying up some loose ends – but not them all

We are tempted to end this book in the middle of the chapter, so as to end in uncertainty, but we won't because we want to *tie up some, but not all, of the loose ends*. You have now reached the last chapter; here we will focus on new material, namely dealing with sleep problems. Worry often happens at night, so we will give you some tips about this in the first section. We will then review the diagram of worry. The final section will focus on staying well and planning for the future.

The wee hours – difficulties in sleeping

To adapt a quote from the creator of Snoopy and the cartoon strip 'Peanuts', namely Charles M. Schulz: 'Sometimes I lie awake at night, and worry about where my life will go wrong. Then a voice says to me, this is going to take more than one night.' For worriers, sleep problems are a very real issue. Indeed, Professor Tom Borkovec, who we have already mentioned, was one of the first to get interested in worry in the early 1980s because of his work on insomnia. He and his team came to the conclusion that one of the main reasons people had difficulty sleeping was not just that they were too tense, but that they were too worried. Here we do not have the space to go into detail about what you should do to get better sleep, but we recommend that those of you with serious sleep problems take a look at another book in this series, *Overcoming Insomnia and Sleep Problems*. It is by Professor Colin Espie, an expert in the psychological treatment of sleep problems, and is well worth reading; you could use it as a close companion to this book.

The ideas to help you sleep better can be broken into four groups. The first are very practical things like checking that your bed is comfy. If it's not, then think about getting a better mattress or a new bed. Is your room dark enough, warm or cool enough and quiet enough? Are there practical steps you need to take to get a better sleep such as buying blackout blinds, or opening or closing windows?

The second group of things relate to forming better patterns and habits. For instance, how much caffeine do you drink during the day and before bed (including fizzy drinks, chocolate and tea)? It could be helpful to stop drinking caffeinated drinks by mid-afternoon and drinking non-caffeinated herbal or milky drinks instead. Do you have a regular sleep pattern, that is, do you go to sleep and wake at a regular time? If not, how much sleep would you like (an average is about eight hours)? Then work out how to get this (eight hours could be 11.00 p.m. to 7.00 a.m. or 10.30 p.m. to 6.30 a.m.). Go to bed when you are feeling tired and stick to a routine of getting up at the same time every day, even when you haven't slept well (don't sleep in). Do you work late using computers or games? Could you think of something else to do to help your mind wind down? Try to have your evening meal early so that it is not resting on your stomach as you go to bed. Do you use alcohol or other drugs to help you sleep? Be wary of using alcohol, since while it may seem to help to get you to sleep, it also stops one from getting good restful sleep. Turn your alarm clock to the wall – you don't really need to know that it's 3.45 a.m. when you wake up. Looking at the alarm clock reminds you that you are awake and makes it harder to sleep. Your alarm clock will do its job and wake you when you need it to. What about exercise? Are you taking enough? Would a walk or a swim help? Avoid exercising too close to bedtime, as we often feel very alert and hot after exercise, making getting off to sleep difficult.

The third group of ideas is about the way you approach the bedroom. It is important to see your bed as a place where you sleep, not worry. So, if you are taken by worry, get up and sit somewhere else until you start to feel sleepy, and then return to bed. This needs some thought beforehand, particularly if we worry about disturbing others. The principle is to find something to do that is not too stimulating or engaging, something that is broadly calming and that we can bring our awareness to. *What things can you think of that might fit the bill?* Sometimes we might get up at 3 a.m. and watch a favourite TV programme that grabs our attention and helps distract from our worry, but now it keeps us up for a different reason, namely to find out what happens next! So, watching some TV can help (nature programmes for instance, (perhaps exploring the differences between black bears and grizzly bears), listening to relaxing music, using a

Mindfulness practice (see Appendix 1), reading a book (art/ photography books are good), drinking a non-caffeinated tea or, as we have been suggesting, writing things down.

The last group are strategies to deal with your worry, such as writing your worries down on a note pad, or making a note of the problems that you are concerned about for the next day. If something is bothering you and there is nothing you can do about it right away, try writing it down before going to bed and then *tell* yourself to deal with it tomorrow. If your mind reviews the day just before you go to sleep, then either do this quietly before going to bed, or write things down if this helps.

Poor sleep will make many of the symptoms of worry much worse; for example, when we are sleep deprived we may feel irritable or struggle to concentrate. Often people cannot escape their worries even when they are asleep because the themes of their worries, or the same daytime worries, appear in their dreams. The evidence from other emotional problems suggests that, if you are able to improve and reduce daytime worry, then worry in dreams should also improve. On a practical note, another thing to do is to note down what your dreams are about. This may help you to understand more about what lies at the heart of your worry (see Chapter 17).

Putting it all together

In the next section you will find the complete version of the worry diagram. We have added the final two components, which appear as arrows pointing towards the belly of the intolerance of uncertainty. These show that life events or stressful things can influence the whole system, as can powerful emotional experiences. These events 'ratchet up' the uncertainty, and, as you will understand, with more uncertainty comes more worry. It reminds us that worry is an everyday event and from time to time we all worry when faced with difficult life circumstances. Examples of life events might include, exams, retirement, ill health, promotion or the birth of a child. Any of these events could ratchet up an individual's intolerance to uncertainty. Strong mood states can also have this effect.

Let's remind ourselves of Tom, who is still at the train station. Track the example through on the diagram.

Situation/Event

If you remember, Tom had difficulties with getting to work and worried about late trains. He had an important meeting to attend and noticed the threat of windy weather on the train system some 300 miles from his home (situation/event). He spotted the uncertainty pretty quickly and thought to himself, *What if my train is delayed and I am late for work?* The uncertainty he experienced fuelled his worry. He cared about his work and believed that it would show him to be uncaring if he did not worry about being late; the beliefs that made up his worry cradle 'instructed' him to worry. His worry was under way and it *telescoped* to all manner of catastrophes. His *Hypothetical Event Worry* revolved

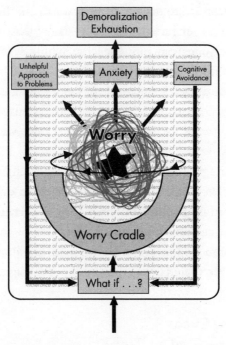

Figure 19.1: The complete picture of worry

around the theme of work; it seemed that at its heart lay the aspiration of being a good and worthwhile person. He 'saw' flashes of his fall from grace, which threatened the idea of his being a worthwhile person. He started to feel more uncertain than ever about his life and his job, which triggered even more worry. He tried desperately to push his worry to the back of his mind. Yet, try as he might, he couldn't seem to shake the worry, which felt very intense. He noticed strong bodily sensations, his heart was thumping in his chest, he also felt tense and edgy. As his worry whirled around, he started to believe that he was losing his mind and the turbo-charger kicked in, making his worry worse and leading him to feel panicky. He felt he couldn't trust himself to make a good decision about how best to get to work and he just avoided solving the problem. He sat down and waited for his worry to subside. He was exhausted and felt down on himself for allowing his worry to get the better of him.

And that was Tom on a good day! Imagine if he had just found out that his girlfriend was pregnant. Although excited, the additional responsibility would have made his job even more important to him. Imagine if he had been talking to his sister, who had told him about possible redundancies at her work. He would be worried for her and unsettled when he got to his own workplace, with redundancy on his mind.

What happened to Tom?

Tom learnt to recognize the triggers for his worry. He discovered that he worried mostly about work and his social relationships, particularly his girlfriend. He began to understand that he was intolerant of uncertainty and started to take small risks to begin to learn to tolerate uncertainty. He even tried being late for work on purpose just to see what would really happen. He learnt that worrying was not the best way to show that he cared about work, and he found out that there were many other ways he could show this. Before he started to work on his worry he believed that problems only ever happened to him, and that if he tried to solve them they would go wrong. He started to recognize that he was solving problems all the time and that actually he was quite good at it. He solved a few medium-sized problems at work, which really helped his confidence. He saw that he valued his work and relationships and understood more about why he had awful images that came with his *Hypothetical Event Worry*. He learnt to spot when he was climbing into the worry elevator, and that his worries were just thoughts and were not real. Rather than trying to push his worry out, he turned to face it and his worry became less problematic. As his worry receded, his anxiety lessened and he felt less tense and irritable. He started to sleep better and to enjoy work more. He continued to take risks and went on a last-minute holiday, without any planning. His relationship improved; as his worry lessened he started to feel closer to his girlfriend as they were able to do more things together. He felt more confident to move on and meet new people. He still worries from time to time, but he can manage that.

Reviewing how you have done

Worry is normal; we all worry. This book will not banish worry since worry is an everyday thing; we all suffer from bouts of worry from time to time, and some of these can be intense although they do not last forever. Do not expect to be worry-free.

In Chapter 6 we asked you to draw up some goals. How have you done? Is there still work left to do, or are you close to reaching them? Do you need to review you goals in the light of the progress you have made? What would you like to achieve now? Complete the questionnaires (on worry or the intolerance of uncertainty) or any of the scales you have used again and compare the scores to those you had at the beginning. What does this tell you? Is there still work to be done? Which part of the programme do you need to return to?

What have you learnt?

Throughout the book we have asked you to pause and reflect on your learning. Can you now collect all this information together? What have you taken from the book? What has stuck in your mind? What has helped you to feel better? What hasn't worked so well? It may be helpful to review the chapters and see what you have taken from each, jotting down all the specific rules, actions and strategies that you have spotted that keep your worry going. Can you draw your own worry diagram? There are several versions of vicious cycles throughout the book – use whatever helps.

Keeping well

For any new skill, in order to stay sharp you need to practise. The new ideas that you have come across in this book are the same in this respect, and so it would be useful if they were built into your routine. You need to keep mentally fit by 'working out' using the worry exercises; in particular, keep pushing yourself into uncertainty. In the annotated diagrams in Appendix 2 we have added the main treatment targets. When you review your worry, what areas of the diagram do you need to work on? What are your Achilles heels?

Lapse and relapse

With any emotional problem we will all have moments when the problem gets a little worse. Just because you have a bad week doesn't mean that the worry is back. In fact, you could have two bad weeks and still this would not mean that your worry was back in the way that it was before. It could be that what you have been experiencing is big event worry and that, in fact, your worry is in proportion to the event. So ask yourself about what has been happening in your life. Also remind yourself of how you used to worry; think about how bad your worry was before you started to do something about it. How does this compare with your worry at the moment? Have you really gone back to square one, or are you just having one of those weeks?

Another thing that happens when people start to feel better is that they forget how bad things actually were before. We talked about change in therapy being like hair growing – sometimes it's almost impossible to notice. Use the questionnaires and ratings scales to help you gauge where your worry is at the moment and decide whether you have suffered a lapse or a relapse.

What might lead to a setback for me?

What life events are coming your way that you know will trigger more worry? Sometimes these revolve around life transitions such as children starting school or walking home alone for the first time, retirement, promotions or starting work. Or a setback can appear before or during predictable events such as exams or family get-togethers. How can you prepare for them? What might help in these circumstances?

Remember that worry is normal and that many of us would worry about these things. Think about how the *worried you* might handle these situations, and then think about how you have learnt to handle them differently. Become aware of your worry, *stand on the bank and notice the flow of your worry* and the factors that influence this. Notice the uncertainty and sit with it rather than worrying. Recognize the rules that instruct you to worry and challenge them, challenge the turbo-charger, recognize when you are climbing into the express worry elevator. Approach problems rather than avoid them, see problems as opportunities to use your problem-solving skills. Your *Hypothetical Event Worry* will remind you of what you value and also of what might threaten this, so face the fear. Rather than sitting on the fence, engage with problems, with worries, with people, with this moment and with life.

What if I still need help?

If you have found the ideas in this book useful but have struggled to apply them to yourself, then maybe drop in to see your family doctor and discuss the options for therapy in your local area. If you want to stick with a CBT approach, then you can ask if there are people trained in CBT locally. According to the National Institute for Health and Care Excellence, CBT is the treatment of choice for worry so we would advise you to see a CBT therapist if at all possible. If you want to find a therapist without going to your GP, you will find more information on how to do so at the back of this book. Tell your doctor or therapist that you have been using this book. Talk to them about what helps and what doesn't.

It takes courage to admit to and work on emotional problems. Therapy is about finding new ways of doing things. This feels risky, but the benefit usually far outweighs the costs. Good luck! We hope that this book has helped you to worry less and to live a little more.

Appendix 1:
Mindfulness-based CBT

In recent approaches and ideas in CBT, there is an emerging trend towards the acceptance of emotional suffering as a process of change. The amount of research in these new areas has grown, but at the time of writing it unfortunately still remains quite thin: there is relatively little research focused on worry. However, for many years therapists have been trying to help worriers by using similar ideas. For example, imagine your worries are clouds floating across your mind. Do not engage with them, do not judge them, just let them be, let them pass without comment. The implication of this idea is very clear for worry. If we could sit with uncertainty and the whirlwind of worry it triggers, and just let the worry be without judging it or paying it too much attention, then we might be able to worry less.

In Mindfulness-based CBT, individuals learn to pay attention to how their mind focuses or becomes aware of experiences. They are taught to notice worry but then to continually reconnect with the present moment, with the here and now. Usually they are instructed to focus on their breathing and use it as an 'anchor' or companion to help them to locate themselves with the here and now. In

Mindfulness, if you stray into engaging with your worry, then the aim is to compassionately bring your mind back to the breath, without judgement or criticism, without expectation or desire, to be here and now with your breath. The value of these ideas is clear: if we were less engaged with worry and were able to stand back and observe the flow without it taking us away emotionally, then worry would not be such a problem – it would become something we observe rather than something we experience.

Our current understanding is that Mindfulness might be best used towards the middle to end of a programme of treatment, once the person has started to understand more about how their worry works and learnt to disconnect a little from it. Over time we may find that Mindfulness can be used earlier, but for now it would appear that it is best used as a way of making sure that we don't fall back into old habits. Indeed, a Mindfulness-based approach might be a very powerful way of keeping people feeling well and their minds fit. If you are interested in learning more about Mindfulness, you'll find some additional information in Appendix 6 (also see Further Reading section).

Appendix 2: Annotated Diagrams of Worry

The first diagram here reminds you of what the different elements are. The second reminds you about what you need to do with each part of the picture of worry to get better.

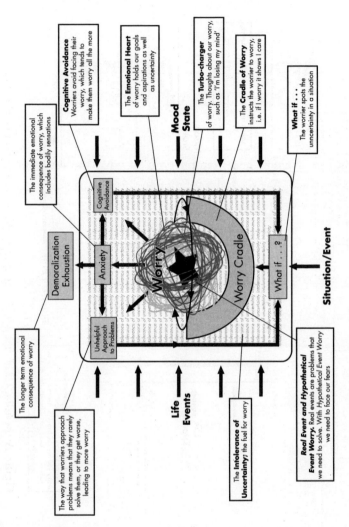

Figure Appendix 2.1: Pulling it all together – a reminder

Appendix 2: Annotated Diagrams of Worry

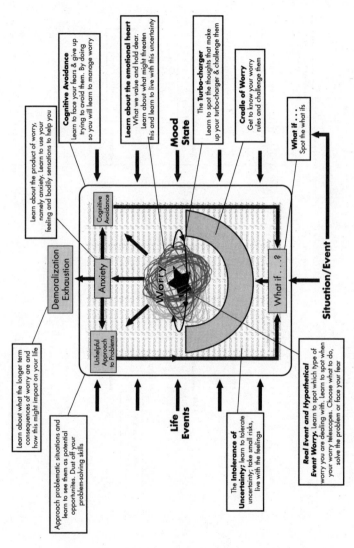

Figure Appendix 2.2: Pulling it all together – what I need to do to feel better

Appendix 3:
Worry Diary

Day/Time	Content	Distress	Worry type
	What was the worry about?	How intense was the worry? How uncontrollable did it seem? Scale: (mild) = 0 to 100 = (very severe)	Is the worry about a real, current problem: does the problem actually exist? Yes/no If no, is it hypothetical? Have I got ahead of myself?

Appendix 4:
Help with the Penn State Questionnaire

Table to help you score your Penn State Worry Questionnaire

Transfer your scores from the Penn State Worry Questionnaire to the second column. Questions numbered 1, 3, 8, 10 and 11 need to be reversed before you add up your total. Use the key below to help you convert your score. A score of 1 would convert to 5, a score of 2 converts to 4, 3 stays the same, a score of 4 converts to 2 and a score of 5 converts to one. Once you have converted your answers for questions 1, 3, 8, 10 and 11, then strike out your original score so that you do not confuse yourself while adding. Then add the total of all sixteen questions. Your score should lie somewhere between 16 and 80; people who have a problem with worry tend to score 57 and above. Repeat the questionnaire once every two weeks to track progress.

KEY

	Not at all typical		Somewhat typical		Very typical
My Score =	1	2	3	4	5
Reversed Score	5	4	3	2	1

Example
My Score

1. _2_ Reversed = _4_
2. _3_
3. _4_ Reversed = _5_
4. _5_
5. _5_
6. _5_
7. _3_
8. _4_ Reversed = _4_
9. _5_
10. _2_ Reversed = _5_
11. _2_ Reversed = _3_
12. _2_
13. _4_
14. _4_
15. _3_
16. _3_

Total _63_

Week No. ——
My Score

1. —— Reversed = ——
2. ——
3. —— Reversed = ——
4. ——
5. ——
6. ——
7. ——
8. —— Reversed = ——
9. ——
10. —— Reversed = ——
11. —— Reversed = ——
12. ——
13. ——
14. ——
15. ——
16. ——

My Total ——

Week No. ——
My Score

1. —— Reversed = ——
2. ——
3. —— Reversed = ——
4. ——
5. ——
6. ——
7. ——
8. —— Reversed = ——
9. ——
10. —— Reversed = ——
11. —— Reversed = ——
12. ——
13. ——
14. ——
15. ——
16. ——

My Total ——

Week No. ——
My Score

1. —— Reversed = ——
2. ——
3. —— Reversed = ——
4. ——
5. ——
6. ——
7. ——
8. —— Reversed = ——
9. ——
10. —— Reversed = ——
11. —— Reversed = ——
12. ——
13. ——
14. ——
15. ——
16. ——

My Total ——

Appendix 5:
Simple problem-solving worksheet

Problem:

Solution Number _____:

If you answer no to any of the following, stop and pick another solution.

1. If I use this solution, will it help me to solve   Yes ☐   No ☐
   my problem?

2. Is this solution practical?   Yes ☐   No ☐

3. What might stop me from using this solution?
   What are the roadblocks? List them here:

4. Can I navigate a way through, around, under or   Yes ☐   No ☐
   over these roadblocks?

5. Is this solution good enough to run with?   Yes ☐   No ☐

6. List the advantages and disadvantages of this solution.

Advantages   Disadvantages

7. Using the scale below, please rate the solution

| Mostly | | Mostly |
| disadvantageous | | advantageous |

5   -4   -3   -2   -1   0   +1   +2   +3   +4   +5

8. Is this solution good enough to put into action?   Yes ☐   No ☐

9. DO IT

Appendix 6:
Useful contacts and information

Internet sites
NICE (National Institute of Health and Care Excellence)

www.nice.org.uk

This website offers information about GAD within the guidance on Anxiety number CG113. Go to the menu, select 'Our guidance', then 'Guidance by type', then 'Mental health and behavioural conditions', then select 'Anxiety'. Alternatively type CG22 into the search facility on this site.

http://www.nice.org.uk/CG113

Professor Michel Dugas

http://psychology.concordia.ca/fac/dugas/downloads_en.html

http://uqo.ca/anxiete

Professor Michel Dugas is a Canadian expert on Generalised Anxiety Disorder. He is now Full Professor of Psychology at the Université de Québec en Outaouais, and Affiliate Professor of Psychology at Concordia University and the Université du Québec à Montréal l, Canada. You will find useful information about GAD on his web pages, including some useful downloadable materials. His materials will eventually become available on his Université de Québec en Outaouais website as well.

Mindfulness

There are many resources online for Mindfulness. Please use an Internet search engine to find information. To help you focus your search you may like to add these two names into your search: Professor Mark Williams and Professor Jon Kabat-Zinn – they are both world-renowned experts on Mindfulness.

The International Association for Cognitive Psychotherapy (IACP)

www.cognitivetherapyassociation.org

IACP is a professional, scientific, interdisciplinary organization whose mission is to facilitate the utilization and growth of cognitive psychotherapy as a professional activity and scientific discipline.

UK

British Association of Behavioural and Cognitive Psychotherapies (BABCP)

Victoria Buildings
9–13 Silver Street
Bury
BL9 0EU

Tel: 0161 797 4484

Fax: 0161 797 2670

Email: babcp@babcp.com Website: www.babcp.com

The website has a list of cognitive behavioural therapists accredited by the organization.

Appendix 6: Useful contacts and information

British Psychological Society

Division of Clinical Psychology
St Andrews House
48 Princess Road East
Leicester
LE1 7DR

Tel: +44 (0)116 254 9568

Fax: +44 (0)116 227 1314

Email: enquiry@bps.org.uk

Website: www.bps.org.uk

MIND

15–19 Broadway
London E15 4BQ

Tel: 020 8519 2122

Fax: 020 8522 1725

Email: contact@mind.org.uk

Website: www.mind.org.uk

Mind is a leading mental health charity in England and Wales. It provides information about Mental Health Problems.

MIND Cymru

3rd Floor, Quebec House

Castlebridge

5–19 Cowbridge Road

East Cardiff

CF11 9AB

Tel: 029 2039 5123

Fax: 029 2034 6585

Website: www.mind.org.uk

NHS Direct

Tel: 0845 4647

Website: www.nhsdirect.nhs.uk

NHS Direct provides information and advice about health, illness and health services, to enable patients to make decisions about their healthcare and that of their families.

Anxiety UK

Zion Community Resource Centre

339 Stretford Road

Hulme

Manchester

M15 4ZY

Website: www.anxietyuk.org.uk

Anxiety UK is a charity that aims to provide support for those living with anxiety disorders by providing in-formation, support and understanding.

Appendix 6: Useful contacts and information

EUROPE

The European Association for Behavioural and Cognitive Therapy (EABCT) has forty-one individual associations from twenty-nine different countries, all committed to the development and promotion of cognitive behavioural therapies. Website: www.EABCT.com

North America

http://www.academyofct.org/i4a/pages/index.cfm?pageid=1

http://www.abct.org/home/

http://www.actcc.ca/en/index.htm

Beck Institute for Cognitive Therapy and Research

1 Belmont Avenue, Suite 700

Bala Cynwyd

PA 19004–1610

Tel: (610) 664 3020

Fax: (610) 664 4437

Email: beckinst@gim.net

Website: www.beckinstitute.org

Center for Cognitive Therapy

PO Box 5308

Huntington Beach

CA 92615-5308

Website: www.padesky.com

Website: www.MindOverMood.com

The Association of Behavioural and Cognitive Therapies is a not-for-profit organization. It serves as a centralized resource and network, enhancing public awareness of cognitive behavior, therapy, disseminating knowledge, and promoting research.

Website: www.abct.org

AUSTRALIA

Australian Association for Cognitive Behavior Therapy

Website: www.aacbt.org

INTERNATIONAL

The Academy of Cognitive Therapy is a not-for-profit organization founded by experts in the field of cognitive therapy, dedicated to providing referrals and educational resources about cognitive therapy to the general public.

Website: www.academyofcognitivetherapy.org

The International Association for Cognitive Psychotherapy (IACP)

IACP is a professional, scientific, interdisciplinary organization whose mission is to facilitate the utilization and growth of cognitive psychotherapy as a professional activity and scientific discipline. Website: www.cognitivetherapyassociation.org

Further reading

Close companion books in the series

Butler, G., *Overcoming Shyness and Social Anxiety* (London: Robinson, 1999).

Espie, C. A., *Overcoming Insomnia and Sleep Problems* (London: Robinson, 2006).

Gilbert, P., *Overcoming Depression* (London: Robinson, 1997).

Fennel, M., *Overcoming Low Self-esteem* (London: Robinson, 1999).

Further self-help reading on worry

Lampe, L., *Take Control of Your Worry: Managing Generalised Anxiety Disorder* (Sydney: Simon & Schuster, 2004).

Leahy, R. L., *The Worry Cure: Stop Worrying and Start Living* (London: Piatkus Books, 2006).

Tallis, F., *How to Stop Worrying* (London: Sheldon Press, 1990).

van der Hart, W. and Waller, R., *The Worry Book: Finding a Path to Freedom* (Nottingham: Inter-Varsity Press, 2011).

Based on a similar psychological understanding of worry, this is a book written from a Christian perspective.

Mindfulness

Zinn-Kabat, J., *Full Catastrophe Living* (London: Piatkus Books, Ltd, 2004).

Problem solving

Nezu, A. M., Nezu, C. M. and D'Zurilla, T. J., *Solving Life's Problems* (New York: Springer, 2007).

Self-help books written from a CBT perspective

Butler, G. and Hope, T., *Manage Your Mind: The Mental Fitness Guide*, 2nd edition (Oxford: Oxford University Press, 2007).

Greenberger, D. and Padesky, C. A., *Mind over Mood: A Cognitive Therapy Treatment Manual for Clients* (New York: Guilford, 2007).

Scholarly and other texts for therapists and health professionals

A central source and influence for this book was Michel Dugas and Melisa Robichaud's *Cognitive Behavioural Treatment for Generalised Anxiety Disorder* (New York:

Routledge, 2006). We would recommend this to therapists and other health professionals. Please also see Michel Dugas's website, listed above.

Bennett-Levy, J., Butler, G., Fennell, M., Hackmann, A., Mueller, M. and Westbrook, D., *Oxford Guide to Behavioural Experiments in Cognitive Therapy* (New York: Oxford University Press, 2004).

Davey, G. C. L. and Wells, A., *Worry and its Psychological Disorders* (West Sussex: John Wiley & Sons, 2006).

D'Zurilla, T. J. and Nezu, A. M., *Problem-Solving Therapy: A Positive Approach to Clinical Intervention* (New York: Springer, 2007).

Westbrook, D., Kennerley, H. and Kirk, J., *An Introduction to CBT: Skills and Applications* (London: Sage, 2007).

Wilkinson, A., Meares, K. and Freeston, M., *CBT for Worry and Generalised Anxiety Disorder* (London: Sage, 2011).

Wilkinson, D. J., *The Ambiguity Advantage: What Great Leaders Are Great At* (New York: Palgrave Macmillan, 2006).

Index

Index

Index